ONCE UPON A HEROINE

450 Books for Girls to Love

ALISON COOPER-MULLIN AND JENNIFER MARMADUKE COYE

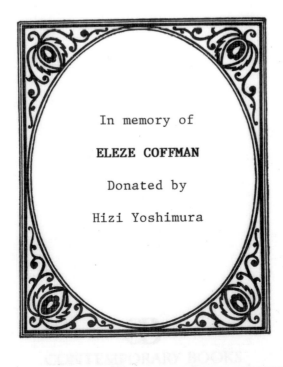

Library of Congress Cataloging-in-Publication Data

Cooper-Mullin, Alison, 1954–
    Once upon a heroine : 400 books for girls to love / Alison Cooper-
Mullin and Jennifer Marmaduke Coye.
      p.   cm.
    Includes indexes.
    ISBN 0-8092-3020-8
    1. Girls—United States—Books and reading.   2. Girls—Juvenile
fiction—Bibliography.   3. Women—Juvenile fiction—Bibliography.
4. Women—Juvenile literature—Bibliography.   5. Children's stories,
English—Bibliography.   I. Coye, Jennifer Marmaduke.   II. Title.
Z1037.C77   1998
[PR830.057]
028.1'6242—dc21

97-32121
CIP

98B7509

The authors gratefully acknowledge the following for permission to reprint previously
published material:

"The Adventures of Isabel," from *Verses from 1929 On* by Ogden Nash. Copyright
1936 by Ogden Nash. By permission of Little, Brown and Company.

From *Gina* by Bernard Waber. Copyright © 1995 by Bernard Waber. Reprinted by
permission of Houghton Mifflin Company/Walter Lorraine Books. All rights reserved.

From *Kate's Castle* by Julie Lawson. Copyright 1992. Published by Oxford University
Press. Reprinted by permission of Stoddart Publishing Co. Ltd.

From *Madeline* by Ludwig Bemelmans. Copyright 1939 by Ludwig Bemelmans,
renewed © by Madeleine Bemelmans and Barbara Bemelmans Marciano. Used by
permission of Viking Penguin, a division of Penguin Books USA Inc.

From *Personal History* by Katharine Graham. Copyright 1997. Published by Alfred A.
Knopf. Reprinted by permission of the author.

Cover design by Kim Bartko
Cover illustration copyright © by Gary Overacre
Author photograph by John Rooney
Interior design by Mary Lockwood

Published by Contemporary Books
A division of NTC/Contemporary Publishing Group, Inc.
4255 West Touhy Avenue, Lincolnwood (Chicago), Illinois 60646-1975 U.S.A.
Copyright © 1998 by Alison Cooper-Mullin and Jennifer Marmaduke Coye
Printed in the United States of America
International Standard Book Number: 0-8092-3020-8
18   17   16   15   14   13   12   11   10   9   8   7   6   5   4   3   2   1

Dedicated with love to our families, with whom we have spent many happy hours reading.

John
and
Emma, Clara, Elizabeth, and Rebecca
AC-M

Michael
and
Jane and Laura
JMC

he books of my childhood were ladders to me. I climbed up them into gardens, forests and make-believe lands. In these places I became other people. As these people, I suffered and laughed and often made up my own endings.

Each time I came down there was more to me than before I climbed up. Such is the way of books.

Jean Craighead George
1973 Newbery Medalist
Julie of the Wolves

CONTENTS

ACKNOWLEDGMENTS

or steering us to new authors and pulling book after book from the shelves, we owe a tremendous debt of gratitude to Marcia Hupp and the staff of the Mamaroneck Library; JoAlyce Newgaard, Dr. Constance Iervolino; Carrieann Bochicchio; the staff of the Greenburgh Library; and the helpful folks at the Bank Street Bookstore and Books of Wonder.

For unstinting assistance, endless patience, and walking the extra mile, we would like to thank a host of family and friends: Nadia Guerrieo, Laurie Bartels, Marcella Berger, Christina Bochicchio, Philip Boffey, Dr. Sidney Borowitz, Greg Brown, Dorrie Casey, Barbara and Phil Coccioletti, Julie Cooper, Dave Elliott, Ron Finklestein, Carl D. Folta, Dale Frehse, John Fulham, Mary Fulham, Larry Goldman, Doug and Stephanie Gould, John Grammer, Kellye Green, Laura Holbrook, Eavan and Chris Hooke, Sandy Hoover, Maury Hopson, John James, Judge Gladys Kessler, Scott Lancaster, Miriam Mahdaviani, Laurie Mandel, Scott Marmaduke, Ellen McConnell, Lisa McElaney, Kathryn McGrath, June

Miller, Abe Morrell, Nadine Mort, Barbara Mullin, Jane and Sam Mullin, Heidi Naumann, Cathy O'Keefe, Nicolas W. Platt, Deborah Porter, Bruce Raben, Nancy Reichley, Sara Reichley, Jim Reynolds, Nadine Scharman, Dr. George Siber, Sandy Smoley, Valerie Straus, and Ty West.

To Ronda Billig, networker extraordinaire, goes a special bouquet of thanks. Time after time, she pulled the rabbit out of the hat.

For his wonderful suggestions and exceptional talent on the Internet, we would like to thank Geoff Swaebe.

Alma Gottlieb deserves special recognition for her part in setting us down this road.

We would like to acknowledge the help and guidance of Susan Ginsburg and Susan Cohen of Writers House and Susan Schwartz and Gerilee Hundt of NTC/Contemporary Publishing Group.

And, of course, we are enormously grateful to our parents, Gloria and Wally Cooper and Carolyn and Arthur Marmaduke, who early on instilled in us the importance of books.

INTRODUCTION

hat book do you remember not being able to put down no matter how many times your parents told you "lights out"? What book did you never get tired of? Was it *Little Women*? Or was it *Anne of Green Gables* or *The Witch of Blackbird Pond* or *Harriet the Spy*?

What made these books so special? Why did we treasure them so much?

We treasured the experience of reading about other girls, kindred spirits who took center stage and held it. In our minds we could star as Anne Shirley cracking her slate over Gilbert Blythe's head or as Kit Tyler defiantly wearing her bright silk dress to a Puritan meeting house. Eudora Welty echoed our sentiments when she said, "I felt every pain and pleasure suffered or enjoyed by all the characters. Oh but I identified!" Over the years not much has changed. Our own daughters have spent long hours as the Ingalls family, pioneering in the backyard, or, like Mary Lennox, finding a secret garden (in our case under the azaleas). When they played doctor, they imagined themselves as Elizabeth Blackwell; when they bandaged their wounded dolls, they became Clara Barton or Florence Nightingale.

Girls are hungry for stories about other girls. In *The Norton Book of Women's Lives*, the writer Phyllis Rose describes her girlhood reading this way: "No sooner did I realize I was likely to grow up to be a woman than I wanted to know what the possibilities were for women's lives. . . . I wanted to be a cowgirl. I was seeking something no term then existed for—a role model. . . . I wanted wild women, women who broke loose, women who lived life to the full."

Role models. Girls want them, and parents want them for their girls. Today's culture makes most parents—including us— very nervous. Reports from the American Association of University Women and from Girls Incorporated, along with powerful books such as Myra and David Sadker's *Failing at Fairness*, Peggy Oren- stein's *Schoolgirls: Young Women, Self-Esteem, and the Confidence Gap*, and Mary Pipher's *Reviving Ophelia* have made real the issues of gender inequity in schools and the erosion of self-confidence in girls. The Sadkers provide page after page of research showing that "Girls are the majority of our nation's schoolchildren, yet they are second-class educational citizens." Orenstein writes, "By sixth grade, it is clear that both girls and boys have learned to equate maleness with opportunity and femininity with constraint."

Every parent hopes that the bright promise shown by a young child will be fulfilled. But the information we're receiving is fright- ening, and the implications for our daughters are downright upset- ting. We kept asking ourselves how we, as parents, could help. One place to start was right in front of us: books. They can provide a framework for our girls to imagine all the different ways their lives can play out. That is why the key question for us was best phrased by Dr. Ellen S. Silber, Director of Marymount Institute for the

Education of Women and Girls: "Yes, a girl can be a great reader, but who is she reading about?"

Generations of women read and loved heroines such as Jo March and Nancy Drew because they were that rare thing—strong-willed, exciting role models. For years it seemed that they might stand alone. As we began to raise our daughters (we have six between us), we started to hunt for other heroines. Initially we were afraid we wouldn't be able to put together a sizable list of worthwhile titles. Happily, we were mistaken. This book is your guide to more than 450 of the best heroines of children's literature.

When we tried to define a heroine to ourselves, we came up with a list of truly sparkling adjectives: intelligent, independent, witty, tenacious, compassionate, courageous. When she talks about her dreams, Jo March says, "I want to do something splendid . . . something heroic or wonderful, that won't be forgotten after I'm dead. I don't know what, but I'm on the watch for it, and mean to astonish you all, some day." Our heroines all take action. They have hopes and plans and the energy to achieve them.

In Vera Williams's *A Chair for My Mother*, the little girl saves pennies to buy her mother a special chair. In Robert Munsch's *The Paper Bag Princess*, Elizabeth outsmarts a dragon and then decides that the prince she saved isn't worthy of her. In Avi's *The True Confessions of Charlotte Doyle*, Charlotte survives murder and mutiny on a ship bound for Boston. In Suzanne Fisher Staple's *Shabanu: Daughter of the Wind*, Shabanu learns to keep her innermost self inviolate when forced into an arranged marriage. In Esther Hautzig's *The Endless Steppe*, Esther fights to stay alive while exiled to Siberia during World War II.

Although our premise is that every girl should be able to imagine herself as the heroine of her own life, we are not trying to say that girls should read only literature about girls. Our daughters loved *Charlie and the Chocolate Factory*, *The Indian in the Cup-*

board, and *Sounder.* We assume they'll grow up to love *Great Expec-*
tations as well as *Pride and Prejudice.* The best literature is universal, which is why we hope this book will also be used by parents of
boys. Just as girls have always met terrific heroes in books, it is an
enriching—indeed necessary—experience for boys to meet great
heroines. We were delighted to receive a letter from author Paula
Danziger that hammered this point home: "I hate saying about any
novel, 'It's a boy book,' 'It's a girl book.' Hopefully, the best books
for girls can also be the best books for boys and vice versa." We
believe your boys will be captivated by *Gina, The Little Riders,*
Alanna, and *Julie of the Wolves.* All the books we've included in this
guide are terrific reading experiences for everyone.

We made our choices based on our in-house market research
team of daughters and on recommendations from friends and family, teachers and librarians. We checked countless book reviews and
children's book award lists. All the final selections had to meet our
own tough standards. We wanted only the best literature—the
right words, the most inspired illustrations. We wanted books
whose titles brought forth again and again our enthusiasm and
affection.

We recognize that you may question some of our selections,
both those we included and those we left out. We chose heroines,
but not all of these heroines are feminists. Think of Sara Crewe in
A Little Princess or Betsy in *Understood Betsy.* These are old-
fashioned reads set in a long-ago world, but we felt the heroines
showed tremendous backbone and spunk. And we couldn't justify
giving up the effervescent Anne Shirley simply because she worries
and worries about having red hair and freckles. Even if the heroine lived in a society that expected her to marry, as Jo March does,
or to be a "little lady," as Caddie Woodlawn is told, we looked for
an uncaged spirit. In all these books, the heroines take the life they
have been given and look it squarely in the eye. The willingness to
be engaged with the world seemed to us to be the hallmark of a
heroine.

On the other hand, we didn't think that *The All of a Kind Family* deserved inclusion. While for the most part it is a sweet story of five sisters, the culminating chapter is a celebration of the long-awaited birth of a boy. No one can miss the implication that five sisters don't add up to one son. Some other finely written books that we remembered fondly from our childhood let us down when we reread them. *Katie John, What Katy Did,* and *Blue Willow* were some of those disappointments. Katie John, who seems like she would be Caddie Woodlawn's first cousin, trades in her harum-scarum ways to do housework. Katy of *What Katy Did* learns patience after a forbidden ride on a swing paralyzes her for many years—a punishment that seems bizarrely disproportionate to her supposed crime. Janey in *Blue Willow* believes that women should stand on the sidelines when men are making the important decisions.

Fairy tales were another thorny issue. A sleeping princess isn't a heroine to us. You won't find "Sleeping Beauty" or "Snow White" listed here, but you will find Robin McKinley's *Beauty*, Patricia C. Wrede's *Dealing with Dragons*, Jane Yolen's *Tam Lin*, and Aaron Shepard's *Savitri*, all well-crafted fables with stalwart heroines. In addition, there are welcome new twists to the shopworn damsels in distress. We think you'll love *The Princess and the Lord of Night*, *Rimonah of the Flashing Sword*, and *Rumpelstiltskin's Daughter*.

Occasionally we'd hear of promising titles that turned out, upon examination, to be so didactic that we couldn't imagine anyone wanting to finish them, let alone reread them. Just because the book has the "right" message doesn't mean it is worth reading. For us to recommend a book, the book must do more than merely describe a girl in a nontraditional role. A great plot integrated with meaningful character development and rich language are what make a book soar. We agree with Natalie Babbitt's statement in an article in the *New York Times Book Review*: "It's as if we cannot resist using the field of children's books for sermonizing. Once in a while a preachy book manages to be a good story at the same time, but that is rare." The excellent books we're including here stand on their own literary merits. The little carpenter of *Annie & Co.*, the busy scientists of *Pond Year*, and the plucky entrepreneur of *Shoeshine Girl* are just a few examples of worthy heroines in exemplary books.

Another area we debated about was artwork. In an amusing but sobering article in the *New York Times*, Jan Benzel tells the story of a friend who called and said, "I've got a real problem with *One Fish Two Fish Red Fish Blue Fish*. Have you *read* it? The only girl in the whole book is brushing hair." We were careful not to make that mistake here. The books we've listed have been illustrated in everything from pen and ink to watercolor to oil, and all of them, we feel, give us great examples of feisty, charming, and exuberant heroines. Jan Brett's lavishly detailed paintings in *Annie and the Wild Animals*, William Steig's clever drawings in *Brave Irene*, James Ransome's glorious illustrations in *Sweet Clara and the Freedom Quilt* will entrance every young reader.

The best part of compiling this book was finding that there has been a virtual explosion of titles showcasing strong heroines. We clearly would not have had such a good time if we had tried to write this book even twenty years ago! For example, if you wanted a book back then that featured a girl who was tough but funny, you were pretty much limited to *Pippi Longstocking* and *Eloise*. Now we also have the marvelous humor of Susan Meddaugh, Roz Chast, Kate Duke, David Small, Roald Dahl, and Joan Bauer, just to name a few. Animal books too now have female protagonists that, outside of the Frances books and Charlotte in *Charlotte's Web*, hardly existed then. Girls can now choose terrific titles with animal heroines from distinguished authors such as Kevin Henkes, Dick King-Smith, and Brian Jacques. And at long last it's possible to enjoy heroines of different races and cultures. From *Abuela* to *Amazing Grace*, from *A Jar of Dreams* to *Jenny of the Tetons*, there are finally some (though never enough) books reflecting our multiethnic society.

Closely linked to this is another area that has truly taken off: biography. When we were growing up, there were a few standard works about such historical figures as Dolley Madison and Florence Nightingale. When we had made our way through this meager selection, we were left frustrated. No more. Our children can read about Grace Hopper, Barbara McClintock, Marian Anderson, Rachel Carson, Georgia O'Keeffe, Bonnie Blair, Sheryl Swoopes, Mary McLeod Bethune. As the Sadkers state in *Failing at Fairness*, when children "read about females who accomplish outstanding deeds, both girls and boys believe that women are capable of great achievement." There are too many inspirational biographies to list here—check the index! Of course, there can always be more books with girls. You still find girls underrepresented in sports stories. And it is still not as easy as it should be to find Hispanic and Asian heroines. We wish we were able to recommend 1,000 titles to you. But the good news is that we aren't as limited as we once were. And that's given us hope.

We've organized this book alphabetically by title within each age category: Preschool (ages three through four), Early Readers (ages five through seven), Independent Readers (ages eight through eleven), and Young Adults (ages twelve and up). We categorized these books based not only on reading level but also by subject matter. Preschool books are simple picture books, centered on home and family. The Early Readers section covers folk tales, school, and beginning chapter books. In Independent Readers you'll find rousing adventures; Young Adult titles explore serious, real-life issues. However, you may find your ten-year-old sneaking off to read picture books, and you may find your six-year-old clamoring for more sophisticated titles. You will have to dip in and out of categories.

The indexes are arranged to help you do just that. You can find titles there by subject—science fiction or pioneers, for example—as well as by author. We have concentrated mostly on fiction, but you will find history, biography, and autobiography well represented. Whenever possible, we have listed the hardcover (cloth) and the paperback publisher(s), and we have included the original copyright date for each book. In addition, we note whenever a book has won a literary award. We did our best to select titles currently in print (we included a very few that aren't), but unfortunately, publishing can be a capricious industry. It is frustrating to discover that a favorite book has gone out of print. At the back of the book we've listed places, in addition to libraries, of course, that carry many of the titles we discuss.

As we researched this book, we began to wonder what books were meaningful to the most successful women—in law, media, science, sports, literature, music, politics, and business—of our time. We became so curious to know that we wrote and asked them! They responded with very special memories of their favorite childhood books. It was thrilling and fascinating for us to receive their letters. Some of the books are remembered affectionately as just plain fun; others were clearly inspirational. We have highlighted the recollections of these distinguished women throughout as a way of reminding parents of the power that great books have to captivate and motivate young girls.

We believe that stories are what we grow on. Our future is shaped by our childhood, and the books of our childhood are such an important part of our journey. We have had tremendous fun discovering these titles and sharing them with our daughters and our friends. We hope these books inspire the young heroines in your life. We think these will be the books they remember, the books they read long after "lights out!"

PRESCHOOL
READ-ALOUDS

AGES THREE THROUGH FOUR

ven the girls in our youngest category are explorers! The world is still so new, so fresh, and these books revel in their innocent adventures. At this stage many authors choose animals as their central characters, and they make endearing heroines.

Courage and confidence begin with a sense of safety and security. The first exploits of preschoolers often take place within the four walls of home or at least within the sight of loving eyes. These books reassure and show the many ways in which we are connected. They mirror the journeys your children are starting.

For little girls the text must be supported by pictures. We loved the variety of illustrations we found in this category—gentle watercolors, funny line drawings, and lavish pastels.

Abuela

Written by Arthur Dorros/Illustrated by Elisa Kleven
Copyright 1991
Cloth: E. P. Dutton
Paper: Puffin
A Reading Rainbow Book
ALA Notable Book

⌐ Cheerful, colorful collages illustrate a fantasy flight that young Rosalba and her grandmother take over Manhattan. Soaring over the city, the two turn somersaults in midair and circle gaily around the Statue of Liberty. The affection they feel for each other is unmistakable, and their giddy outing reflects their intrepid spirits. Sprinkled with Spanish phrases, this happy story concludes as Rosalba and Abuela get ready for another adventure, stepping eagerly onto a little boat in the park. "*Vamos* . . . Let's go."

The Adventures of Isabel

Written by Ogden Nash/Illustrated by James Marshall
Text copyright 1963
Illustrations copyright 1991
Cloth: Joy Street
Paper: Little Brown & Co.

> Isabel met an enormous bear,
> Isabel, Isabel, didn't care . . .
> Isabel, Isabel didn't worry,
> Isabel didn't scream or scurry.

⌐ In fearless Isabel, the master of nonsense verse has created America's most heroic preschooler. The inimitable Isabel coolly disposes of ravenous bears, nasty witches, hideous giants, and other "bugaboos." What's her secret? Listen to your little one squeal as you turn the pages to find out. Marshall's zany illustrations add to the fun.

Amanda's Perfect Hair
Written by Linda Milstein/Illustrated by Susan Meddaugh
Copyright 1993
Cloth: William Morrow
Paper: Tambourine/Morrow
⌒ Amanda's wildly gorgeous mane of blond hair is the first thing
and, it seems to Amanda, the *only* thing people notice about her.
She's tired of people talking about her hair! She's tired of the trou-
ble it creates! What an infuriating situation! Finally Amanda takes
charge, takes the scissors, and takes on a new look.

Amazing Grace
Written by Mary Hoffman/Illustrated by Caroline Binch
Copyright 1991
Cloth: Dial Books for Young Readers
Paper: Scholastic
A Reading Rainbow Book
⌒ The children in Grace's class tell her that she can't be Peter Pan
in the school play because she's a girl and because she's black. But
Grace really wants this part. Luckily she has a very special mother
and grandmother, who tell her, "You can be anything you want,
Grace, if you put your mind to it."
    There are spectacular illustrations of Grace playacting her
favorite roles: Joan of Arc, Mowgli, Hiawatha, Anansi. The story
and the artwork are perfectly in sync here, making this an uplifting and beautiful book. *Boundless Grace* is the wonderful sequel.

Angelina Ballerina
Written by Katharine Holabird/Illustrated by Helen Craig
Copyright 1983
Cloth: Crown
⌒ Angelina is the sprightly mouse heroine of the series of books
that begins with this title. Her enthusiasm, her verve, her bounce

make her such fun to read about. Angelina always has a mission; in this book it is to become a famous ballerina. The whimsical and cheerful illustrations capture her lively charm.

Anna Banana and Me

Written by Lenore Blegvad/Illustrated by Erik Blegvad
Copyright 1985
Cloth: Margaret K. McElderry Books
Paper: Aladdin

⌒ A timid little boy admiringly tells the story of his brave best friend, Anna Banana. She can do *anything*. A born leader, Anna Banana thinks up the most daring games, builds the greatest sand-castles, and tells the scariest tales. Her courage is catching, and at the book's end the little boy triumphs over his fears. It's nice to see a girl inspiring a boy!

Annie & Co.

Written and Illustrated by David McPhail
Copyright 1991
Cloth: Henry Holt

⌒ "I want to go out in the world and fix what needs fixing," lit-tle Annie tells her father. So he helps her fix up her pony cart, mak-ing places for her tool chest, a picnic basket, and her sign, "ANNIE & CO. WE FIX ANYTHING." And off she trots. She doesn't need to go far before her repair services are required, first by a cellist, then by a clown, then by a mayor, then by a goose. In Annie, McPhail has created a resourceful girl who knows how to mend just about any-thing. Would that we were all so capable!

Annie and the Wild Animals

Written and Illustrated by Jan Brett
Copyright 1985
Cloth: Houghton Mifflin

Paper: Houghton Mifflin

~ Annie is bereft when her cat, Taffy, disappears. She misses having her pet and is determined to find a new one. The enterprising little girl bakes corn cakes and leaves them in the woods to lure a new animal to her home. A moose, a wildcat, a bear, a stag, and a wolf all arrive, but she decides that none of them would make a cuddly, friendly pet. Ultimately, though, there's a happy ending for Annie when Taffy reappears with three new kittens.

Aunt Isabel Makes Trouble
Written and Illustrated by Kate Duke
Copyright 1996
Cloth: E. P. Dutton

~ When it's time for a story, there's no one like Penelope's Aunt Isabel. Just the promise of one of her wonderful stories is enough to entice Penelope home from a day in the park. Aunt Isabel even lets Penelope jump in and help, providing the story with twists and turns until the final page. Penelope asks that there be, of course, a heroine named after herself, and Aunt Isabel obliges with the adventures of Lady Penelope, the star pitcher of the East Woods nutball team. The story-within-the-story is loads of fun—whenever you think there can't possibly be further trouble for our heroine, Penelope and her aunt ingeniously concoct another predicament for Lady Nell to overcome. The superb watercolor pictures are crammed with delights for young eyes.

We're introduced to Penelope and her aunt in Duke's earlier book, *Aunt Isabel Tells a Good One*. Make them both part of your library!

The Balancing Girl
Written by Berniece Rabe/Illustrated by Lillian Hoban
Copyright 1981
Paper: E. P. Dutton

⁓ From her wheelchair Margaret can balance a twenty-block tower. She can wheel along with a book on her head. She can create elaborate castles, and indeed "she can balance herself and hop on her crutches." Her classmate Tommy is downright jealous and forever knocking over Margaret's efforts. When the time comes for the school carnival, all the children are eager to participate. Margaret comes up with a clever idea that capitalizes on her special skill and ends up earning more money for the school than any other booth. Even Tommy is impressed. Without a hint of condescension, the book keeps its friendly focus on Margaret's abilities.

A Bargain for Frances
Written by Russell Hoban/Illustrated by Lillian Hoban
Copyright 1970
Cloth: HarperCollins
Paper: HarperTrophy

⁓ Is there a child anywhere who doesn't identify with Frances? She's an irrepressible badger who epitomizes childhood. This title in the Frances series happens to be our favorite. Here Frances is hoodwinked by her so-called good friend Thelma. Frances has been saving her pennies to buy a beautiful china tea set, but Thelma tricks Frances into buying her crummy plastic tea set instead. And there are no backsies! When Frances realizes she's been had, she comes up with a plan to show Thelma what friendship should really be about.

There are other fine books about Frances that your little ones will treasure. In *A Birthday for Frances* she learns to cope with a baby sister's birthday party. In *Bedtime for Frances* she learns that the dark isn't that scary.

Beast
Written and Illustrated by Susan Meddaugh
Copyright 1981

PICABO STREET

~

Silver Medalist,
Downhill, 1994 Olympics, Lillehammer
World Champion,
Combined Downhill, 1993; Downhill, 1995
Gold Medalist,
Super Giant Slalom,
1998 Olympics, Nagano

urious George was my favorite book as a young girl. There was not really one specific story that I liked better than another, just the character himself and all of his adventures. It was my favorite book because I saw a lot of his temperament and curiosity in myself, especially as a child. I was always trying to figure out what was *really* going on with everything. It was not like I tried to start trouble; on the contrary, I just needed to gather all the information about any particular thing. I did not care what I had to do to get the information. Also, George was a very smart character who would rather figure things out himself than *be told* what to do and when. I am the same, with my mind always cranking over something, trying to figure it out. Most of the time we both find ourselves in a difficult situation due to our overwhelming drive to assist someone or something. In the end, George always figured out the solution and aided the cause. I always liked that fact and try to do the same.

Cloth: Houghton Mifflin
Paper: Houghton Mifflin

⌒ Anna isn't scared. Everybody else is scared of the big beast that's lurking about the house. Everybody else falls apart. Only Anna sets out to discover what the beast is really like. She discovers a big furry beast, all right, but a timid beast who couldn't hurt a fly. Totally adorable.

Blueberries for Sal

Written and Illustrated by Robert McCloskey
Copyright 1948, 1976
Cloth: Viking
Paper: Puffin
Caldecott Honor Book

⌒ This wonderful book deserves its reputation as a classic.

Two mothers, one human, one bear, take their children to Blueberry Hill. Little Sal and Little Bear prefer to sit and eat berries while their mothers work. Pretty soon they've lost their moms, and then they mix up their moms! Can Little Sal find her mother? Does a mother always know her child? There is just the right amount of suspense before the story reaches the absolutely correct conclusion.

Cannonball Simp

Written and Illustrated by John Burningham
Copyright 1966
Cloth: Candlewick Press
Paper: Candlewick Press

⌒ "Simp was what most people would call an ugly little dog. She was fat and small and had only a stump for a tail." No one wants to take her in. Thrown out on her own, Simp has several close calls before she finds herself consoling a circus clown about to lose his job. Simp comes up with a plan that not only turns his tired act around but earns her the home she's been looking for. Burningham's vigorous ink and gouache illustrations convey Simp's hardy spirit.

A Chair for My Mother

Written and Illustrated by Vera B. Williams
Copyright 1982
Cloth: Greenwillow
Paper: Greenwillow
Caldecott Honor Book
Boston Globe–Horn Book Award
A Reading Rainbow Book

~ This is a lucky little family. Not because of money—indeed the lack of it is apparent—but because Mama, Grandma, and the young narrator love and care for each other so much. Mama works hard as a waitress, and the family's goal is to buy her a fat, soft, comfortable chair she can sink into when she comes home. Every bit of loose change goes into a big jar; when the little girl helps her mother at the diner, her pay goes into that jar as well.

There's a real celebration when Mama finally gets her chair. You'll feel like snuggling in, too! The brightly colored illustrations also express a strong, joyful sense of family and neighborhood. We're sure that you will want to read more about Rosa in the sequels, *Something Special for Me* and *Music, Music for Everyone*.

Chester's Way

Written and Illustrated by Kevin Henckes
Copyright 1988
Cloth: William Morrow
Paper: Puffin
ALA Notable Book

~ A close friend claims that she read this book to her boys at least 900 times! We know why. Chester and Wilson, two nice, timid mice, are as alike as two peas in a pod. They always get out of bed on the same side, and they always double-knot their shoes. Then Lily moves in. Lily has her own dashing way of doing things. She wears exotic disguises, she carries a loaded squirt gun, and she plasters Band-Aids all over herself to look brave. When Chester and Wilson are surrounded by bullies, guess who comes to the rescue? A fast friendship develops, and the boys' humdrum days are over. Nine hundred encounters with these characters may not be enough!

Christina Katerina & the Box

Written by Patricia Lee Gauch/Illustrated by Doris Burn
Copyright 1971
Paper: Putnam

⌐ If your houses are anything like our houses, your children have appropriated every cardboard box. Ours have been turned into taxicabs, castles, boats, sleds, cages for wild animals, and ticket booths. In other words, all the marvelously inventive things that Christina Katerina turns hers into! We'd have to say that our girls unanimously consider Christina Katerina a true soulmate. We're betting yours will also.

Chrysanthemum

Written and Illustrated by Kevin Henkes
Copyright 1991
Cloth: Greenwillow
Paper: Mulberry Books

⌐ As Shakespeare said, "What's in a name?"

"Chrysanthemum thought her name was absolutely perfect. And then she started school." All the children tease her about her flowery name with so many letters. Chrysanthemum is miserable. But when the idolized music teacher reveals her name—Delphinium!—the children are envious and suddenly want to change their names to Marigold, Carnation, and Lily of the Valley. Just as in real life, a sympathetic adult is sometimes needed to give a shot of courage to a young girl suddenly unsure of herself.

Henkes's writing and illustrations have an easy charm that we find irresistible. One of our all-time favorites!

Contrary Mary

Written and Illustrated by Anita Jeram
Copyright 1995
Cloth: Candlewick Press
Paper: Candlewick Press

⌒ You can't help smiling in recognition at the little mouse who loves to do just the opposite of what's expected. She reads her book upside down, walks on her hands, and flies her kite along the ground. Contrary Mary has a field day doing everything backward. Her patient and clever mother knows how to play along and end Mary's game on just the right note. Silly fun for every young reader.

The Country Bunny and the Little Gold Shoes

Written by Du Bose Heyward/Illustrated by Marjorie Hack
Copyright 1939
Paper: Houghton Mifflin

⌒ When we were browsing in one of our favorite bookstores in New York, Books of Wonder, the helpful staff said, "*Please* don't forget to include *The Country Bunny*." So of course we went right home to reread it. And guess what? It's about a pretty liberated rabbit who raises her twenty-one children to be responsible and self-reliant so that she can get a job. The job she wants is to be one of the five Easter Bunnies. To get it, she has to have certain qualities— she must be fast, clever, wise, and kind. When Mother Cottontail proves she is brave as well, Grandfather Easter Bunny rewards her with a pair of little gold shoes. Surprisingly ahead of its time, this nugget is perennially in print.

Daisy Dare
Written and Illustrated by Anita Jeram
Copyright 1995
Cloth: Candlewick Press
Paper: Candlewick Press

⌐ Daisy mouse is never scared. So far she's taken any dare her friends dream up. She'll eat a worm, walk on a high wall, stick out her tongue at Miss Crumb. But what about taking the bell off the cat's collar? Can she do it? Bouncy drawings and simple text tell this funny story of a girl with tons of gumption.

Dance, Tanya
Written by Patricia Lee Gauch/Illustrated by Satomi Ichikawa
Copyright 1989
Cloth: Philomel Books
Paper: Putnam

⌐ The illustrations in this book are among the loveliest we know. They are delicate and charming. Tanya is a little sister. Perhaps you know one—she's the one always watching her big sister from the sidelines. Tanya's big sister studies ballet, but Tanya is too young for lessons. How is she supposed to let her mother know she is a dancer, too? The story ends just as you would hope. A sweetie pie of a book.

The beguiling sequel is *Bravo, Tanya*.

Doctor Kiss Says Yes
Written by Teddy Jam/Illustrated by Joanne Fitzgerald
Copyright 1991
Cloth: Firefly Books

⌐ The benevolent Doctor Kiss is always on call. After Doctor Kiss's parents tuck her in at bedtime, she's off to make her rounds. Tonight a squire fetches her to a striped tent where a wounded knight lies. A fair damsel tells the good Doctor Kiss how the brave knight was hurt on the battlefield. Doctor Kiss listens carefully and examines the poor knight's scraped knees. Aha! She knows just what to prescribe. Bandages are one of her secrets, as are counting to a thousand and getting some sleep. In fact the cure is amazingly like Doctor Kiss's own bedtime ritual. A quirky and charming flight of fancy.

Emma's Christmas: An Old Song Re-Sung & Pictured

Written and Illustrated by Irene Trivas
Copyright 1988
Cloth: Orchard Books
Paper: Orchard Books

⌐ In an exuberant, silly, and imaginative twist on the familiar carol "The Twelve Days of Christmas," we find Emma, the farmer's daughter, refusing the prince's hand in marriage. Determined to win her, he starts showering her with presents. He begins with a partridge in a pear tree, but those gifts have an amazing way of adding up! By the twelfth day she has thirty drummers, forty maids a-milking, thirty-six calling birds, forty golden rings . . . well, you get the picture. At the end his persistence has won her heart, but Emma can't muster any enthusiasm for a move to the castle. She's supremely happy living in the country. It's nice to see her noble suitor obligingly compromise and become her Farmer Prince. The comical illustrations complement the uproariously funny tale.

Emma's Vacation

Written and Illustrated by David McPhail
Copyright 1987
Cloth: E. P. Dutton

⌐ Emma, the resourceful bear in a series of books, goes on a vacation with her family. Her parents cram into one day a drive to the top of a mountain and rides on a boat, a bus, a train, and a rocket ship. The next day Emma insists on staying at their cabin and enjoying Mother Nature. Her parents are taken aback until Emma teaches them to appreciate life's simple pleasures. This is a satisfying story accompanied by droll and charming watercolors.

Two other Emma books worth reading are *Fix-It* and *Emma's Pet*.

Encore for Eleanor
Written and Illustrated by Bill Peet
Copyright 1981
Cloth: Houghton Mifflin
Paper: Houghton Mifflin

⁓ What is a poor elephant to do when she is too old to perform at the circus? Bill Peet, one of our most prolific writers of children's literature, has given us this optimistic story of Eleanor, who happily discovers that even if she can't manage stilts anymore, she has other surprising, creative talents. Bravo!

Even That Moose Won't Listen to Me
Written and Illustrated by Martha Alexander
Copyright 1988
Cloth: Dial Books for Young Readers
Paper: Dial Books for Young Readers

⁓ Nobody listens to Rebecca. It's so frustrating! There's a moose in the backyard eating the garden, but her busy family ignores Rebecca's warnings. Undaunted, she gamely tries several gentle tricks to scare him off, but when he gets too near the rocket ship she's building, she *really* gets mad. Rebecca is a spunky little heroine who takes charge and shows up her family in a most amusing way.

Geraldine's Blanket
Written and Illustrated by Holly Keller
Copyright 1984

Paper: Mulberry Books/William Morrow

⌐ There is a treasured blankie in many a young life. Olympic champion Bonnie Blair confesses in her autobiography (see Index) that she cherished hers until she was fourteen! Geraldine is similarly attached to a blankie, but her parents keep telling her she's way too old to keep taking it with her everywhere. To entice her away from it, they give her a beautiful doll. But Geraldine is one step ahead of them: she turns the blanket into a doll dress. Empowering and delightful all at once.

Ginger Jumps
Written and Illustrated by Lisa Campbell Ernst
Copyright 1990
Cloth: Simon & Schuster
Paper: Aladdin

⌐ During every performance Ginger, a timid circus dog, watches the crowds and wonders when she will find a family she can belong to. Her rival Prunella, the snooty star of the high-diving act, always upstages her. One day when Prunella unexpectedly stumbles, a single laugh rings out, and Ginger realizes it belongs to the newest and littlest clown—why, *that's* who she's been waiting for! Determined to win the attention of the little clown, Ginger bravely races past Prunella to the tippy-top of the frighteningly high platform for a climactic jump right into the welcoming arms of her own girl at last.

Happy Winter
Written and Illustrated by Karen Gundersheimer
Copyright 1982
Paper: HarperTrophy

⌐ The two busy sisters in this book know exactly what to do with a winter day. They make snow angels, play dress up, bake a cake, create birthday presents for Mom, read their favorite books, soak in a steamy tub, and watch the stars come out. Sweetly told

in verse and crammed with delicious illustrations, this simple story
is a read-aloud favorite.

Harriet and the Roller Coaster
Written and Illustrated by Nancy Carlson
Copyright 1982
Cloth: Carolrhoda Books
Paper: First Avenue Editions

⌒ George has Harriet very nervous when he dares her to go on
the roller coaster. But she won't back down now; she's not going to
give him the satisfaction. Higher and higher they climb. Once over
the top, Harriet decides that she likes it so much, she wants to ride
it all day. Guess who gets scared and watches her from a bench?
Clear, bright watercolors illustrate this risk-taking lesson.

There are many Harriet books you'll have fun with. In particularly you might want to check out *Harriet in the Garden*, in which
baseball-playing Harriet lands herself in a spot of trouble.

Heckedy Peg
Written by Audrey Wood/Illustrated by Don Wood
Copyright 1987
Cloth: Harcourt Brace
Paper: Harcourt Brace
Christopher Award

⌒ Here's a book that's dear to our hearts for an obvious reason:
Mom is the hero! After the children do everything they're not supposed to do and disaster predictably ensues (Well, what do you
expect? They didn't listen to their mother!), only Mother's wit and
wisdom saves them all from being a tasty lunch for the terrifying
Heckedy Peg. Near the end there's a wonderfully dramatic moment
when Mother nobly rises up and says, "I've got my children back,
Heckedy Peg. Now you'll be sorry you ever took them."

An extra-special mention needs to be made about the stunning illustrations on every page. This is one of those exciting books

in which the fairy-tale story and the spectacular paintings meld into a real work of art.

Here's Pippa!
Written by Betty Boegehold/Illustrated by Cyndy
      Szekeres
Copyright 1973, 1975
Cloth: Alfred A. Knopf
Paper: Bullseye Books

⌢ The copies we own of this book are positively dog-eared! Spunky Pippa Mouse and her woodland friends, Ripple Squirrel, Weber Duck, Gray Bird, and Cricket, have just the right sort of playful adventures for a young child: Pippa ice-skates, swims, gets a pet, builds a door, and has a birthday party. The simple pencil drawings add to the merriment. When you put down this book, you and your toddler will be smiling.

Hog-Eye
Written and Illustrated by Susan Meddaugh
Copyright 1995
Cloth: Houghton Mifflin

⌢ Could there be a small someone in your life who is prone to a version of "the dog ate it"? When do you believe her? Well, the very intelligent little piggy in this story has the ultimate shaggy dog story for not getting to school on time. Or does she? One morning she finds herself on the wrong school bus and suddenly at the mercy of a big, bad wolf. She smartly saves herself from the soup pot and the wolf with her special hog-eye curse. The peerless Susan Meddaugh wrote and illustrated this extremely funny book, and it is one of the best read-alouds we know.

I Like Me!
Written and Illustrated by Nancy Carlson
Copyright 1988

Cloth: Viking Penguin
Paper: Puffin

～ Whole shelves of pop psychology books on self-esteem could be replaced with this little volume! A pleasantly plump pink pig exuberantly declares that she has a best friend—herself! She goes on to show enthusiastically how she loves to take care of herself, ride her bike *really* fast, and cheer herself up when the chips are down. The line that makes everyone we know grin is "When I get up in the morning I say, 'Hi, good-looking!'" How can you resist?

If Anything Ever Goes Wrong at the Zoo
Written by Mary Jean Hendrick/Illustrated by Jane Dyer
Copyright 1993
Cloth: Harcourt Brace
Paper: Voyager/Harcourt Brace

～ First-class illustrations decorate this totally terrific story. Leslie earnestly informs the zookeepers that if anything ever goes wrong at the zoo the animals are more than welcome at her house. They all solemnly promise to keep her offer in mind. When the zoo floods, guess what arrives at Leslie's hilltop house? Leslie immediately puts her plan into action—the elephants go in her garage, the monkeys on the swing set, the alligator in the bathtub, and the lion in the closet. Leslie's ark saves the day!

Imogene's Antlers
Written and Illustrated by David Small
Copyright 1985
Cloth: Crown
Paper: Crown
A Reading Rainbow Book

～ You know you're in for a treat when you open this book to read: "On Thursday, when Imogene woke up, she found she had grown antlers." Imogene is unperturbed by this new development,

CLAIRE V. BROOME, M.D.

*Deputy Director, Assistant Surgeon General,
United States Public Health Service Centers
for Disease Control and Prevention*

s a child I was a voracious and uncritical reader. Fortunately, the nuns in my rigid parochial school were willing to turn a blind eye as I read a book a day totally unrelated to what was going on in the classroom. A book from childhood that has stayed with me is the *Just So Stories* by Rudyard Kipling. The incredible love of words, simple, complex, and definitively mispronounced; the encouragement to play with words; the free flight of imagination have stayed with me through the years and created warm touchstones with my family and the wider world of literature. To me, this first glimpse of the magic of what one can do with words easily outweighs the politically incorrect colonial perspective and Kipling's superbly wrongheaded disdain for biology (the latter despite my scientific career).

and the comedy erupts as her frantic family gets hysterical. Unflappable Imogene, though, continues to move serenely through her day. Small's uproarious illustrations are perfect for this wacky tale. This is a surefire hit with a laugh-aloud finish.

Jessica
Written and Illustrated by Kevin Henkes
Copyright 1989
Cloth: Greenwillow
Paper: Puffin

◌ Maybe you had an invisible friend; maybe one of your children does. If so, this book is sure to ring some bells.

Ruthie Simms is never alone, because Jessica is always there. Ruthie's parents keep saying, "There is no Jessica," but that's ridiculous. Of course there is a Jessica, to eat with and play with and go to bed with. But what about school? Can Jessica go with Ruthie? A delightful surprise awaits Ruthie at school and the reader at home.

Julius, the Baby of the World
Written and Illustrated by Kevin Henkes
Copyright 1990
Cloth: Greenwillow
Paper: Mulberry Books
ALA Notable Book

◌ All this fuss over her new baby brother! Lilly is appalled. Julius is useless, messy, and smelly. Can't her parents see that? Can't they stop all this crooning and cooing? Lilly's attitude earns her plenty of time in the "Uncooperative Chair." It isn't until her stuck-up cousin pronounces Julius to be totally disgusting that Lilly has a complete about-face and heroically leaps to his defense. Funny, funny stuff for a new elder sibling.

Just Us Women
Written by Jeannette Caines/Illustrated by Pat Cummings
Copyright 1982
Paper: HarperTrophy
A Reading Rainbow Book

⌒ A leisurely road trip during which you read the map, you set the pace, and you get to go all by yourself with your favorite aunt is a pretty special event. Here a lucky little girl and her aunt Martha mosey down the East Coast to North Carolina. They make all the stops they want to along the way and talk to their heart's content. The free and easy holiday these two share is also nicely detailed in the warm, humorous artwork.

Kate's Castle
Written by Julie Lawson/Illustrated by Frances Tyrrell
Copyright 1992
Paper: Stoddart Kids

⌒ Instead of "The House That Jack Built," read your daughter this version about a young girl at the beach on a perfect sunny day. A small sample should give you a taste of the poetic treats in store:

> This is the staircase of twisting shells
> That twirl and swirl in spiralling curls
> Way up the tower of treasurely finds—
> Moon snails and agates and sea urchin spines—
> Kept in the castle that Kate built.

The shimmering watercolors will make you "ooh" and "aah."

Kate's Giants
Written by Valiska Gregory/Illustrated by Virginia
 Austin
Copyright 1995

Cloth: Candlewick Press
Paper: Candlewick Press

⌒ For calming children's nighttime fears, this book is tops. In Kate's room there is a small door leading to the attic, and every night she imagines big, scary things sneaking through it. Her parents say, "If you can think them up, then you can think them out." Kate summons all her courage, and sure enough, that works. But then she wonders, might it be possible to think up *friendly* things? Sure enough, that works, too!

As the wonderful illustrator wisely says, "If only we all, like Kate, could turn our fears into fun."

Katy and the Big Snow
Written and Illustrated by Virginia Lee Burton
Copyright 1943
Cloth: Houghton Mifflin
Paper: Houghton Mifflin

⌒ "Katy liked to work. The harder and tougher the job the better she liked it." Katy is a big red tractor. In the summer she's a bulldozer, and in the winter she's a snowplow. When the biggest blizzard of all times hits Geoppolis and the city comes to a halt, Katy is ready.

Like its precursor, *The Little Engine That Could*, this classic was one of the first books to open up the traditional "boys' world" of work and machinery. Burton carried this off as well in her equally famous *Mike Mulligan and His Steam Shovel* (remember, the heroic steam shovel is named Mary Anne). We would have welcomed more books like these all along!

Koala Lou
Written by Mem Fox/Illustrated by Pamela Lofts
Copyright 1988
Cloth: Harcourt Brace
Paper: Voyager/Harcourt Brace

MEM FOX

~

Children's Book Author, Koala Lou

hen I write for girls (aged between birth and about seven years old), I'm most anxious to provide them with lively stories showing women and girls as feisty, can-do people. For reasons of sexism, racism, religionism, class-ism, and Euro-centrism I'd hesitate to draw attention to a single novel I read as a child. God forbid that today's girls should read the nonsense I was reading when I was their age!

The only texts I'd comfortably recall and recommend, which I loved to distraction, are some of the Old Testament stories (in the King James version of the Bible) like those of Ruth and Esther; the original Mowgli stories by Rudyard Kipling in their un-Disney-fied form; and the legends, fairy stories, and folktales of the world. Their heroism inspired me. Every troublesome task was dealt with in a magnificent and brilliant fashion. No one said, "It can't be done." Apparently insurmountable difficulties were overcome by courage, wisdom, and ingenuity. These stories certainly fired me up.

Before I wrote this contribution I hadn't realized how much influence my early reading had had on my expectations of life. I'm now aware that I've lived by many of the principles of my heroes and heroines. Their dreams and mine became the same. And many of those shared dreams have, in the manner of all good fairy stories, come true.

⌐ Everybody loves Koala Lou. Most of all—and best of all—her mother loves Koala Lou. But as lots and lots of brothers and sisters arrive, Koala Lou worries that her mother doesn't love her anymore. She concocts a splendid scheme to regain her mother's attention: she, Koala Lou, will enter the Bush Olympics and win the gum-tree-climbing contest! When her plan seems to go awry, Koala Lou discovers that her mother's love is absolute, unconditional, and guaranteed.

Children can't wait to chime in with the book's cheerful refrain, "Koala Lou, I DO love you!" This is a wonderful read-aloud selection.

The Library
Written by Sarah Stewart/Illustrated by David Small
Copyright 1995
Cloth: Farrar Straus & Giroux

⌐ Eccentric Elizabeth is a classic bookworm: she is *never* without a book. But what is she going to do when she has no more room for her books? Told in catchy verse, this cheery story of a single-minded heroine is complemented by Small's droll illustrations.

The Little Engine That Could
Written by Watty Piper/Illustrated by George and Doris Hauman
Copyright 1930
Cloth: Platt & Munk/The Putnam & Grosset Group
Paper: Putnam
A Reading Rainbow Book

⌐ Surely you know all about this book. It's as sunny and merry as you remember. When the happy little train breaks down on her way over the mountains, the toy passengers try to flag down assistance. But no one will help until the kind little blue engine arrives.

It's a big job, but she cheerfully rises to the challenge. She puffs and chugs until her job is done. "I think I can—I think I can" turns to "I thought I could. I thought I could." A must!

The Little Old Lady Who Was Not Afraid of Anything
Written by Linda Williams/Illustrated by Megan Lloyd
Copyright 1986
Cloth: HarperCollins
Paper: HarperTrophy

⌒ Clever word repetition builds the suspense in this sweetly scary picture book. One windy autumn night, the little old lady who was not afraid of anything hears a loud CLOMP CLOMP from a disembodied pair of shoes. Then a WIGGLE WIGGLE from a pair of pants, then a SHAKE SHAKE from a shirt, then a . . . well, you'll catch on! She not only bravely faces down this spooky assortment but cleverly puts them to good use, too. A great Halloween read.

Lon Po Po: A Red-Riding Hood Story from China
Translated and Illustrated by Ed Young
Copyright 1989
Cloth: Philomel Books
Paper: PaperStar
Caldecott Medal
Boston Globe–Horn Book Award Winner

⌒ Three little sisters are on their own when a wolf, disguised as their grandmother, knocks on the door. He hopes to make a delectable dinner of the children, but the eldest daughter, Shang, is far too quick for him. This tale comes from an ancient oral Chinese tradition; its much younger European counterpart is the familiar "Little Red Riding Hood." Ed Young has beautifully illustrated this story in washes of gleaming pastels; the faces of the girls slyly peek out through the colors as they outwit the wolf.

Lottie's Circus
Written by Joan W. Blos/Illustrated by Irene Trivas
Copyright 1989
Cloth: William Morrow

～ The circus comes to town—right in Lottie's backyard. "First you make believe, and then something special happens," explains Lottie to her pet cat, assorted dolls, and stuffed animals. A whole circus happily parades itself through Lottie's daydream: she sells the tickets, builds the bleachers, pops the popcorn, tames the lion, swings from the trapeze, walks the high wire. . . . Don't miss Lottie's daring, darling, three-ring, one-girl greatest show on earth!

Louanne Pig in Making the Team
Written and Illustrated by Nancy Carlson
Copyright 1985
Cloth: Carolrhoda Books
Paper: Carolrhoda Books

～ Louanne is hoping to be on the cheerleading squad. Arnie wants to be a football star. Everything flip-flops when the football coach puts Louanne on his team and Arnie gets picked to lead the cheers. Uncluttered pictures help tell this story of two friends who learn not to pigeonhole themselves.

Lucy's Picture
Written by Nicola Moon/Illustrated by Alex Ayliffe
Copyright 1994
Cloth: Dial Books for Young Readers
Paper: Puffin

～ Everyone in nursery school is painting pictures, but even the brightest paints won't work for Lucy. She needs something very special for her grandfather, and so she happily sets to work creating a collage. Using twigs and cloth and sand and feathers, Lucy makes a beautiful landscape that Grandpa can really appreciate. For Lucy's grandpa is blind and relies on touch to "see" her picture. The artwork throughout is pleasingly collagelike, showing off a busy and thoughtful girl.

Madeline
Written and Illustrated by Ludwig Bemelmans
Copyright 1939
Cloth: Viking
Paper: Puffin

DR. ELLEN BAKER

⌐

NASA Astronaut

 have always been an avid reader. Books are filled with interesting people and new and different ideas. I can travel to distant lands and distant times while reading a good book. In a book I can find relaxation, comfort, joy, tragedy, excitement, mystery, and intrigue.

The Madeline books by Ludwig Bemelmans have long been a favorite of mine. Madeline—kind, smart, brave, and curious—is also a favorite of my daughters. It has been great fun sharing cherished books of my girlhood with my children, and it is wonderful to see that these books are special for them as well. Perhaps one day I'll share them with my granddaughters.

⌒ Madeline is a spunky little girl whose bravery and Gallic charm have been holding young listeners rapt for decades. Bemelmans's distinctive, lovely, scribbly drawings of Parisian street scenes are unforgettable. Children adore reciting these couplets by heart, so much so that anyone who's ever read this more than twice can join in on "To the tiger in the zoo / Madeline just said, 'Pooh-pooh.'" In other books (*Madeline's Rescue, Madeline and the Bad Hat, Madeline and the Gypsies*) Madeline goes on to have many more adventures; her impish appeal is timeless.

The Maggie B.
Written and Illustrated by Irene Haas
Copyright 1975
Cloth: Margaret K. McElderry Books
Paper: Aladdin

⌒ Margaret Barnstable makes a bedtime wish that, for one special day, she will sail the open seas as captain of a very splendid ship. When she wakes up, there she is, captain of the *Maggie B.* with her little brother James as crew. This is an enchanting good-night story of dreams that come true; the illustrations are especially dear. We've baked "Maggie B. Peaches" for our girls and *tried* to sing her sea shanties.

Maggie's Whopper
Written by Sally Hobart Alexander/Illustrated by Deborah
        Kogan Ray
Copyright 1992
Cloth: Simon & Schuster

⌒ Fishing on the lake with her Great-Uncle Ezra is one of Maggie's greatest joys. This time she's determined to catch a whopper as big as her brother Tom's. The only thing that troubles her is the thought of Old Thatch, a 300-pound bear who prowls the surrounding woods. Great-Uncle Ezra reassures her that Old Thatch wants berries and minnows—not them. But when Maggie finally lands her whopper, she turns to find Old Thatch heading straight for Great-Uncle Ezra! Will she know how to save him? This little picture book packs a big punch!

Make Way for Ducklings
Written and Illustrated by Robert McCloskey
Copyright 1941
Cloth: Viking
Paper: Viking
Caldecott Medal

BARBARA K. GIBBS

⌒

Director, Cincinnati Art Museum

 book that was important to me at a very early age was Robert McCloskey's *Make Way for Ducklings*. In *Make Way for Ducklings*, the mother duck must lead her eight ducklings single-handedly from their nest by the Charles River through the dangerous streets of Boston to meet up with their father in the Public Gardens. Though the ducklings follow by instinct, it always seemed to me that the mother's self-confidence and bravery inspired the policeman and others to rally to her aid. I'm sure my crusader tendencies can be traced back to the example set by that determined, courageous mother duck.

⏤ With its soft brown pencil drawings of eight fluffy, quacking ducklings, this is one of the most reassuring books ever written. These children never have a doubt about who's taking good care of them. Mrs. Mallard is absolutely in charge of her brood. She chooses the right place to hatch her ducklings, she teaches them to swim and dive, to walk in a line, to come when they are called, and to keep safely away from bikes and scooters. When the time comes to move to a new home in the Boston Public Gardens, Mrs. Mallard stops traffic so her family arrives unharmed. Children *beg* for this at bedtime!

Mama Zooms!
Written and Illustrated by Jane Cowen-Fletcher
Copyright 1993
Paper: Scholastic

⏤ "Every morning Daddy puts me in Mama's lap and we're off!" In her zooming machine, Mama zooms her little one hither and yon, becoming a racehorse, a ship, a buckboard wagon, a spaceship. Halfway through, the reader is taken by surprise—Mama's zooming machine is a wheelchair. Warmly illustrated, this is a highly unusual book, showcasing an imaginative and courageous mama.

Margarete Steiff: Toy Maker
Written by Carol Greene
Copyright 1993
Cloth: Children's Press
Paper: Children's Press

⏤ How many of us ever knew there was a woman behind the fabulous Steiff stuffed animals? Margarete Steiff was born in Germany in 1847 and was stricken with polio when she was just eighteen months old. "Who will take care of Margarete after we die?" her parents would ask. But they needn't have worried. Starting with one little felt elephant, Margarete developed and ran one of the world's most famous toy companies.

Because of its special appeal to toddlers, we decided to include this beginning biography in this section. (All other biographies start in "Early Readers.") It is illustrated with many period photographs of Germany and, of course, all those lions and leopards and teddy bears!

Mary Mary
Written by Sarah Hayes/Illustrated by Helen Craig
Copyright 1990
Cloth: Margaret K. McElderry Books

⌒ The giant who lives on the top of the hill terrifies the town. All except for Mary Mary, that is. As contrary as the little girl in the nursery rhyme, Mary Mary dares to do what no one else will. She marches right up to the giant's door. The giant proves to be a rather sad, messy, muddled fellow. Mary Mary looks around and bluntly sizes up the situation: "What you need . . . is managing." She manages that giant right into happiness with an unexpected, amusing solution. Outstanding.

Moira's Birthday
Written by Robert Munsch/Illustrated by Michael
       Martchenko
Copyright 1987
Paper: Annick Press

⌒ Birthday fever has struck! Without her parents' knowledge, Moira has invited the entire elementary school to her party. When her parents open the door, they're met by a stampede. They're aghast! How can they feed these kids? Who's going to clean up the mess? What will they do with 200 presents? Moira is always one step ahead of her parents—she's got the answers to every objection. Classic Munsch hilarity.

My Mama Had a Dancing Heart
Written by Libba Moore Gray/Illustrated by Raul Colon
Copyright 1995
Cloth: Orchard Books
New York Times Best Illustrated Children's Book

⌐ "My mama had a dancing heart and she shared that heart with me." Lines like that make all the reading we did for this book worthwhile. The young woman who tells this story is now a ballerina, and she looks back lovingly at all the dancing times she had with her mama in the spring rain, in the summer waves, in the fall leaves, and in the winter snow. Jubilantly illustrated, it is also poetically written, in toe-tapping language that will make you want to get up and kick your heels.

My Working Mom
Written by Peter Glassman/Illustrated by Tedd Arnold
Copyright 1994
Cloth: William Morrow

⌐ "It isn't easy having a working mom"—especially if your mom is a witch! Mom is really, really busy at her job, flying off to meetings and brewing mysterious concoctions in her lab. But this little girl finds her mom never lets her down: Mom gives birthday parties that are literally out of this world, always shows up to cheer at soccer games, and lets the kids hitch a ride on her broomstick. All in all, the little girl guesses, she wouldn't have it any other way. The amusing pictures also cast a lighthearted charm.

Nessa's Fish
Written by Nancy Luenn/Illustrated by Neil Waldman
Copyright 1990
Cloth: Atheneum
Paper: Aladdin

⌒ In the Arctic, a little girl and her grandmother go ice fishing. When her grandmother becomes ill, Nessa must watch through the night to protect her and their cache from predators. Impressively, Nessa remembers everything she has been taught to frighten away wolves, foxes, and bears. The illustrations, in icy pastels, are lovely.

There is an equally pretty sequel, *Nessa's Story*.

Nora and the Great Bear

Written and Illustrated by Ute Krause
Copyright 1989
Cloth: Dial Books for Young Readers
Paper: Puffin

⌒ In Nora's tiny village the long winter evenings are spent discussing the fearsome Great Bear. More than anything, Nora wants to join the hunters in their search for this fabled beast. She learns all of a hunter's skills: strength, cunning, and patience. When the annual hunt fails to find the Great Bear, Nora has an idea. She puts down her weapons and calls softly to the Great Bear. Tracks appear. Following them, she is soon hopelessly lost. A shadow falls on the snow: the Great Bear himself has come to lead her home. Nora is proud to have accomplished what adults have only talked about.

Nora's Stars

Written and Illustrated by Satomi Ichikawa
Copyright 1989
Paper: Putnam

⌒ Doesn't every child secretly believe that toys can come alive? One night, after Nora is tucked into bed at her grandmother's country estate, the dolls and stuffed animals start to jump out of their old trunk and dance about the room. They all run outside, and when Nora says she would love to play with the stars, the toys fly up into the night and gather them for her. They sprinkle the stars

ELLEN TAAFFE ZWILICH

Carnegie Hall Composer's Chair
1983 Pulitzer Prize for Music

he first book that was mine was given to me when I was about five, when I had just begun to read. It was a book about Gigi, a merry-go-round horse at the Prater in Vienna, and the adults either don't know or have forgotten that the merry-go-round horses can speak. Not only do the children have favorite merry-go-round horses, but the horses have favorite children. Gigi's favorite is a little girl named Lily. When Lily rides him, he goes faster, and sometimes he even leans toward the ring so she can reach it. (By the way, Gigi's father was the Wind, and his mother was the Vienna Woods.) During the war the merry-go-round and the horses fall into disrepair and Gigi is taken away on a boat. Gigi undergoes all kinds of awful transformations until finally he ends up far away on someone's lawn, painted a different color. Lily grows up and one day visits this place. When she sees the carousel horse outside, she fondly recalls her merry-go-round days, but when Gigi speaks to her and says, "Lily, it's me, Gigi," Lily can't hear him. She's become an adult.

I have no idea who wrote this story, but I can close my eyes and remember how the book smelled and how it felt in my hands. I guess all creative people hope that they never lose the gift of hearing the horses speak.

over her quilt and turn it into a shimmering cape. But then Nora notices that the sky looks too dark, too sad. She takes her cape and shakes the stars back into the sky. All is now right with the world. An enchanting story of selflessness, told with exquisite magical watercolors.

One Windy Wednesday
Written by Phyllis Root/Illustrated by Helen Craig
Copyright 1996
Cloth: Candlewick Press
~ When a blustery wind comes along and blows the quack out of the duck into the lamb, and the baa out of the lamb into the pig, Bonnie Bumble knows she has a job to do! She gets right to work and sets everything straight. Author Phyllis Root and artist Helen Craig (of *Angelina Ballerina* fame) have scored here with a perky story that hits the mark with toddlers.

Owl Moon
Written by Jane Yolen/Illustrated by John Schoenherr
Copyright 1987
Cloth: Philomel Books
Caldecott Medal
A Reading Rainbow Book
~ In this poetic, reverent book a little girl and her pa walk through the winter forest late at night to go owling. Along the way she wants to talk, especially when she is uncertain about what might be hiding in the shadows, but she knows that if an owl is to show itself she must be silent and stoic. She's rewarded when a magnificent owl comes swooping down around them. What makes this book extra-special is the tender trust between father and daughter and the mysterious midnight world of the woods.

The Paper Bag Princess
Written by Robert N. Munsch/Illustrated by Michael
        Martchenko
Copyright 1980
Cloth: Annick Press
Paper: Annick Press

⌒ This is the book that stunned at least one of our daughters and sparked, we hope, a small feminist awakening. The princess doesn't marry the prince? The princess doesn't want the prince? This is a very funny tale of a resourceful and clever girl who outsmarts a dragon to save her prince but drops him with no regrets when his true nature is revealed.

The Patchwork Quilt
Written by Valerie Flournoy/Illustrated by Jerry Pinkney
Copyright 1985
Cloth: Dial Books for Young Readers
Christopher Award
Coretta Scott King Award
A Reading Rainbow Book

⌒ Grandma holds fast to the old ways. Mama offers to buy her a new quilt, but Grandma insists on making one, one full of memories and meaning. Tanya is enchanted with Grandma's plan, and together they find the scraps that will tell their family story. Even when Grandma becomes ill, Tanya continues to work. Three generations of women finally complete Grandma's masterpiece. Pinkney's award-winning artwork lovingly portrays this affectionate family and the determined little girl who first believed in Grandma's quilt. There is a nice sequel, *Tanya's Reunion*, that takes Tanya back to her grandmother's farm.

The Piggy in the Puddle
Written by Charlotte Pomerantz/Illustrated by James Marshall
Copyright 1974

Cloth: Simon & Schuster
Paper: Aladdin
A Reading Rainbow Book

⌐ If you want to get the giggles, race out to get this book. It bubbles over with singsong daffiness as the little piggy refuses to obey her parents and leave her lovely mud puddle. Eventually her sensibilities prevail and her family dives in, too. An antic and goofy story that will be read aloud again and again and again!

The Purse

Written and Illustrated by Kathy Caple
Copyright 1986
Paper: Sandpiper

⌐ Katie keeps her money in a Band-Aids box. She loves the "clinkity, clinkity, clinkity" sound of the coins. It makes her feel rich! When her big sister persuades her to buy a grown-up purse, Katie is delighted until she realizes she has no money and nothing to go "clinkity, clinkity, clinkity." Resourceful Katie finds steady employment from her parents, doing one odd job after another. Soon she has saved enough for another Band-Aids box that will fit nicely inside her new purse. Light and believable.

Sally Ann Thunder Ann Whirlwind Crockett

Retold by Caron Lee Cohen/Illustrated by Ariane
    Dewey
Copyright 1985
Cloth: Greenwillow
Paper: Mulberry Books

⌐ Here's a tall tale of a lady "made of thunder with a little dash of whirlwind." She can outscream an eagle, outclaw a mountain lion, and jump over the Grand Canyon with both eyes shut. When Mike Fink, the biggest, baddest man around, boasts that he can scare her teeth loose, it's clear he's never met Sally Ann Thunder Ann Whirlwind Crockett. A rollicking read!

Sheila Rae, the Brave
Written and Illustrated by Kevin Henkes
Copyright 1987
Cloth: Greenwillow
Paper: Mulberry Books

⟶ Poor Louise. She's just the scaredy-cat little sister to the brave and fearless Sheila Rae. Nothing intimidates Sheila Rae—not monsters in the closet, cracks in the sidewalk, bullies on the playground, or big dogs at the end of the block. When Sheila Rae rashly tries a new way home from school, timid Louise secretly follows her. Sheila Rae's nerves of steel desert her when she realizes she is lost, but Louise unexpectedly comes to the rescue. Now there are *two* brave sisters.

Sing, Sophie!
Written by Dayle Ann Dodds/Illustrated by Rosanne
        Litzinger
Copyright 1997
Cloth: Candlewick Press

⟶ Sophie is a rootin', tootin' guitar-playing cowgirl who loves to sing. She strums her guitar and makes up hilarious holler-along songs that will crack up your young listeners. Her talents aren't appreciated around the old homestead, though, until a thunderstorm sends the baby into a crying fit and only Sophie's serenades can soothe him. Finally folks start paying proper attention to Sophie's tunes. A great giggly read-aloud.

Sisters
Written and Illustrated by David McPhail
Copyright 1984
Cloth: Harcourt Brace
Paper: Voyager/Harcourt Brace

⟶ Here is a gentle story of two sisters that celebrates all the ways in which they are different and alike. "One liked baseball. The other found it boring. . . . They fought over the piano . . . and made up over tea." The pen-and-ink illustrations by the author are both charming and realistic. Different or alike, the sisters love each other just because they are sisters, just for being themselves.

The Squiggle

Written by Carole Lexa Schaefer/Illustrated by Pierr
   Morgan
Copyright 1996
Cloth: Crown
ALA Notable Book

⌒ We think this one, set in China, could become a classic. A nursery school class is walking in a slow, straight line to the park. The last little girl in line spots a piece of string. In her hands it becomes a dragon dancing, the great wall of China, the path of a circus acrobat, the ripple in a pool. Her classmates watch, enchanted, and laughingly grab on to the string to make a "slither-slish, push-a-pat, snap, tah-dah, crack crickle hiss . . . squiggle of a line" for the rest of their walk. The imaginative art is rendered beautifully on oatmeal-colored paper.

Stellaluna

Written and Illustrated by Janell Cannon
Copyright 1993
Cloth: Harcourt Brace
Paper: Voyager/Harcourt Brace
A Reading Rainbow Book

⌒ Children's books usually feature mice or kittens or big fuzzy bears, not bats! These glorious illustrations prove how a gifted artist can change our perceptions. The heartwarming story of a baby bat, Stellaluna, who is separated from her mother and befriended by a family of birds has proved enormously popular. Children love Stellaluna's plucky ways and find her gift for friendship very touching.

Stephanie's Ponytail

Written by Robert Munsch/Illustrated by Michael
    Martchenko
Copyright 1996
Cloth: Annick Press
Paper: Annick Press

⌒ Stephanie isn't interested in doing what others do. She wants to be unique. Because no one else in her class wears a ponytail, she decides to wear one. Her unimaginative classmates copy her. She moves her ponytail to the side. They copy that. Whatever she tries, they copy. Frustrated, she tricks them all in a side-splitting finale.

Tar Beach

Written and Illustrated by Faith Ringgold
Copyright 1991
Cloth: Crown
Paper: Random House
Caldecott Honor Book
Coretta Scott King Award
New York Times Best Illustrated Children's Book
A Reading Rainbow Book

⌒ From the tar roof of her apartment building, Cassie Louise Lightfoot can look out and feel "like I owned all that I could see." She dreams of flying free among the stars, over New York City and the sparkling George Washington Bridge. She imagines that flying will liberate her to right the racial injustices her African-American family has felt. More than anything, generous Cassie wants to give her family all they need to be happy. Her father would own a building, her mother would laugh, and they would all have ice cream every night.

Ringgold first created this magical story as a "quilt painting," and the original is in the collection of the Guggenheim Museum.

Tell Me a Story, Mama
Written by Angela Johnson/Illustrated by David Soman
Copyright 1989
Cloth: Orchard Books
Paper: Orchard Books

⌒ This is one of the sweetest bedtime books imaginable. A little girl begs her mama for a story "about when you were little." Mama can't start a sentence without her little girl finishing it, for these are all favorite stories that the two have clearly shared over and over. Mama had a temper, Mama stood up to the mean old neighbor lady, Mama and Aunt Jessie took a train trip all by themselves, Mama brought a puppy home. . . . The little girl knows these treasured childhood tales by heart.

The watercolor illustrations of this loving African-American family are perfect. Cuddle up with this one.

Three Days on a River in a Red Canoe
Written and Illustrated by Vera B. Williams
Copyright 1981
Cloth: Greenwillow
Paper: Mulberry Books
A Reading Rainbow Book

⌒ Jaunty, happy illustrations accompany the itinerary of a river journey taken by a little girl, her cousin Sam, and their mothers. They paddle, they build campfires, they put up tents, they cook, they see rainbows, moose, waterfalls, and crayfish—you just might find yourself looking in the classifieds to see if any red canoes are for sale!

Thunder Cake
Written and Illustrated by Patricia Polacco
Copyright 1990
Paper: PaperStar

ESMERALDA SANTIAGO

⁓

Author, When I Was Puerto Rican *and*
Becoming American

 had no books as a child. We were poor, and books were a luxury we could only dream about. That is not to say that my ten sisters and brothers and I were without stories.

At night, when the doors and windows were bolted and the kerosene lamps flickered, Mami and Papi told Juan Bobo's goofy escapades, or about the vain Cucarachita Martinez, or related the travels of Don Quijote de la Mancha and his faithful friend Sancho Panza. They told us about dancing princesses, magic lamps, and caves filled with treasure that opened if one spoke the right words . . . their adventures were as real to me as the earth I walked on.

Those mysterious nights of my childhood in Puerto Rico, when Mami or Papi's voice filled the air with possibility, were the beginning of my love for words and of the power they convey to enrich and transform a life.

Today, while my house is filled with books, they cannot begin to compare to the voices I still hear in my head. . . . They are the sounds of love, of one generation passing knowledge to the next. I treasure them, just as I hope my children, in addition to treasuring the books they hold dearest, will remember the hours I made up tales to amuse and instruct them, sometimes just to have them near, enraptured, in story.

⁓ If, after you've sung "My Favorite Things," your little ones are still terrified of thunderstorms, you must read them this book. Polacco wrote it, she says, because when she was little she "feared the sound of thunder more than anything."

One day at Grandmother's farm the sky rumbles, and the little girl dives right under the bed! Her grandmother teaches her how to count when she sees the lightning to figure out how far away the storm is. She'll then be able to tell how long they have to gather the ingredients to make Thunder Cake. All around the farm they go, racing against the storm to get the eggs from the chickens, the milk from the cow, the chocolate from the dry shed. When they are safely inside and the cake is in the oven, Grandmother tells her how brave she was. The little girl realizes the truth in her words and from then on "never feared the voice of thunder again." Polacco's lively folk-art illustrations convey both the excitement of the threatening storm and the endearing affection between these two generations.

Tillie and the Wall
Written and Illustrated by Leo Lionni
Copyright 1989
Cloth: Alfred A. Knopf
Paper: Dragonfly Books
A Reading Rainbow Book

⁓ Lionni is a staple of preschool story hours. His simple tales are pitched just perfectly to our little ones, and his appealingly playful collages hold their attention. Children love to hear about Tillie, the youngest mouse, who is the only mouse to wonder about the big wall. Who is on the other side? How can she get there to find out? Several unsuccessful attempts do nothing to discourage her, and when, at last, she tunnels her way to the other side of the wall, she's met by mice just like her who celebrate her amazing arrival with a party. She's feted just as grandly upon her return home. A sweet treat for all.

To Climb a Waterfall
Written by Jean Craighead George/Illustrated by Thomas
　　　Locker
Copyright 1995
Cloth: Philomel Books

⌐ This book evokes the wonder and grandeur of the great Hudson River painters. It offers a quiet lesson in observing and learning from the natural world as a girl climbs to the top of a waterfall. George's words guide us through Locker's beautiful paintings without upstaging their mystery and magic. The love these collaborators feel for Kaaterskill Falls (in the Catskill Mountains) is more than apparent. As Locker says, it is his favorite place on earth.

Together
Written by George Ella Lyon/Illustrated by Vera Rosenberry
Copyright 1989
Cloth: Orchard Books
Paper: Orchard Books

⌐ Sometimes it is the simplest of poems that can make your heart soar. Here two best friends, one white girl and one African-American, show how much better life is when you go through it "together." Calling back and forth to each other, they imagine that they can build a house, make ice cream, fight fires, catch fish. Illustrated with fanciful, festive pictures, this is a book you and your children will always treasure.

Trouble with Trolls
Written and Illustrated by Jan Brett
Copyright 1992
Cloth: Putnam

⌐ Full of beautiful colors and incredible detail, Jan Brett's sumptuous illustrations are often the reason you pick up her books. She is, however, a talented storyteller as well. Here Treva and her dog,

Tuffi, are crossing a mountain to visit her cousin when pesky trolls try to kidnap Tuffi. Clever Treva outwits the trolls over and over in a gratifying story.

Tumble Tower
Written by Anne Tyler/Illustrated by Mitra Modarressi
Copyright 1993
Cloth: Orchard Books

~ Do you play Tom Chapin's music at your house? Do you know his song "Happiness Is Living in a Neat Mess"? That would be Princess Molly's theme. She lives in a tower that, in a kind understatement, could be called disheveled. Her clean, neat, tidy parents and her prissy brother don't understand her at all. But one night there's a flood, and the only safe haven is Molly's room. She can give the prince her old pajamas, feed her parents her leftover snacks, read them books from under her pillow, and have the cat and her six kittens snuggle in with the royal family to keep them warm. After that, everyone is a bit more casual! We know one little girl who appreciated this book (by noted adult author Anne Tyler) so much she said, "This is great. Even her hair is messy!"

Under the Moon
Written by Dyan Sheldon/Illustrated by Gary Blythe
Copyright 1994
Cloth: Dial Books for Young Readers

~ The cover of this hauntingly beautiful book shows a young girl looking up out of her pup tent at the moon. It is Jenny, who while digging in her backyard has unearthed an ancient arrowhead. That night, as she clutches it in her sleep, she has a powerful dream that takes her back to when the only people on the continent were Native Americans. When Jenny lifts the flap of her tent, she sees smoke coming from tepees and a circle of people sitting around a campfire. She spends the night listening to their stories of long ago, "when the land was as large and as open as the sky. When there were stories in the stars and songs in the sun." In the morning, she knows she must honor them by putting the arrowhead back where it belongs. Blythe's luminous oil paintings (we wish we could own one) will move you as much as the poetic text.

A Very Noisy Girl
Written by Elizabeth Winthrop/Illustrated by Ellen Weiss
Copyright 1991
Cloth: Holiday House

⁓ The constant din that Elizabeth creates—by jumping on the furniture, banging on the drums, pounding up and down the stairs—so rattles her mother that she pleads with Elizabeth not to be "such a noisy girl." Elizabeth disappears into her room, and when she comes out for lunch she pretends to be a very quiet little dog. Her mother plays along with her and begins to wish out loud that Elizabeth would come back: "It's much too quiet." When Elizabeth stops her game of pretend, her mother admits that having a noisy girl is really lots of fun. You'll celebrate with Elizabeth as she cartwheels into her mother's lap.

The Wednesday Surprise
Written by Eve Bunting/Illustrated by Donald Carrick
Copyright 1989
Cloth: Clarion Books
Paper: Houghton Mifflin

⁓ We admit to a fondness for any book about reading. This one, though, is particularly inspiring. On Wednesday nights, when Grandma comes to Anna's house, they go upstairs together to read. They're preparing a big surprise for Dad's birthday. When the house is decorated and the presents are ready, Anna and Grandma give Dad the gift they have worked so hard on: Anna has taught Grandma to read. Everyone is beaming as Grandma says, "Maybe I will read everything in the world now that I've started."

When I Was Little:
A Four-Year-Old's Memoir of Her Youth
Written by Jamie Lee Curtis/Illustrated by Laura Cornell
Copyright 1993
Cloth: HarperCollins
Paper: HarperTrophy

⁓ Integrated with Laura Cornell's joyous watercolors, each sentence in this "memoir" becomes a sight gag. (Our favorite is the picture of the little girl in time-out for painting a boy's face green and yellow!) Together the words and illustrations capture the world as seen from four—and also as four is seen from forty! You never know, a four-year-old in your life might be inspired to write her own autobiography.

EARLY
READERS

AGES FIVE THROUGH SEVEN

ith the onset of school comes the beginning of real independence. Although the family may still serve as a comforting, warm touchstone, these plots deal with girls assuming responsibility, choosing their own friends, and making their own decisions. These books are celebratory—they cheer and applaud the pluck and persistence the heroines display.

By now children are certainly ready for folktales. The distinction between real and make-believe is reasonably clear to a six-year-old, and she relishes the extravagant battles between good and evil at the heart of these traditional stories. The tales we've included feature wide-awake princesses who slay their own dragons as well as some very funny versions that twist around the familiar standards.

Books in this group still have beautifully drawn illustrations, but they have much fuller text. These titles do double duty: you can read them aloud to your children, and many are suitable for beginning independent reading. Also in this category we find our first biographies and historical novels based on real-life heroines, reinforcing the "can do" theme.

Aani and the Tree Huggers

Written by Jeannine Atkins/Illustrated by Venantius J. Pinto
Copyright 1995
Cloth: Lee & Low Books

ᴑ Based on real events in India in the 1970s and illustrated in the style of Indian miniature paintings, this is the story of young Aani and the village women who stopped the destruction of their forest. When the cutters come with their machines, Aani and her friends beg them to leave the land alone. They need the fruit and berries for food, the wood for tools, the roots of the trees to stop erosion. The cutters won't listen until Aani makes a powerful silent protest: she wraps her arms around a tree and won't let go.

Amelia Earhart: Courage in the Sky

Written by Mona Kerby/Illustrated by Eileen McKeating
Copyright 1990
Paper: Puffin

ᴑ "Amelia's favorite books were *Peter Rabbit*, *Black Beauty*, and all kinds of adventure stories. Almost always, the heroes in those adventures were boys. Amelia didn't think this was fair. . . . Just once, she wished for an adventure story about a girl. Amelia Earhart wrote that adventure story with her own life."

Kerby has written an appealing biography for youngsters. Although it may require reading aloud, the dramatic subject matter will hold even a six-year-old's attention. She was the first woman to fly across the Atlantic. She was the first person in the world to cross it twice. She was the first person to attempt to fly around the world at the equator.

The words Earhart once wrote to her husband could serve as a motto to all girls: "I want to do it because I want to do it. Women must try to do things as men have tried. When they fail, their failure must be but a challenge to others."

Note: Older readers will enjoy *Sky Pioneer* (see Index).

An American Army of Two
Written by Janet Greeson/Illustrated by Patricia Rose
    Mulvihill
Copyright 1992
Cloth: Carolrhoda Books
Paper: First Avenue Editions

⌒ "Yankee Doodle" became the favorite marching song of the Patriots during the Revolutionary War, and its popularity has never waned. During the War of 1812, it was the signal to British soldiers that American troops were on the move. The New England coast was hit particularly hard by British blockades, and Rebecca and Abigail Bates, living in a lighthouse in Scituate, Massachusetts, were keenly aware of the danger they were in. On one eventful day they spy the British rowing toward shore to commandeer the town's meager supplies. The town is defenseless, but the two sharp-witted girls hide in a grove of trees and frighten the British off by playing "Yankee Doodle" on a fife and drum.

Annie and the Old One
Written by Miska Miles/Illustrated by Peter Parnall
Copyright 1971
Cloth: Little Brown & Co.
Paper: Little Brown & Co.
Newbery Honor Book

⌒ Told in simple language, this is a poignant and profound story of a young Navajo girl who grows to understand the spiritual ways of her people.

Annie cannot accept her grandmother's announcement that, when Annie's mother has finished the new rug on the loom, she will "go to Mother Earth." Annie resolves to stave off her grandmother's death by making sure her mother will not have time to weave. She misbehaves in school so her mother will be summoned by the teacher. She frees the sheep so her mother will have to spend hours rounding them up. When these subterfuges fail and the weaving continues, Annie resorts to pulling the threads out of the loom while her mother sleeps. Finally, her wise grandmother makes her understand that Annie cannot hold back time. She must respect the cycle of life. In Annie, the author has given us a brave girl who learns to handle a difficult situation with exceptional grace.

Author: A True Story
Written and Illustrated by Helen Lester
Copyright 1997
Cloth: Houghton Mifflin

⁓ An absolutely charming book, lightly self-mocking, about hurdles met and overcome.

Even as a toddler, Helen Lester *loved* to write. She made grocery list after grocery list for her mother. When she started school, she had the prettiest penmanship in the class, but it was backward. She was a "mirror writer," and it took lots of work before she could write in the proper direction. Although that problem was solved, she still found writing stories frustrating—sometimes she just couldn't come up with a single idea. She became a teacher and taught second grade for ten years before trying her hand at writing children's books. There are lots of wastebaskets illustrated here as the author fills them up with ideas that somehow don't pan out. Success deservedly comes to her (she's the popular author of *Tacky the Penguin* and many other titles), but she cheerfully acknowledges her missteps along the way.

Don't keep this book away from older children—they adore it too.

Best Enemies
Written by Kathleen Leverich/Illustrated by Susan Condie
      Lamb
Copyright 1989

Cloth: Greenwillow

Paper: Alfred A. Knopf

⌒ Nobody likes to remember it, but everyone's been there. We've all had a "best enemy." Priscilla's is a girl named Felicity Doll. Felicity is always there, trying to undermine Priscilla. She steals her sweater, her desk, and her brand-new pencil case. She makes fun

LEE SMITH

⌒

Author, Fair and Tender Ladies *and* Oral History

 y favorite book from childhood was *Misty of Chincoteague*—not only because it is a wonderful novel, but also because Marguerite Henry stayed at my grandmother's boarding house on Chincoteague Island (off Virginia's Eastern Shore) while she was writing it. So it is filled with the salty air and ocean breezes and long summer days I associate with visiting my beloved grandmother. Reading it again and again, I could almost feel the crunch of crushed oyster shells beneath my bare feet as I walked to the store, or how the saddle stuck to my legs as I rode the island ponies through the marsh. And since I was a young writer-in-the-making, *Misty of Chincoteague* helped me to see how familiar scenes from my own real life could be the stuff of fiction. Marguerite Henry had sat in the same old wicker front-porch swing that I had—surely I could write a book someday, too!

of her shoes. She horns in on her birthday party. Priscilla rallies
again and again, refusing to let Felicity get the best of her.

Our girls adored this book. They found it hysterically funny
and dead-on accurate. Yours will too!

P.S. More good news: there are two sequels, *Best Enemies
Again* and *Best Enemies Forever*.

The Best-Loved Doll

Written by Rebecca Caudill/Illustrated by Elliott Gilbert
Copyright 1962
Cloth: Henry Holt
Paper: Henry Holt

⟋ Which doll should Betsy take to the party to win a prize?
Belinda, who wears a bride's dress of white taffeta; Melissa, who is
over a hundred years old; or Mary Jane, who can run a sewing
machine? She can't take Jennifer. Her hair is tangled, her nose is
cracked, her cheeks are covered with tape. Or can she? Betsy's decision and what happens at the party will gladden the hearts of all
girls who are supremely loyal to their own best-loved dolls.

The Best Present

Written and Illustrated by Holly Keller
Copyright 1989
Cloth: Greenwillow

⟋ Some rules don't seem fair, such as the rule that says you have
to be ten years old to visit someone at the hospital. Rosie's grandmother is there, on the seventh floor, and eight-year-old Rosie is
determined to see her. She tries to disguise her age by unbraiding
her hair and donning a hat and gloves, but the hospital guard is not
deceived. A dejected Rosie can't do anything but slip the flowers
she's brought to the elevator man and hope they get to Grandma.
When Grandma comes home, she hugs Rosie close, brushing aside
Rosie's disappointment: "It was very brave of you to try." Rosie's
stout effort was really the "best present" of all.

Betsy-Tacy
Written by Maud Hart Lovelace/Illustrated by Lois Lenski
Copyright 1940
Cloth: HarperCollins
Paper: HarperTrophy

⌒ This book falls into the category of best-loved books. Properly speaking, Betsy and her best friend, Tacy, are not heroines. They are just two very recognizable five-year-old girls growing up together throughout a series of ten books. The setting is a simpler, slower time, and the focus is on the most ordinary everyday events. These are great beginning chapter books, immensely appealing to young readers. Many women we know remember with pleasure the hours they spent with Betsy and Tacy.

When we looked at the book jacket, we found two quotes worth sharing. Actress and singer Bette Midler wrote, "I read every one of these Betsy-Tacy books twice. I loved them as a child, as a young adult and now, reading them with my daughter, as a mother. What a wonderful world it was!" Columnist and novelist Anna Quindlen, who lists herself as a lifetime member of the Betsy-Tacy Society, said, "Betsy-Tacy fans never die. They just reread."

The Big Balloon Race
Written by Eleanor Coerr/Illustrated by Carolyn Croll
Copyright 1981
Cloth: HarperCollins
Paper: HarperTrophy
A Reading Rainbow Book

⌒ The characters in this easy reader are drawn from real life: Carlotta Myers was the most famous aeronaut of her time. This story opens at the big balloon race of 1882 when Carlotta's daughter, Ariel, becomes an unwitting stowaway after falling asleep in the *Lucky Star*'s basket. Ariel is chagrined to find herself aboard, because her added weight will make it harder for her mother to win. The two of them team up to make the best of this unexpected situation, tossing out sandbags, the anchor, and all the odds and ends they can lay their hands on. With Carlotta's engineering expertise and Ariel's plucky last-ditch efforts, this mother-daughter duo wins the day. High-flying fun.

Birdy and the Ghosties
Written by Jill Paton Walsh/Illustrated by Alan Marks
Copyright 1989
Cloth: Farrar Straus & Giroux
Paper: Sunburst

⁓ Birdy has been gifted with second sight. It's true: the second time she looks at things, Birdy sees so much more. One morning there are loud voices outside the seaside cottage door, ghosties demanding that Birdy's father row them across the water. He is too afraid of the spirits to refuse, and he and Birdy ready the boat to ferry their invisible passengers. When her father asks Birdy what the phantoms look like, she can't bring herself to scare him with the horrible truth. Instead, to ease his mind she concocts a description of a glittering regal family. As she talks, her words free the ghosties from their ugliness, transforming them into the beautiful noble creatures she's invented. Written in lilting prose and illustrated in ethereal watercolor washes, this is a captivating folktale.

Another lyrical story about Birdy is *Matthew and the Sea Singer*.

Bloomers!
Written by Rhoda Blumberg/Illustrated by Mary Morgan
Copyright 1993
Cloth: Atheneum
Paper: Aladdin

⁓ In 1851 Amelia Bloomer was the editor of a journal that advertised the first clothes for women that did not involve tight corsets, cumbersome petticoats, or long gowns. They were called *bloomers,* after her, and in them women felt liberated as they were able to walk and breathe much more freely. Susan B. Anthony and Elizabeth Cady Stanton adopted them, and soon bloomers became the symbol of women's rights. Witty illustrations accompany this short, lively history of the heroines brave enough to wear the "unladylike" outfit that helped foment a revolution.

Brave Irene

Written and Illustrated by William Steig
Copyright 1986
Cloth: Farrar Straus & Giroux
Paper: Farrar Straus & Giroux

~ "I can get it there!" Irene stoutly reassures her sick mama. She must rush. The duchess needs the beautiful ball gown Mama has made—and she needs it tonight. How will Irene do it? The snow is piling up, and the wind is whirling. "Go home!" the ill-tempered wind shouts at her. But Irene won't give up. Even when she is half-buried in a snowdrift, even when she twists her ankle, even when the wind steals the dress and Irene is left with nothing but the box, she trudges on. She wrestles that wind all the way to the palace, where Steig gives his brave heroine the supremely happy ending she deserves.

The Bridge Dancers

Written by Carol Saller/Illustrated by Gerald Talifero
Copyright 1991
Cloth: Carolrhoda Books
Paper: First Avenue Editions

~ A shaky, swaying old footbridge is the only connection between Maisie's mountain home and the houses across the gorge. Maisie's never been across the bridge, and it terrifies her. Her older sister, Callie, isn't afraid, though—she dances out onto it, laughing as it dips and swings. When their mama is called to deliver a baby, a storm blows in and Callie brazenly decides to chop firewood. The ax slices her leg, and Callie begs Maisie to cross the bridge and get their mama. The reader thinks she knows what Maisie will do, but her unexpected solution is in fact far more realistic. When Mama comes home, she approves of Maisie's good sense: "I guess there's more than one way to cross a bridge."

Busybody Nora
Written by Johanna Hurwitz/Illustrated by Lillian Hoban
Copyright 1976
Cloth: William Morrow
Paper: Puffin

∽ Nora and her little brother, Teddy, live in a big apartment building in New York City. Nora has friends throughout the building, in large part because she's made it her business to get to know everybody. What she'd really like the most is for the whole building to do something special together, something like, oh . . . say, a party! And when a determined little girl sets her mind on something, you just know she'll make it happen. Simple, easygoing fun for the young reader.

The Cabin Faced West
Written by Jean Fritz/Illustrated by Feodor Rojankovsky
Copyright 1958
Cloth: Coward McCann
Paper: Puffin

∽ Jean Fritz is acclaimed for her biographies of famous people, but here she excels with the warmhearted story of an ordinary little girl, her own great-great grandmother, Ann Hamilton. Although Fritz has embroidered some of the details of Ann's life, the essential events are true.

Ann is a very lonesome ten-year-old living with her pioneer family in the Pennsylvania wilderness. She misses town life in Gettysburg; most of all, she misses having a friend. There isn't a single girl around Hamilton Hill for her to play with and confide in. Her family keeps saying "some day" things will be better. Those are the two words Ann comes to hate most. But after a terrible storm, and a thrilling visit from General George Washington, she surprises herself by "thinking 'some day' just like the others."

Caterina, the Clever Farm Girl
Written by Julienne Peterson/Illustrated by Enzo
      Giannini
Copyright 1996
Cloth: Dial Books for Young Readers

⌒ This is a witty retelling of a Tuscan folktale with delightful illustrations wherein clever Caterina confounds a king.

Unlike the miller's daughter in "Rumpelstiltskin," this nifty heroine doesn't need any help from anyone to solve the king's crafty riddles. She relies on her own quick mind for the answers. The king is so impressed that he marries Caterina and seats her beside him as he settles disputes for his people. Because Caterina speaks up when she disagrees with him, the king's touchy pride is wounded and he banishes her. Caterina's not the type to give up, though. She has another sly trick up her sleeve, and when she's played it out, the repentant king laughingly realizes that neither he nor his kingdom can do without her.

A refreshing and funny story.

Clara Barton: Angel of the Battlefield
Written by Rae Bains/Illustrated by Jean Meyer
Copyright 1982
Cloth: Troll Associates
Paper: Troll Associates

⌒ Perfect for younger readers (probably as a read-aloud), this is a commendable biography of the painfully shy girl who grew up to be a valiant nurse during the Civil War and the founder of the American Red Cross. Clara, born on Christmas Day in 1821, was an extremely bright child and the pet of her adoring family. When Clara was eight, her parents sent the precocious girl to boarding school, hoping it would cure her shyness. Although Clara loved her studies, boarding school did nothing to alleviate her timidity, and she returned home after one semester. From her brothers Clara learned to hammer a nail, throw a ball, tie a square knot, and ride a pony. From her father, she acquired her lifelong love of geography, maps, and travel. When her older brother fell off a roof and broke his back, eleven-year-old Clara took two years off from school to nurse him. No task was too difficult for Clara to handle.

By concentrating on Barton's girlhood days, the author has done an excellent job of turning this icon into a real person that children can understand.

A Clean Sea: The Rachel Carson Story
Written by Carol Hilgartner Schlank and Barbara Metzger/
Illustrated by David Katz
Copyright 1994
Paper: Cascade Pass

⟶ Today endangered animals and threatened ecosystems are part of most primary grade curricula, thanks to the pioneering work of marine biologist Rachel Carson. *A Clean Sea*, which seems targeted for classroom use, is just as terrific at home. Strong, punchy graphics decorate the multicolored pages of this visually appealing biography, and the authors cover the highlights of Carson's remarkable career in a clear and simple style. Young readers really respond to both the anecdotes from her childhood and the environmental crusade she launched.

Note: *Listening to Crickets: A Story about Rachel Carson* (see Index) is a fuller treatment of Carson's life for older readers.

Clever Gretchen and Other Forgotten Folktales
Retold by Alison Lurie/Illustrated by Margot Tomes
Copyright 1980
Cloth: HarperCrest

~ Alison Lurie, a highly regarded novelist and critic, was one of the first to compile a collection of stories, each one having a strong female protagonist. In her introduction she writes, "In the fairy tales we know best today, the heroes seem to have all the interesting adventures. . . . As for the heroines, things just happen to them. . . . But there are thousands of folktales in the world that are not at all like this." She's chosen fifteen of her favorites to retell, including Clever Gretchen, who outwits the Devil; Mitilca, who is a soldier for the sultan; and Molly Whuppie, who fools a giant. Lurie hopes that one day these resourceful heroines will "be as well known as Cinderella and Snow White are now." We hope so too.

The Courage of Sarah Noble
Written by Alice Dalgliesh/Illustrated by Leonard Weisgard
Copyright 1954
Cloth: Atheneum
Paper: Aladdin
Newbery Honor Book

~ In 1707, eight-year-old Sarah accompanies her father into the wilderness while he builds a home for their large family. Everyone else was too frightened to come, but Sarah stepped forward to help. She is scared too, of course, but she steels herself by remembering her mother's words: "Keep up your courage, Sarah Noble."

When the house is ready and her father travels back to get the family, Sarah stays with their Indian neighbors. Now her courage is truly tested, for although Sarah has made friends among the Indians, it seems quite another thing to live on her own with them for several months. Sarah's unusual true story is about facing one's fears gracefully and with dignity.

Dial-a-Croc

Written by Mike Dumbleton/Illustrated by Ann James
Copyright 1991
Cloth: Orchard Books
Paper: Orchard Books

⌐ When your child is old enough to start setting up a lemonade stand, she'll be old enough to appreciate Vanessa and her unlikely business partner. After venturing into the outback, Vanessa returns home with a crocodile and puts her plan in motion. A classified ad brings in all kinds of jobs. It turns out that more people than you could have imagined have a use for a crocodile! Soon they are rolling in money—there's enough to buy a house with a crocodile-shaped swimming pool and a helicopter. But when her pal gets homesick, Vanessa does the right thing. This is a tongue-in-cheek tale that's especially easy to read, with highly amusing watercolors.

Elizabeth Blackwell: First Woman Doctor

Written by Carol Greene/Illustrated by Steven Dobson
Copyright 1991
Cloth: Children's Press
Paper: Children's Press

⌐ This perfect first introduction to a great feminist pioneer is profusely illustrated with photographs and engravings.

Elizabeth Blackwell, who started life as a shy girl worrying about doing something important, ended up making history. Twenty-nine medical schools said no when she applied. But on November 4, 1847, Blackwell began as a student at Geneva Medical College and went on to graduate as America's first woman doctor. She continued her studies in Paris, hoping to become a surgeon, until a serious eye infection dashed this ambition. Blackwell then went to New York City and opened a hospital for poor women and children. To complement it, she started a nursing school and a medical college for women. Her efforts more than proved to the world that women had much to contribute to medicine. The statistics of her hospital speak for themselves: "In 1865, her hospital treated 31,657 people. Only five died."

Note: *The First Woman Doctor* by Rachel Baker (see Index) is a much more detailed biography.

DR. MARY ELLEN AVERY

～

*Thomas Morgan Rotch Distinguished Professor of
Pediatrics, Harvard Medical School
Physician-in-Chief Emerita,
Children's Hospital, Boston*

 loved *David Copperfield*! Dickens's books are full of the plights of children. He was a profound child psychologist as well as a powerful social reformer. I also read *Arrowsmith*, perhaps a curious role model, but Sinclair Lewis depicted him as someone who felt medical science was terribly important. *Of Human Bondage* clearly got me focused on children and making changes that might be helpful. And I always read the funny papers. I still do. I like to keep laughing!

Eloise
Written by Kay Thompson/Illustrated by Hilary Knight
Copyright 1955
Cloth: Simon & Schuster

⁓ Nobody would call Eloise a good girl. Grown-ups might call her a holy terror, but irrepressible Eloise knows how to live! Ensconced in the top floor of the Plaza Hotel (her picture hangs in the lobby to this day), she imperiously orders room service, rings for the Valet to press her sneakers, crashes fancy parties in the Grand Ballroom, and is a severe nuisance at the front desk. When not terrorizing the hotel, she's drawing on her bottomless imagination to supply her with new, wonderfully unorthodox activities. Eloise is the one child who would *never* complain of boredom. As she herself declares, "Oh my Lord / There's so much to do."

The Emperor and the Kite
Written by Jane Yolen/Illustrated by Ed Young
Copyright 1967
Cloth: Putnam
Paper: Sandcastle
Caldecott Honor Book

⁓ Ed Young's traditionally styled Chinese papercut illustrations and Jane Yolen's unerring knack for telling a good story make this a very special book. It is the story of Djeow Seow, a tiny Chinese princess who is always overlooked—even forgotten entirely—by her father, the emperor. When evil men imprison her father in a tower, everyone else wails and wrings their hands, but the brave little princess uses her kite to lift baskets of food to the emperor. Then Djeow Seow assembles a rope of vines and grasses strong enough for her father to climb down. He bows low before her and "never again neglected a person—whether great or small."

Eve and Her Sisters: Women of the Old Testament
Written by Yona Zeldis McDonough/Illustrated by Malka H. Zeldis
Copyright 1994
Cloth: Greenwillow

MEREDITH VIEIRA

~

ABC News Correspondent
Cohost, The View

loise was the first female hero I ever met in literature, and to this day she remains the most unforgettable. As a little girl I loved her for all the things she wasn't: she wasn't pretty, or shy, or neat, or afraid of grown-ups . . . or good, most of the time. Eloise was her own potbellied little person, and Oooooooooooooo I absolutely admired her independence. And here was a child who valued make-believe as much as I! It's funny . . . I don't remember ever finding it sad that Eloise had no father to speak of and a mother who was never there. From my vantage point—the suburban home with two parents and a picket fence—Eloise's world at the Plaza seemed incredibly exotic. I guess I just wanted to be her . . . or at least be a bit like her. Back in the fifties, girls with spunk weren't the norm in children's literature. Maybe that's why I held her so dear. Maybe that's why, when my own daughter Lily Max was born four years ago, I ran out and bought her first present: *Eloise.*

~ Although the author and illustrator concede the "patriarchal vision" of the Old Testament, they were haunted by the personal stories of women from the Bible. Here are the tales of fourteen biblical heroines. The great Deborah is a judge and warrior; Jael is a fierce defender of her people. Esther bravely unveils the secret of her heritage to her husband King Ahasuerus, pleading for the lives of

Elizabeth Dole

~

President, American Red Cross

 he heroines I enjoyed enormously as a young girl were found in the Bible stories my grandmother, Mom Cathey, read to me and my friends on Sunday afternoons. As we sat around her chair and enjoyed the lemonade and cookies she made for us, the lives of Mary, Mother of Jesus; Ruth; Esther; and Lydia came alive in the words and illustrations she shared with us. I still read and study these same heroines and their incredible example for daily living.

Jews in his kingdom. A shrewd Abigail undoes the harm caused by her husband's unguarded tongue. The vignettes are short and simple, and the bold paintings that accompany each story are arresting.

The Fantastic Drawings of Danielle
Written and Illustrated by Barbara McClintock
Copyright 1996
Cloth: Houghton Mifflin

~ Set in turn-of-the-century Paris, with the prettiest Kate Greenaway–type illustrations imaginable, this is the story of Danielle, a young artist, and her photographer father. While her father photographs street scenes, the imaginative Danielle draws fantastic animals and flowers. Her father, however, cannot make his photography pay, and when he falls ill, his determined daughter resolves to take his place. She gamely struggles with the unfamiliar, cumbersome camera. Discouraged and disheartened, she looks

ALICE S. HUANG, PH.D.

～

Dean for Science, New York University

avorite childhood books bring images of a horse named Black Beauty or wild horses on the island of Chincoteague. But a lasting impression comes not from a girls' book per se but from the Bible. When I was twelve, my father gave me my very own Holy Bible (illustrated); it was only four by six inches with its onion-thin pages edged in red and a black leather closure. In it was inscribed: May our beloved Ali "continue to increase in wisdom and stature, and in favor with God and man" Luke 2:52.

In that book, especially in the Old Testament, I found all the women that I ever wanted to emulate. Beginning with Eve so full of curiosity and thirst for knowledge, I moved on to the model of womanhood exemplified by Judith, Ruth, and Rachel. There was also the wealthy Queen of Sheba, who sought wisdom from Solomon, as well as the selfish Delilah, who betrayed Samson. And finally there was Esther, the brave woman who saved her own people. Each of these women is presented with a distinctive personality and comes through as strong, smart, and real. They were wonderful for a young girl to know. I hope that as I move on in life there will be a Ruth at my side.

up to see a painter, Madame Beton, who kindly invites her into her studio and listens to her troubles. As luck would have it, Madame Beton needs an assistant, and to the eager Danielle this is the

JUDITH JAMISON

Artistic Director,
The Alvin Ailey American Dance Theater

y favorite book is the Bible. I grew up in
Philadelphia and attended Mother Bethel, the
African Methodist Episcopal Church, the first
black church in America. I went there every Sunday from
birth until I went to college at Fisk University and that
church is the reason the Bible is such an integral part of my
life. During the week, a neighbor would hold a Bible class
and I would go with my friends and we would read and talk
about what those verses meant to us. In school, from the
time I was eight years old, I was the Bible reader at
assemblies.

All around me were Bible-reading, God-fearing people.
Everyone knew the 100th Psalm and the Lord's Prayer the
way they knew the Pledge of Allegiance. My grandfather
was a Baptist minister, and the Bible was simply part of our
general conversation. My grandmother quoted Bible verses
all the time. I remember her saying "Put on the whole armor
of God." She meant that, in the battles I would fight on this
earth, faith would be my strongest ally. I am proud to have
them as ancestors. Recently I wrote a letter to my dancers
after a tour in Zurich and I saluted them with words from
the Bible: "I lift you up." It means, I am praying for you.

I don't think of the Bible as just a book; I think of it as
the book.

FAYE WATTLETON

～

President, Center for Gender Equality

ecause I did not grow up in a family that placed a high priority on literature, my reading experiences were focused mainly on schoolwork and . . . the Bible. Within the Bible, however, are stories of inspiration, especially in the lives of the women of the Old Testament. Their belief in God, loyalty and commitment to their faith, yet independence of spirit, helped to shape the values that I hold today. Ruth and Esther were examples of such qualities.

answer to her prayers. At last she not only can help her father but can also learn what she needs to become the artist she's always dreamed of being.

Felita
Written by Nicholasa Mohr/Illustrated by Ray Cruz
Copyright 1979
Paper: Bantam/Skylark
～ Worried about the schools and safety, Felita's parents decide to move to a better neighborhood. Felita must leave her busy, vibrant street where she knows and is known by everyone. On her new street there are no Puerto Ricans. The girls who set out to befriend her are quickly curbed by their mothers; Felita and her family are shunned and tormented until they finally return to their old neighborhood.

Interspersed with this story are episodes of growing up that might be shared by any young girl. The realistic portrayal of a close-knit Puerto Rican family working to succeed sets this book apart. You'll want to catch the sequel, *Going Home*, as well.

Firetalking
Written by Patricia Polacco/Photographs by Lawrence
        Migdale
Copyright 1994
Cloth: Richard C. Owen Publishing
⌒ Patricia Polacco, author and illustrator of *Thunder Cake* (see Index) and numerous other fabulous children's books, shares here the stories behind her stories. We learn about her Ukrainian grandmother, who became the inspiration for *Rechenka's Eggs*; her favorite cat, who lives on in *Mrs. Katz and Tush*; her best friend, who's the model for the little boy in *Chicken Sunday*.

Photographs on every page help show the reader the intricate steps she takes to write and illustrate her books. Children will also be fascinated to learn how Polacco struggled in school, yet grew up to write some of their favorite stories. The title of this book comes from the happy evenings Polacco spent as a girl listening to her grandparents tell stories around the fireplace—"firetalking" her grandmother called it. Polacco says, "I am lucky . . . so very lucky! I love my life. Can you imagine doing what you love every day?"

The Four Gallant Sisters
Written by Eric A. Kimmel/Illustrated by Tatyana
        Yuditskaya
Copyright 1992
Cloth: Henry Holt
⌒ The heroines in this fairy tale are four orphaned sisters who, disguised as men, have apprenticed themselves to learn various trades so that they can make their own way in the world. After seven years of training, they are master craftspeople and easily

obtain work at court. When the prince's intended bride is captured by a dragon, the sisters boldly sail off to stage a valiant rescue. Their brave deeds earn them the open admiration of the bride's four brothers. You won't be surprised at the traditional ending that's in store, but you will be pleased by the intelligent, courageous actions of these four gallant sisters.

The Gadget War

Written by Betsy Duffey/Illustrated by Janet Wilson
Copyright 1991
Cloth: Viking Penguin
Paper: Puffin

~ Kelly Sparks is pretty cool. The third-grade kids all admire the string of endless gadgets that she creates. Each invention starts with a problem that Kelly scientifically identifies and then solves. When a new boy, Albert Einstein Jones, appears in class, Kelly immediately spots that he's going to be a competitor—and a problem. The two square off, and the gadget war begins. It quickly escalates, as Kelly's arsenal expands to include a fake pencil, a spy snooper, a slime slinger, and a food-fight catapult. Albert fights back, but peace breaks out after the two wreak havoc in the cafeteria. Good, simple fun.

Georgia O'Keeffe

Written and Illustrated by Mike Venezia
Copyright 1993
Cloth: Children's Press
Paper: Children's Press

~ Venezia has a mind that naturally understands children. In his Getting to Know the World's Greatest Artists series, he appeals to their sense of humor while making sure they absorb all the right information. He mixes his silly cartoon drawings with short, useful text and many reproductions of the artist's paintings. It's an offbeat approach that has worked in our houses with amazing success.

His *Georgia O'Keeffe* showcases many of this important twentieth-century artist's paintings. He describes her love of the desert, her use of color, her flirtation with New York City, her choice of subject. O'Keeffe was a provocative woman: "She often found beauty in things that most people would ignore or never even notice, and was able to show that beauty in her paintings."

Note: *Inspirations* (see Index), which examines the lives of four female modern artists, including O'Keeffe, will interest older readers.

A Gift for Mama
Written by Esther Hautzig/Illustrated by Donna Diamond
Copyright 1981
Cloth: Viking
Paper: Puffin

~ Don't you always tell your children that a handmade gift is the best of all? Sara's mother does, but Sara is tired of making presents. She knows exactly what she wants to buy her mother for Mother's Day: the most beautiful black satin slippers in Vilna, Poland. Resourceful Sara earns the money by mending and darning every day after school, but her mother can't hide her disappointment over a store-bought gift. Mama learns a lesson when the extent of Sara's hard work is revealed. This is a touching family story from the author of *The Endless Steppe* (see Index).

A Gift for Tia Rosa
Written by Karen T. Taha/Illustrated by Dee DeRosa
Copyright 1986
Paper: Bantam
A Reading Rainbow Book

~ Carmela has a special neighbor, Tia Rosa, who is almost a grandmother to her. Tia Rosa has taught her to knit and they have spent many happy hours together. But Tia Rosa is growing increasingly frail. After a stay in the hospital, she comes home, but is still very ill. Carmela devotes her free time to keeping Tia Rosa company. But Carmela's joy at having Tia Rosa back is short-lived.

After Tia Rosa's death, Carmela is despondent because she never had a chance to make her a gift. Her mother explains, "Tia Rosa didn't want her kindness returned. She wanted it passed on." When Tia Rosa's grandchild, Rosita, is born, Carmela realizes she has a way to give Tia Rosa a gift after all. Sweet and touching.

Gina
Written and Illustrated by Bernard Waber
Copyright 1995
Cloth: Houghton Mifflin
Paper: Houghton Mifflin

⌐ Goofy boys, roughhousing boys, boys who pay girls absolutely no attention. Everywhere Gina looks in her new apartment building, that is all she sees. What Gina is dying for is a friend and she figures there has to be a way to break into the neighborhood gang. One day she tells the doubtful boys that she'd like to play baseball, too. When they see her throw, see her bat, they all start to scream, "Come on over and play on our team." Suddenly Gina is surrounded by a horde of admiring buddies who now follow *her* lead.

Waber's kids are always believably scruffy and comic. He's chosen to tell this story in catchy verse. Sure to be a home run with your crowd.

Gina Farina and the Prince of Mintz
Written and Illustrated by Nancy Patz
Copyright 1986
Cloth: Harcourt Brace

⌐ "That girl has a mind of her own . . . and her heart's always set on adventure." Gina Farina bakes the most luscious, splendiferous pies and barters her baking skills for a chance to see the world with a group of traveling players. When they meet the cranky Prince of Mintz, Gina Farina not only boldly refuses his command to bake exclusively for him but also smartly maneuvers him into being a "happy, helpful and not at all grumpy" Prince. Stories such as this one usually end with a wedding, but here Gina Farina continues on her way, traveling back to visit her friend the Prince every seven years, a satisfying topsy-turvy ending.

Girls to the Rescue
Edited by Bruce Lansky
Copyright 1995
Paper: Meadowbrook Press

⌐ As he says in his introduction, Lansky understands that "singing 'Someday my prince will come' in the shower is a big waste of water." He has collected ten easy-to-read stories from around the world that feature bright and courageous girls. Some retell older tales, some are original, all are appealing. In a Spanish tale, Carla's father has been hoodwinked by a greedy merchant, but he's paid back in kind by clever Carla. In a Japanese story, Kimi rescues her braggart brother from an ogre. In a funny tale set in Ireland, Princess Meghan outsmarts the entire royal court.

This book will grab the attention of even the most reluctant reader. Three other volumes complete this lively set.

Gittel's Hands
Written by Erica Silverman/Illustrated by Deborah Nourse
    Lattimore
Copyright 1996
Cloth: Bridgewater Books

⌐ With its lovely Marc Chagall–like paintings, this is a Jewish variation of the Rumpelstiltskin story. Gittel is the dutiful daughter of a doting father who "boasted and bragged about her to every-

JULIA CHILD

～

Chef and Author

I read a great deal as an early teenager, but nothing that could be considered "great" books. My solo reading was mostly real trash. My mother read to us a great deal of serious stuff like *Ivanhoe* and so forth. I entertained myself with other things.

I remember one summer when I was at the Santa Barbara girls' camp called Asoleato Heehiho, the camp had a whole set of the G. Henty books—fifteen or twenty of them. I gobbled all of them, and the stories were very much the same: the hero or heroine with a wicked stepmother, who came through all kinds of trials, always suffering but doing "the right thing."

They were very satisfying to the imaginative ego, because you as a reader always won out against terrible adversity. I don't remember any details at all except that I thoroughly enjoyed them, and I wonder if they still exist.

one he met." Without consulting Gittel, he makes a deal with Reb Raya, the hay merchant, for Gittel to embroider a beautiful matzo cover from an old rag and a piece of thread, prepare a holiday feast from table scraps, and make a silver cup from a coin. Of course, poor Gittel can do none of these things. It is a gratifying moment for the reader when Gittel at last speaks up for herself and her father looks at her with a new and *real* kind of pride.

Grandma Moses: Painter of Rural America
Written by Zibby Oneal/Illustrated by Donna Ruff
Copyright 1986
Paper: Puffin

⁓ This easy-to-read biography conveys Grandma Moses's spirit loudly and clearly.

The first large picture Anna Mary Moses painted was born of necessity—she'd run out of wallpaper! Although she had loved painting as a child, the demanding pace of a farm wife, mother, and entrepreneur had left her no adult opportunity for artistic pursuits. It wasn't until she was in her seventies that she finally had the time to paint her famous primitives. Always modest, always plain speaking, she thought anyone could pick up a brush and create. "Could you sweep this floor? You could. But you'd have to get about doing it. That's how it is with paintin'." By the time of her death at age 101 she had received the acclaim of presidents and the affection of an adoring public.

Happily Ever After
Written by Anna Quindlen/Illustrated by James
        Stevenson
Copyright 1997
Cloth: Viking

⁓ Who says you have to choose between baseball and fairy tales? Not Kate! The star shortstop of the Deli Demons loves them both. When she wonders what it would be like to be a princess, Kate is startled to find herself locked in a tower, laced up in a long pink dress, with a crown slipping over her forehead and a simpering prince calling to her from below. In short order, she rescues herself from the castle, teaches a witch to sing "The Hokey Pokey," and gets a baseball game going between the ladies-in-waiting and the serving maids.

Pulitzer Prize–winning journalist Anna Quindlen has written a droll comedy, with an unflappable heroine who plays and reads "happily ever after."

Hattie and the Wild Waves
Written and Illustrated by Barbara Cooney
Copyright 1990
Cloth: Viking Penguin
Paper: Puffin

∽ Graced by the author's own elegant illustrations, this is an evocative story, set at the turn of the century, about taking yourself and your dreams seriously.

Hattie wanders along the beach at her beautiful summer home and wonders about her destiny. From her earliest days Hattie has loved to paint. As the years go by, filled with the pleasant idylls of a wealthy family, she watches her sister and brother choose their more conventional paths and finally realizes, "The time had come . . . for her to paint her heart out." An affecting book with a quiet message every child should hear.

I'm in Charge of Celebrations
Written by Byrd Baylor/Illustrated by Peter Parnall
Copyright 1986
Cloth: Atheneum
Paper: Aladdin

∽ A young girl living in the desert is astonished when people suggest she might be lonely. Lonely? How could that be? The narrator of Baylor's eloquent prose poem gives us a litany of the wonders around her and describes how she bestows every natural phenomenon with its own festival day. "Last year," she says, "I gave myself one hundred and eight celebrations—besides the ones that they close school for." There is Dust Devil Day, Coyote

Day, Time of the Falling Stars, and best of all, the New Year's party she holds on the spring morning when the cactus blooms. This imaginative book is an enriching experience for any girl.

Insects Are My Life
Written by Megan McDonald/Illustrated by Paul Brett
    Johnson
Copyright 1995
Cloth: Orchard Books
Paper: Orchard Books

⌐ The bespectacled heroine in this story, Amanda Frankenstein, is crazy about insects. She enthusiastically studies them and watches them and mimics them. Amanda knows quite a lot and plans to be an entomologist, but it's not just her passion for bugs that sets this little girl apart from the crowd. She's somebody who sticks to her guns. Whether she's being teased by her brother or her classmate nasty old Victor, Amanda knows exactly what she likes. Amanda gets a nice reward when she meets a soul mate, Maggie, who grins and says, "Reptiles are my life!"

Jamaica Louise James
Written by Amy Hest/Illustrated by Sheila White Samton
Copyright 1996
Cloth: Candlewick Press
Paper: Candlewick Press

⌐ Jamaica Louise is cool and bold and an artist to boot. Her grandmother works in the token booth at a subway station. She leaves before dawn every morning and comes back at night to tell stories about the people she's seen. On Grammy's birthday, Jamaica comes up with a *completely awesome* present that surprises Grammy and all of her subway riders. It even earns her a plaque from the mayor!

This book's bright, vibrant design has a hip, jazzy, urban feel that is totally infectious. Don't miss it!

Kate Shelley and the Midnight Express
Written by Margaret K. Wetterer/Illustrated by Karen Ritz
Copyright 1990
Cloth: Carolrhoda Books
Paper: Carolrhoda Books
A Reading Rainbow Book

⌒ This is the gripping real-life drama of Kate Shelley's daring railroad rescue. In 1881, in the midst of a raging storm, the bridge near Kate's Iowa house collapses, sending two workmen into the floodwaters. The *Midnight Express* is due to cross the bridge within an hour—unless Kate can stop it. How she crawls along the broken rails in the dark and leads the search party to the spot where the drowning men are clinging for life makes for exciting reading. Kate became a national heroine and received many honors, but she "liked the one from her railroad friends best. Whenever she rode the train home, they stopped it to let her off right in front of her own house."

Keep the Lights Burning, Abbie
Written by Peter and Connie Roop/Illustrated by Peter E. Hanson
Copyright 1985
Cloth: Carolrhoda Books
Paper: Carolrhoda Books
A Reading Rainbow Book

⌒ While her father is away on the mainland buying food and medicine, a tremendous storm lashes the Maine island where young Abbie lives. Mindful of her responsibilities, Abbie struggles for many days to take care of her sick mother and little sisters and, most important, to keep the lighthouse lamps lit. Many lives are in her hands. This simply told but dramatic, true story is a lesson in bravery and fortitude.

The King's Equal
Written by Katherine Paterson/Illustrated by Vladimir Vagin
Copyright 1992
Cloth: HarperCollins
Paper: HarperTrophy

⌐ Newbery Medal author Katherine Paterson penned this exceptional fairy tale for Vladimir Vagin, a renowned Russian artist, to illustrate. His elaborate, decorative paintings set off the court scenes of the arrogant Prince Raphael, who can never be crowned king unless he marries a woman who is his equal.

Far away in the high mountains there lives a poor young peasant, Rosamund, bravely struggling to make ends meet under the harsh taxes and edicts of the prince. A magical wolf comes to her aid and sends her to announce herself at court. When the prince sees her, he is smitten and declares Rosamund worthy to be his wife, but she calmly replies that she is "*more* than equal" to the prince. She sends Raphael off to her mountain hut for a year while she rules in his stead. Rosamund sagely undoes the damage the selfish prince had wrought, endearing herself to the people. When the chastened prince returns, his humble demeanor wins her hand at last. Full marks for this original tale and its intelligent heroine.

Koko's Story
Written by Dr. Francine Patterson/Photographs by Dr. Ronald
      H. Cohn
Copyright 1987
Paper: Scholastic

⌐ Project Koko began in 1972, when Francine Patterson began teaching Koko, a one-year-old gorilla, American Sign Language. By the time Koko was five, she could sign various sentences, including "Sorry. Need hug" and "Time quiet chase" (her phrase for hide-and-seek), as well as "Pour that hurry drink hurry." Koko could even put quarters in the soda machines at Stanford University, where she lived and worked with Dr. Patterson. Children will love reading about all of Koko's exploits and laugh at her explicit reaction to foods she doesn't like: "Dirty stink!"

The appealing photographs depict the love between Dr. Patterson and Koko as well as the serious scientific research. Animal lovers everywhere will also want to read *Koko's Kitten*.

Leah's Pony

Written by Elizabeth Friedrich/Illustrated by Michael Garland
Copyright 1996
Cloth: Boyds Mills Press

∼ How can one little girl stop the Depression from claiming her family's farm? Leah knows her papa must auction off the cattle, the chickens, the truck, and the tractor to pay the bank. But she has one thing of value she is willing to sacrifice—her pony. With the dollar she earns, Leah goes to the auction and bids on the tractor. In a tender and dramatic scene, the neighbors fall silent. Indeed, they close ranks around her so that the tractor can be hers.

Her generous act sparks a chain reaction. The family's belongings are all bought for pennies by their friends and returned to Leah and her parents.

This is a lovely story showing that even a little girl can make a difference. The handsome oil paintings set off the text with distinction.

Least of All

Written by Carol Purdy/Illustrated by Tim Arnold
Copyright 1993
Paper: Aladdin

∼ Is Raven Hannah really too little? Too little to hold the horse's reins on the way home from church? Too little to carry the milk pails? Too little to stack the wood? Sometimes it seems that's all anybody says. At last, Raven Hannah is given a real job—to churn the butter. While she works at this lonely chore, Raven holds a Bible on her lap and teaches herself to read. At Christmas, her family is overcome with emotion when Raven reads the Nativity story aloud to them, for no one else in her family has ever learned to read. Everyone, especially Raven, knows that she is not too little anymore.

Lilly's Purple Plastic Purse
Written and Illustrated by Kevin Henkes
Copyright 1996
Cloth: Greenwillow
ALA Notable Book

⌒ Lilly adores school. She loves everything about it, especially her wonderful teacher, Mr. Slinger. Lilly hangs on his every word and announces that she plans to be a teacher when she grows up. However, when Lilly brings her brand-new purple plastic purse to school, she cannot restrain herself from opening and closing and rattling and waving it about her. And Mr. Slinger is not amused.

This exuberantly illustrated book is a delight to read. Young schoolchildren know just how Lilly feels and don't mind at all learning a subtle lesson in manners. Henkes triumphs again!

Lily and Miss Liberty
Written by Carla Stevens/Illustrated by Deborah Kogan Ray
Copyright 1992
Paper: Little Apple

⌒ All the schoolchildren in Lily's class are raising money to pay for the pedestal of the Statue of Liberty. Lily's immigrant family is very poor and cannot give her anything, but Lily refuses to be left out of this patriotic effort. She must come up with a way to help! With a burst of inspiration, Lily designs paper crowns to look like the one of Miss Liberty and, like a true entrepreneur, sells enough so that she feels she has made a real contribution. Directions for making Lily's crowns are included.

Little House in the Big Woods
Written by Laura Ingalls Wilder/Illustrated by Garth
 Williams
Copyright 1932
Cloth: HarperCollins
Paper: HarperTrophy

～ This is the first book in the series that takes Laura from a five-year-old in the Wisconsin woods to a young bride in South Dakota. There are nine titles in all. As Laura grows up, the books grow with her so that the later books may be more suitable for older readers.

There are exquisite details of the day-to-day life of a pioneer family: how Ma and Pa fought a grass fire or how Pa and Laura hung a door in their log cabin. Laura seems to have remembered

CHERYL TIEGS

～

Model, Designer, Businesswoman

 very summer I would go to the library and check out the Little House series. I was fascinated with how they lived "at one" with nature. This by no means made their lives easy . . . but it meant they had to focus on their priorities. This value of being in touch with your surroundings and being self-reliant has stayed with me all my life. I just finished reading it to my young son.

everything about her amazing childhood: the songs Pa played on the fiddle, the Indians on the prairie, the grasshoppers that destroyed their crops, the long winter that nearly starved them out.

You simply can't read these books often enough. As little girls we were all absorbed in Laura's story. Coming back to this as mothers, we had a new admiration for Ma's fortitude, her strength, and especially her ability to raise four self-reliant daughters who never flinched at misfortune.

The Ingalls family saga is an incredible document of American history. The astonishing aspect, the heart of these books, is how the family endures and surmounts what sometimes seems to be relentless hardship. Laura's affectionate memoir is nothing less than inspirational.

The Little Riders

Written by Margaretha Shemin/Illustrated by Peter Spier
Copyright 1963, 1988
Paper: Beech Tree Books

⌒ Like the little mounted soldiers that grace the church steeple in her Dutch town, Johanna is a fighter. The Nazis who occupy her village want to melt down the little riders for bullets, but Johanna and her grandparents rescue the figurines for safekeeping. When the Nazis begin a search for them, Johanna makes a desperate attempt to hide her beloved statues. She finds help from a most unexpected quarter. This is a fast-paced, heart-stopping read, and Johanna is a quick-witted and sensitive heroine.

Little Sure Shot: The Story of Annie Oakley

Written by Stephanie Spinner/Illustrated by Jose Miralles
Copyright 1993
Paper: Random House

⌒ Contrary to the Irving Berlin musical, Annie Oakley never threw a match in her life. Certainly not to get a man! In fact,

Annie's shooting ability *impressed* Frank Butler, and they seem to have made their marriage a true partnership.

Born in 1860, it was hunger that first drove Annie to learn how to shoot. Her family needed food and nine-year-old Annie picked up the rifle to hunt. Soon she was regularly supplying her family and local restaurants with game. After an older sister invited her to move to Cincinnati, Annie practiced in the shooting galleries, then entered a contest against expert marksman Frank Butler. They successfully teamed up—as performers and as husband and wife. Annie's fame in particular kept growing until she became the star attraction of Buffalo Bill's Wild West Show. Lots of lively descriptions of her stunts make this crackerjack reading for any kid.

Mae Jemison: Space Scientist
Written by Gail Sakurai
Copyright 1995
Cloth: Children's Press
Paper: Children's Press

⌒ When Mae Jemison announced to her kindergarten teacher that her ambition was to be a scientist, the teacher condescendingly replied, "Don't you mean a nurse?" As Jemison tells people now, "Don't be limited by others' limited imaginations." She certainly wasn't!

When the shuttle *Endeavour* orbited Earth in September 1992, Mae Jemison became the first African-American woman in space. Her resume already included an undergraduate degree from Stanford, a medical degree from Cornell, two years in the Peace Corps, and a medical practice in Los Angeles. One of fifteen chosen by NASA (out of a pool of two thousand!), Jemison underwent the rigorous training necessary to become an astronaut. On board the *Endeavour*, she conducted numerous experiments that would expand our knowledge of space travel. The many photographs feature Jemison hard at work. Inspiring.

Mandy
Written by Barbara D. Booth/Illustrated by Jim
   LaMarche
Copyright 1991
Cloth: Lothrop, Lee & Shepard

⟶ Because she is deaf, dark nights are the scariest times for Mandy. The dark makes her feel so alone and vulnerable. She can't sign to her friends, she can't read anyone's lips, she can't hear people approaching. But when Grandma loses her cherished silver brooch in the woods, Mandy determines that not even her fear of the nighttime will stop her from searching for it. She slips out of the house without letting Grandma know. Lightning flashes and wind whips the trees, but Mandy presses on. The expressive illustrations are by renowned artist Jim LaMarche.

Marie Curie: Brave Scientist
Written by Keith Brandt/Illustrated by Karen Dugan
Copyright 1983
Paper: Troll Associates

⟶ Brandt does a splendid job of bringing the childhood of Marie Sklowdowska alive for today's young readers. Marie's family struggled against increasing poverty and devastating illness, but nothing could extinguish Marie's insatiable desire to learn. She would become so engrossed in her studies that she could not be distracted—as an adult, Marie liked to tell the story of how her brothers and sisters stacked a pyramid of chairs behind her as she read. Marie never noticed a thing until she stood up and the chairs crashed around her!

When the time finally came for Marie to attend university, Poland's schools were closed to women. She and her sister Bronya devised a plan whereby Bronya would study at the Sorbonne while Marie worked to support her. Bronya would then pay for Marie to go to Paris and begin her work. First in her class in physics and second in her class in mathematics, Marie determined to find a life in science.

Children are fascinated by her incredible story. Older readers will find more detail in *Marie Curie and the Discovery of Radium* (see Index).

Martha Speaks

Written and Illustrated by Susan Meddaugh
Copyright 1992
Cloth: Houghton Mifflin
Paper: Houghton Mifflin
New York Times Best Illustrated Children's Book
ALA Notable Book
A Reading Rainbow Book

⌒ It is impossible to say which is our favorite Martha book— *Martha Speaks* or one of the sequels, *Martha Calling* (copyright 1994) and *Martha Blah Blah* (copyright 1996). Whether or not you have a beloved canine companion in your life, we think you'll agree that these books provide nonstop belly laughs. When Martha's owners feed her a bowl of alphabet soup, the letters float up to her brain, and—presto!—Martha talks. Unfortunately, she doesn't stop. "You people are so bossy. Come! Sit! Stay! You never say please. . . . Yo, Rinty! Good dog. How's the flea problem? . . . I've seen this program. Want me to tell you what happens?" Naturally, this rather gets on her family's nerves. Martha is so insulted that she won't speak to them, but when a burglar comes to the house and gives her some alphabet soup to keep her quiet, Martha snaps into action and saves the day.

In *Martha Calling*, Martha wins a telephone contest with totally loony results. In *Martha Blah Blah* she loses her ability to speak when the soup company decides to save money by taking the letter *a* out of its alphabet soup. As you know by now, we are serious Meddaugh fans. Her work is consistently good-hearted with a high degree of the ludicrous. Treat yourself and your children!

Mary Cassatt
Written and Illustrated by Mike Venezia
Copyright 1993
Cloth: Children's Press
Paper: Children's Press

⌒ Here's another title in the successful *Getting to Know the World's Greatest Artists* series (see Georgia O'Keeffe earlier in this chapter). Venezia is back with more of his special brand of art and giggles. In a brief sketch of Mary Cassatt's life, punctuated with the author's signature comic asides and illustrated with eighteen reproductions of her work, the reader learns that Cassatt was an unconventional girl, who defied parental authority to become a painter. After forming a firm friendship with Degas and experimenting with techniques to create beautiful pastel colors, she went on to be recognized as America's premier Impressionist painter. Her talent for making "ordinary, everyday scenes important" is Cassatt's special legacy.

Mary McLeod Bethune
Written by Patricia and Fred McKissack
Copyright 1992
Cloth: Children's Press
Paper: Children's Press

⌒ Mary McLeod Bethune was her parents' fifteenth child but their first to be free-born and the first in her family to be educated. The fruits of her learning became evident when the cotton clerk finally had to stop cheating her father because Mary could read the scales. From there her accomplishments were astounding.

In 1904 she opened a school for African-American girls that stands today as Bethune-Cookman College; she served on the National Child Welfare Commission for President Hoover; she was a friend and adviser to President Roosevelt, acting as his director of the newly created Office of Minority Affairs; she helped integrate Johns Hopkins Hospital; and she was part of Mrs. Roosevelt's team that wrote the UN charter. Truly a woman to be honored, she never failed to exhort young women to reach for the stars. This biography, filled with photographs, does Bethune justice.

Master Maid: A Tale of Norway
Written by Aaron Shepard/Illustrated by Pauline Ellison
Copyright 1997
Cloth: Dial Books for Young Readers

〜 Leif is a know-it-all young man who spurns everyone's advice. Ignoring the dire warnings of his father, he insists on hiring himself out to a nasty troll and lands himself in big trouble. The work looks easy, and Leif is blithely sure he can handle it. The troll's capable Master Maid knows better, though, and generously tells Leif the secret tricks to getting these jobs done. Nevertheless, each time, Leif brashly thinks that he knows best and tries to complete the job his way. Of course he can't, and each time he has to admit the Master Maid was right. When the troll decides that Leif is ready to be chopped up for stew, it is the Master Maid who speedily arranges their narrow escape. A wedding follows, but when she is asked if she will love, honor, and obey, Leif smartly interjects, "Never mind that! It's best if *I* obey *her*." Lively illustrations accompany this fresh retelling of a Norwegian folktale.

Mieko and the Fifth Treasure
Written by Eleanor Coerr
Copyright 1993
Cloth: Putnam
Paper: Yearling

〜 Five treasures are required to paint Japanese word pictures: a fine sable brush, an inkstick, an inkstone, a roll of rice paper, and beauty in the heart.

After the bomb drops on Nagasaki, Mieko's hand is badly scarred. Full of hate, she fears she has lost the fifth treasure forever. Her parents send her to live on her grandparents' farm so that she can heal physically and spiritually. Mieko is withdrawn and unhappy until her friendship with another little girl, Yoshi, gives her the confidence to enter a calligraphy contest. Her new friendship has crowded out the hatred in her heart so that once again her brush strokes fly over the rice paper. Sensitively written, this is a fine introduction to a difficult subject.

Mirette on the High Wire
Written and Illustrated by Emily Arnold McCully
Copyright 1992
Cloth: Putnam
Paper: Putnam
Caldecott Medal
New York Times Best Illustrated Children's Book
A Reading Rainbow Book
～ This is for the daredevil in every girl! Bellini, the famous tightrope walker who crossed Niagara Falls, stopping midwire to cook an omelet, has come to live at Mirette's mother's boarding-house in Paris. When Mirette discovers who he is, she insists on learning his amazing tricks. But Bellini has a shameful secret—he has lost his nerve. In a riveting climax, it is Mirette who vanquishes his fear. Persistence and bravery are the winning themes of this book. We also loved its Toulouse-Lautrec–style illustrations.

Mischievous Meg
Written by Astrid Lindgren/Illustrated by Janina Domanska
Copyright 1960
Cloth: Viking
Paper: Puffin
～ Meg doesn't know the meaning of the word *bored*. She's forever thinking up exciting "pretends" that keep her and her sister,

Betsy, busily occupied and often in trouble. The river on their Swedish farm becomes the Nile; the roof of their woodshed becomes a mountain for a picnic; the well becomes the perfect place to play Joseph and his brothers. You'll chuckle again and again at the messes Meg gets herself into. Her high spirits are never dampened for long, though. She's back in the next chapter, ready for more. Written with a keen awareness of how children really behave, this is an old-fashioned, delightful read from the fertile imagination that brought us *Pippi Longstocking*.

Miss Rumphius
Written and Illustrated by Barbara Cooney
Copyright 1982
Cloth: Viking Kestrel
Paper: Puffin
American Book Award
New York Times Best Book of the Year

⌒ As a little girl, Alice Rumphius wants to emulate her grandfather. She, too, will travel to faraway places and live by the sea. He tells her that is good but not enough. She must also do something to make the world more beautiful. What that might be Alice can't imagine, but she promises her grandfather anyway.

Near the end of her long, interesting life, Alice has kept all the promises she made so long ago. Now she turns to her grandniece and reminds her that she, too, must do something to make the world more beautiful.

This is a wonderfully illustrated story of advice lovingly given and received, handed down through generations. Wouldn't it be nice if everyone had a Great-Aunt Alice?

Molly the Brave and Me
Written by Jane O'Connor/Illustrated by Sheila Hamanaka
Copyright 1990
Paper: Random House

⌒ When our girls started to read on their own, we were always scrambling to find easy-to-read books that featured girls. This title, with "real chapters," made our kids feel grown up and proved very popular. The simple story focuses on a familiar second-grade scenario: that scary first sleepover. Beth's friend Molly sure seems fearless, and Beth is nervous that if she sleeps over Molly will find out how timid Beth really is. Fortunately, things have a way of working out, and Beth discovers she really is a "kid with guts!" A satisfying title from the Step into Reading series.

Molly's Pilgrim

Written by Barbara Cohen/Illustrated by Michael J. Deraney
Copyright 1983
Cloth: Lothrop, Lee & Shepard
Paper: Yearling
A Reading Rainbow Book

⌒ As Molly's narrow-minded classmates learn in this eloquently written story, America's pilgrims are still coming to our shores.

When the teacher asks that each child bring in a Pilgrim or Indian doll for the Plymouth Plantation model they are building in class, Molly anxiously seeks help from her mother. Molly's never heard of Thanksgiving, but as she tries to explain it to her mother, her mother's face lights up in recognition. They have just come from Russia to escape the Cossacks who burned their synagogue. They are pilgrims, too!

This is one of the best books about understanding and acceptance that we've come across. If you can find it at your library, there is a lovely video too.

Mufaro's Beautiful Daughters

Written and Illustrated by John Steptoe
Copyright 1987
Cloth: Lothrop, Lee & Shepard

Paper: Mulberry Books
Caldecott Honor Book
Boston Globe–Horn Book Award
Coretta Scott King Award
A Reading Rainbow Book

~ Set in Africa, this is a retelling of a Zimbabwe folktale about two sisters and their rivalry and how generosity and kindness always triumph. Manyara's puffed-up pride leads to her downfall: she ends up as the servant to her laudable sister, the queen. A pleasing and worthy fable with lush, rich illustrations that are a feast for the eyes.

Muggie Maggie

Written by Beverly Cleary/Illustrated by Kay Life
Copyright 1990
Cloth: William Morrow
Paper: Avon

~ Maggie stages a small rebellion in third grade when she refuses to learn to write in cursive. Why should she? She can use the computer or she can print. What's the big deal? But her rebellion begins to box her in when she can't read what's on the board or what's in the notes she's carrying as message monitor. She begins to secretly study cursive. When she peeks at the notes, she's amazed to discover they're all about her! A stubborn girl and a supportive teacher come together in a most satisfying conclusion. Of course, there are lots of trademark Cleary chuckles along the way. A perfect early chapter book.

My Grandmother's Journey

Written by John Cech/Illustrated by Sharon
        McGinley-Nally
Copyright 1991
Cloth: Simon & Schuster
Paper: Aladdin

～ Gramma tells her granddaughter, Korie, that her life's story is "a tale full of twists and turns like a path through the woods." During the Russian Revolution, Gramma lost her father, mother, and three brothers. She and her husband lost their house, land, and all their belongings. They lived on the run, working and sleeping where they could. World War II brought further hardships—and one miracle. Korie's mother was born in a forest, and when strangers saw her their hearts softened. With their baby, their "gift of hope," they finally made their way to freedom. The harsh realities of Gramma's life are offset by Gramma's warm tone as well as the joyous and buoyant illustrations. A touching tribute to a real-life grandmother.

My Name Is Maria Isabel

Written by Alma Flor Ada/Illustrated by K. Dyble Thompson
Copyright 1993
Cloth: Atheneum
Paper: Aladdin

～ When Maria Isabel's thoughtless teacher discovers she has two Marias in her classroom, she fixes on a simple solution. Maria Isabel can just become "Mary." That's convenient for the teacher but heartbreaking to Maria Isabel. She loves her name, Maria Isabel Salazar Lopez, because it connects her to her adored grandparents. She's lost without it. When the teacher assigns an essay called "My Greatest Wish," Maria Isabel seizes the chance to tell her teacher just how she feels. Children will sympathize with the heroine in this gracefully written story.

Nadia the Willful

Written by Sue Alexander/Illustrated by Lloyd Bloom
Copyright 1983
Cloth: Alfred A. Knopf

～ When Hamed, Nadia's beloved older brother, is lost in the desert, he is mourned by everyone in their bedouin tribe. But

Nadia's father is so overcome with his grief that he forbids Hamed's name to be spoken ever again.

Nadia, whose reputation as a stubborn and easily angered girl has earned her the nickname Nadia the Willful, chafes under this strict rule. She misses her brother so much that she can't help telling stories about him. It is the only way she knows to console herself. In the end she is able to bring this comfort to her father, who renicknames her Nadia the Wise.

We liked this title so much that we included it despite its being out of print. We had no trouble finding it on library shelves though, and wish you the same luck.

Nobody Owns the Sky: The Story of "Brave Bessie" Coleman

Written by Reeve Lindbergh/Illustrated by Pamela Paparone
Copyright 1996
Cloth: Candlewick Press
Paper: Candlewick Press

~ The author, daughter of Anne Morrow and Charles Lindbergh, had never heard of the first African-American aviator, Bessie Coleman, until 1987, on the anniversary of her father's flight. She writes that, "Bessie was an incredibly brave person who was hardly noticed, while my parents got so much publicity that it was difficult for them to live their normal lives. I saw a crazy imbalance and wanted to set things right." She does so with this book, told in verse. Bessie's dreams of flying began as a child in the Texas cotton fields where she worked. People mocked her ambitions because she was the wrong gender and the wrong race. But Bessie never listened to the naysayers. An inspirational story, nicely illustrated, of a girl who let nothing stop her.

Nothing Ever Happens on 90th Street

Written by Roni Schotter/Illustrated by Kyrsten Brooker
Copyright 1997

Cloth: Orchard Books

⌒ Eva is stuck on the stoop, looking at her empty assignment book, wondering how she can possibly fill it by "writing about what you know." After all, *nothing* ever happens on 90th Street! Each of Eva's eccentric neighbors has a bit of useful advice to offer and Eva starts to work through her writer's block. When the quiet street suddenly erupts with farcical action, Eva eagerly scribbles her eyewitness account into her journal. When calm prevails again, the neighbors lament, "If only someone had written it all down." "I did," Eva pipes up, "But just wait. It'll be even better . . . after I rewrite it."

Full of slapstick humor, zany illustrations, and unstudied counsel, this is a frolicsome read for any budding author.

Now I Will Never Leave the Dinner Table
Written by Jane Read Martin and Patricia Marx/Illustrated by
    Roz Chast
Copyright 1996
Cloth: HarperCollins

⌒ The two authors, who have written for "Saturday Night Live," have teamed up with matchless New Yorker cartoonist Roz Chast to produce a scathingly funny book about sibling rivalry. Patty Jane Pepper has decided to stay at the dinner table forever because her bossy sister, Joy, who is babysitting her, won't let Patty Jane leave until she has eaten her spinach. Patty Jane thinks Joy is a drip. Unlike Patty Jane, Joy does not like to do spider art and does not like mud. Will Patty Jane grow old at the table? Tune in tomorrow for Patty Jane's inventive, offbeat solution.

The first book about Patty Jane and Joy, *Now Everybody Really Hates Me*, is every bit as entertaining.

The Old Woman Who Named Things
Written by Cynthia Rylant/Illustrated by Kathryn Brown
Copyright 1996

Cloth: Harcourt Brace & Company

⌒ An unconventional offering from a talented writer, this book is about taking risks—no matter what your age.

Once there was an old woman, a very lonely old woman who had outlived everyone she knew. Because it hurt so much to lose them, she had cut herself off from making new friends. To pretend that she has company, she names the things around her: her car is Betsy; her chair is Fred; her bed is Roxanne. When a shy, brown puppy appears at her gate, the old woman begins feeding him, but refuses to name him. One day the puppy doesn't show up. The old woman finds herself worried and anxious over his whereabouts. Ultimately, she decides to come out of her shell to find the puppy and to give him a name—Lucky—in honor of "how lucky she had been to have known" her "old, dear friends." Off-beat and thought provoking.

On the Pampas
Written and Illustrated by Maria Cristina Brusca
Copyright 1991
Cloth: Henry Holt
Paper: Owlet

⌒ An idyllic rendering of a young girl's summer, this loving memoir is filled with the bustling activities of her grandparents' Argentinean *estancia*. The lucky narrator and her adventurous cousin Susanita have the run of the great ranch, galloping on their ponies, learning to lasso, branding the cattle, hunting for the huge *nandu* eggs. They have a heyday learning to be gauchos. The bright, festive watercolors highlight the holiday mood. All in all, this book portrays a summer to envy.

One Morning in Maine
Written and Illustrated by Robert McCloskey
Copyright 1952
Cloth: Viking Kestrel

Paper: Puffin

⌒ By sticking to a child's-eye view of life, this classic book, in its umpteenth printing, has won many fans. The simple story revolves around Sal, a little girl with a very wiggly tooth. After it falls out, she races down the beach to show her father. To her great consternation, she drops the tooth, and neither she nor her father can find it. How will Sal ever be able to make a wish without her tooth? Sal takes a gamble that, since seagulls lose their feathers the way children lose their teeth, a wish on a feather might do the trick. A particular hit with five- and six-year-olds, McCloskey's benevolent world beckons readers again and again.

Only Opal: The Diary of a Young Girl

Portions Selected from Diary by Jane Boulton/Illustrated by
    Barbara Cooney
Copyright 1994
Cloth: Philomel Books
Paper: PaperStar

⌒ A reader can only marvel at the real-life story of Opal White-ley and hope that she has even one-tenth of Opal's inner resources. In 1905, when she was just five, Opal's parents died and she went to live with an Oregon family. Opal started her diary then, on the backs of envelopes given to her by a neighbor. She kept it up through the nineteen different lumber camps she lived in, and she held on to the scraps that remained after her foster sister tore the diary into pieces. When she was twenty, Opal took them to an editor, and in 1920 her diary was published. It caused an overnight sensation.

Opal's poignant words are extraordinary. She doesn't shirk from describing her bleak, lonely life, and yet that is not what the reader remembers. Opal's gift was to find an innocent joy in nature and to write movingly about it. She carries a mouse in her pocket that she calls Felix Mendelssohn, she names the cow Elizabeth Barrett Browning, and she christens the pig who follows her to school

Joan Benoit Samuelson

*Women's Marathon Gold Medalist
1984 Olympics, Los Angeles
Women's Winner, Boston Marathon, 1979, 1983*

 would have to say that my favorite book as a child was *One Morning in Maine* by Robert McCloskey. Just the other morning, our son came into our bedroom to ask if I would read his favorite book. *One Morning in Maine* was in his hands.

One Morning in Maine is about two sisters, Sal and Jane. It is more about Sal than Jane. Sal and Jane grow up on the coast of Maine with their parents. Sal loses her tooth in the clam flats while showing her father her loose tooth (Sal's father is digging clams at the time). Needless to say, Sal is growing up.

Sal has a real zest for life and a love for nature and the outdoors. Her healthy outlook on life is refreshing, and her positive attitude is contagious. Her energy seems limitless and inspirational. I have always been able to relate to Sal's affinity for the Maine lifestyle. I now realize how blessed I am to live in Maine and to be able to raise a family here.

Other favorite books include *Pippi Longstocking, Mrs. Piggle-Wiggle,* and *Madeline.* All of these girls/women have a real sense of being and love for adventure. They are very independent and creative in their thinking. Their concern and appreciation for those around them is very evident in the way they interact and touch the lives of others.

Peter Paul Rubens. "When I feel sad inside I talk things over with my tree. I call him Michael Raphael. It is such a comfort to nestle up to Michael Raphael. He is a grand tree. He has an understanding soul." Touching and mystical, this is the kind of book that leads to great discussions.

There is a complete version of the diary called *Opal: The Journey of an Understanding Heart* (Crown) that is suitable for older readers.

Phoebe the Spy
Written by Judith Berry Griffin/Illustrated by Margot Tomes
Copyright 1977
Paper: Scholastic

⁓ It's easy to dismiss Fraunces Tavern as "just one of those places where George Washington slept." Until, that is, you know the true story of a very courageous little girl connected with this historic site that still stands near the southern tip of Manhattan Island.

In 1776, Samuel Fraunces owned what was then called the Queen's Head Tavern. Samuel and his thirteen-year-old daughter, Phoebe, were among the few free African-Americans in the colonies. Loyal to the Revolutionary cause, Samuel suspects a plot against General Washington's life, but knows no details. To discover the traitor, he sends Phoebe to work as the housekeeper in Washington's New York headquarters. Fortunately, Phoebe's sharp eyes don't miss a thing—we all have a lot to thank her for.

A Picture Book of Florence Nightingale
Written by David A. Adler/Illustrated by John and
        Alexandra Wallner
Copyright 1992
Cloth: Holiday House
Paper: Holiday House

⌒ Informative and easy to read, Adler's popular picture books fill a niche for the beginning reader. Until your child is ready for the more in-depth biographies and autobiographies we've recommended in our older categories, these are one good place to start. The series includes heroines such as Anne Frank, Helen Keller, Rosa Parks, Eleanor Roosevelt, Sojourner Truth, and Harriet Tubman. This entry is a fine introduction to the remarkable woman who revolutionized nursing.

Born into a wealthy family, Florence Nightingale wanted no part of the easy life she could have inherited. She felt a calling to serve. After much quarreling, her parents gave in to Florence's insistence that she train to be a nurse. When the Crimean War broke out in 1854, Florence sailed to Turkey with a group of nurses under her charge. She spent her nights walking through the wards with her lantern, checking on her patients. The grateful soldiers nicknamed her "The Lady with the Lamp." The indomitable Nightingale went on to institute nurses' training and spearhead hospital reform.

Pink Paper Swans
Written by Virginia Kroll/Illustrated by Nancy L. Clouse
Copyright 1994
Cloth: William B. Eerdmans

⌒ Color collages dance their way across the pages of this beautiful book. During the long, hot city summer, Janetta, a lively little African-American girl, sits outside her apartment building and watches her neighbor, Mrs. Tsujimoto, create her origami menagerie. Janetta is fascinated by this magic art and thrilled when Mrs. Tsujimoto makes a paper swan just for her. But the next summer Mrs. Tsujimoto fails to appear on the stoop. A worried Janetta knocks on the door to find out if she's all right and discovers that arthritis is making it impossible for Mrs. Tsujimoto to fold her paper and keep her livelihood. Janetta sizes up the situation and tells her, "You be the mind. I'll be the fingers." The wonderful partnership that blossoms leaves you feeling good all over.

Pond Year
Written by Kathryn Lasky/Illustrated by Mike Bostock
Copyright 1995
Cloth: Candlewick Press
Paper: Candlewick Press
⌐ Messing in the muck of a nearby pond is the most fun these two six-year-old "scum chums" can imagine. Each season is special. In the spring they build twig rafts and catch tadpoles. During the summer, they race crawdaddies and swear eternal allegiance as pond buddies. In September they look for muskrats, and in the winter they ice-skate over the sleeping pond. *Pond Year*'s great watercolors and terrific text buzz with the exuberance of these little scientists.

The Princess and the Admiral
Written by Charlotte Pomerantz/Illustrated by Tony Chen
Copyright 1974
Paper: Feminist Press
Jane Addams Children's Book Award
⌐ On the eve of her country's celebration of a hundred years of peace, savvy Princess Mat-Mat learns that a fleet of warships is about to descend on her defenseless Tiny Kingdom. Her advisers are despairing. But the ingenious princess concocts an original plan to trap the enemy in the mouth of the riverbed.

Their admiral is completely humiliated, especially when he realizes he's been done in by a mere girl! However, Princess Mat-Mat is as magnanimous in victory as she has been shrewd in strategy. She has the admiral conducted safely back to his emperor but extracts a promise that he will not "make unkind remarks about women and girls." An exemplary leader and an entertaining feminist tale.

DR. SYLVIA A. EARLE

~

Marine Biologist
Former Chief Scientist, National Oceanographic
and Atmospheric Association
Director, Deep Ocean
Exploration and Research, Inc.

 nimal stories won my heart early on. I befriended all of the dogs in Albert Payson Terhune stories, tracked along wooded pathways with Ernest Thomas Seton, and late at night when I was supposed to be sleeping, with a flashlight creating a glowing haven under my bedcovers, read *Black Beauty* and all the books about birds and trees and fish that I could find on our bookshelf at home and the school library. I devoured encyclopedias! I so loved nonfiction that it took many years for me to warm up to the idea that great truths can be conveyed by telling great stories. Years later, when I began writing books and stories myself, I hoped that kids would read them and want to take care of wilderness and wildlife just as I was inspired to do when I read tales by explorers such as William Beebe (*Half Mile Down, Arcturus Adventure, Log of the Sun*) and later Hans Hass (*Diving to Adventure*) and Jacques Cousteau (*The Silent World, The Living Sea*).

The Princess and the Lord of Night
Written by Emma Bull/Illustrated by Susan Gaber
Copyright 1994
Cloth: Harcourt Brace & Company

⌐ A princess who gets everything she wants . . . Sounds like a dream come true, right? Not for this princess. She's been cursed by the Lord of Night, who has decreed that if ever she wanted something she couldn't have, the king and queen would die and the kingdom would be shattered. On her thirteenth birthday, she wakes up knowing what she really wants and knowing that she will have to get it for herself. Thus begins her magical journey to shed the evil enchantment. Her generosity along the way repays itself when she finally confronts the Lord of Night. This original fairy tale, with its intelligent heroine, is complemented by resplendent illustrations.

Princess Florecita and the Iron Shoes
Written by John Warren Stewig/Illustrated by K. Wendy Popp
Copyright 1995
Cloth: Alfred A. Knopf

⌐ Stunningly illustrated, this is a Spanish fairy tale that turns "Sleeping Beauty" upside down. Princess Florecita hears a bird singing of a bewitched sleeping prince and cannot rest until she has rescued him. Her arduous journey through dense forests and across snowy mountains shows her to be a princess of uncommon strength and courage. A welcome change from the usual hackneyed princess role!

Princess Furball
Written by Charlotte Huck/Illustrated by Anita Lobel
Copyright 1989
Cloth: William Morrow
Paper: Mulberry Books

～ This is a retelling of the Cinderella story with a much more resourceful princess at the center! When the king promises her hand in marriage to an ogre, the princess stalls him by demanding three dresses, one as golden as the sun, one as silvery as the moon, another as glittering as the stars. In addition, she needs a coat made of a thousand different kinds of fur. When the king actually has these gifts made, the princess has no choice but to run away. How she adroitly uses these items to her advantage makes very enjoyable reading.

Princess Prunella and the Purple Peanut
Written by Margaret Atwood/Illustrated by Maryann
     Kovalski
Copyright 1995
Cloth: Workman

～ For pure read-aloud pleasure, it is hard to top this book by the noted adult author Margaret Atwood. This is an alliterative tale of a proud and prissy princess who thinks she is perfect. She gets her comeuppance, learns her lesson on the perils of pride, and becomes praiseworthy. Everyone has a grand time perusing these pages!

The Rag Coat
Written and Illustrated by Lauren Mills
Copyright 1991
Cloth: Little Brown & Co.

～ Minna's father is a coal miner in Appalachia. When he dies, there is so little money that Minna can't buy a coat for school. To make ends meet, her mama and her friends make quilts. While they are working on a pattern called Joseph's Coat of Many Colors, Minna reveals that she wishes she had such a coat. The "Quilting Mothers" never hesitate; they dig into their ragbags and quilt her one.

SARA LEVINSON

～

President,
National Football League Properties, Inc.

I always loved fairy tales. Fairy tales were a great way for me to transport myself to another time and place. And, growing up with four brothers and sisters, this escape was something I truly treasured!

I remember the giant *Grimm's Fairy Tales* book that adorned the bookshelf in my bedroom. My favorite fairy tale was the "Princess and the Pea." Although this tale may be considered "politically incorrect" in today's society—back then it was all that I could dream of.

As I was a light sleeper, I always related to the Princess's dilemma. I always hoped that this would one day happen to me. I remember putting various objects under my mattress at night and hoping for a more restless night than usual. I wanted to prove to my twin brothers that I was a Princess. My older sister would swear that she saw me up all night. We both wanted to convince my brothers that I was a Princess.

Unfortunately, they always claimed that they heard me snoring. Of course, I was not convinced of this. How could I, a Princess, snore? Impossible! So, my two very snide brothers placed a tape recorder under my bed one night.

Well, they were proven right. I snored. Despite what my brothers uncovered that night, I have and always will believe in Princesses.

When her coat is finally finished, Minna proudly shows it off at Sharing Day. The reaction from her classmates is not what she'd hoped for, until she explains how each scrap has a special story behind it. Beautiful watercolors help tell this beautiful tale of cooperation.

The Rajah's Rice: A Mathematical Folktale from India

Adapted by David Barry/Illustrated by Donna
  Perrone
Copyright 1994
Cloth: W. H. Freeman & Co.

〜 "Powers of two, as mathematicians call doubling, are very powerful indeed. Taking the number 2 and doubling it 64 times (the number of squares on a chessboard) results in the number 18,446,744,073,709,551,616, enough grains of rice to fill the great volcano, Mt. Kilimanjaro."

Who understands this? Not the rajah, and not the villagers. Chandra does. When the rajah offers her any reward she chooses for healing his sick elephants, wise Chandra merely asks that he place two little grains of rice on a chessboard and then double that amount for every square. The rajah smirks at such a foolish request. At the end of the first row, Chandra has one teaspoon of rice; at the end of the second row, she has one bowl; at the middle of the fifth row, she has nearly a palace full of rice, and the rajah's storehouses are empty.

You don't run across mathematically savvy heroines every day. Chandra's unusual story is told nicely, and the vivid folk art illustrations show off the Indian setting. Well done!

Ramona the Pest

Written by Beverly Cleary/Illustrated by Louis Darling
Copyright 1968

Cloth: William Morrow

Paper: Camelot

⌐ "She was not a slow-poke grownup. She was a girl who could not wait. Life was so interesting she had to find out what happened next."

Irrepressible Ramona has been charming children for three decades. This is the first of the five tip-top Ramona titles. (The others are *Ramona and Her Mother, Ramona and Her Father, Beezus and Ramona,* and *Ramona Quimby, Age 8.*) She's off to her first day of kindergarten, where she is enchanted by her pretty teacher, Miss Binney, and sits glued to her seat because Miss Binney told her to "sit here for the present." She sits and sits, waiting for that present. Older children collapse into giggles not only because they get the joke but also because they recognize themselves.

MURIEL SIEBERT

⌐

President and Chairwoman,
Muriel Siebert & Co.
First Woman Member,
New York Stock Exchange

When I had just learned to read and was sick in bed with a cold, my father brought me the first of many volumes of the Bobbsey Twins. These books still resonate for me today because they told the stories of two very tenacious young ladies (and their twin brothers) who got involved in all sorts of intrigue and adventures. In the end, their perseverance paid off. I can relate to that!

And that's the key to Ramona's popularity. She's a real little kid, living a working-class suburban life, with predicaments so familiar and a perspective so genuine that children immediately identify with her. It is clear that the author has total recall for the highs and lows of growing up. Ramona is frank, funny, and a pleasure to read about.

SHERYL SWOOPES

～

Forward, Houston Comets
1996 Olympic Gold Medal, Basketball,
Atlanta, Georgia

first picked up Ramona at the public library. I could relate to her—she was so funny! But I felt a little bit sorry for her, too. She was a loner in a way. Although I had lots of friends in school, after school I was usually alone, making up games in my head and thinking up things to do. This seemed to me just what Ramona did.

Ramona always kept my attention. She was always into mischief—I like to create mischief, too. She was funny and I like to be funny. She was stubborn and I can be hardheaded. She was different and that appealed to me. I didn't want to be like everyone else. Ramona sounded just like me.

I didn't really read that much as a child, but if a book caught me I wouldn't let it go. My baby boy may be the same way. He already has a whole shelf full of books. Of course, right now, he's more interested in chewing than reading— he'd rather eat *Green Eggs and Ham* than listen to it!

Revolutionary Poet:
A Story About Phillis Wheatley
Written by Maryann N. Weidt/Illustrated by Mary O'Keefe
    Young
Copyright 1997
Cloth: Carolrhoda Books
Paper: Carolrhoda Books

ᴖ Phillis Wheatley was the first African-American to publish a book. Stolen from her home in Africa when she was probably just seven years old, she came to Boston as a slave in 1761. She was sold to the prosperous Wheatley family who, against the manner of the day, taught her to read and write. Recognizing her precocity, they taught young Phillis Greek, Latin, geography, astronomy, and history. Phillis was moved to write poetry and first saw her work published in the Newport newspaper in 1767. Undeterred by setbacks, she continued writing and publishing throughout her short life, garnering praise not only across America but in Britain as well. This unusual story of the gifted woman often called "the mother of black literature" is a well-presented, readable biography.

A Ride on the Red Mare's Back
Written by Ursula Le Guin/Illustrated by
    Julie Downing
Copyright 1992
Cloth: Orchard Books
Paper: Orchard Books

ᴖ Famous science fiction writer Ursula Le Guin was inspired to write this fantasy when she was given a little red wooden horse from Sweden. In it a little girl courageously rescues her young brother from ugly trolls. Aided by her toy horse, which thrillingly comes to life, she trudges through the long, dark Scandinavian night to make her way to the trolls' mountain hideaway. While the red mare distracts the trolls, the girl tricks the guard and slips into the cave.

There, amid rot and decay, she finds her brother, who is already in danger of turning into a troll, and leads him home to safety. "My brave daughter," whispers the grateful mother at the close of this satisfying tale.

Rimonah of the Flashing Sword:
A North African Tale

Written by Eric A. Kimmel/Illustrated Omar Rayyan
Copyright 1995
Cloth: Holiday House

～ Yes, there's an evil stepmother, yes, there's a magic mirror, yes, there's a princess, and yes, this does resemble "Snow White" . . . but in this North African story the heroine brandishes a flashing sword and fearlessly fights for her life. Rimonah has fled to the desert to escape the vicious sorcery of her stepmother. She hides first with a bedouin tribe and becomes famous for her daring horsemanship. When the queen discovers her whereabouts, Rimonah flees again, this time to the hidden cave of the forty thieves. By now a fierce warrior, Rimonah joins their band as they bravely skirmish against the royal soldiers. The vengeful queen finally gets the upper hand when Rimonah, weakened from battle wounds, unsuspectingly slips a poisoned ring on her finger. Rimonah falls instantly into a deathlike sleep but of course is awakened by the proverbial kiss of a prince. Rimonah knows she will never be safe until the wicked queen is defeated. She rescues her father and sends the queen to her deserved demise. Exotic artwork swirls dramatically throughout this splendid retelling of an ancient Egyptian folktale.

Rumpelstiltskin's Daughter

Written and Illustrated by Diane Stanley
Copyright 1997
Cloth: William Morrow

⌒ What would have happened if the miller's daughter *hadn't* married the king? He really wasn't very pleasant, always demanding that she keep spinning straw into gold. A sensible girl might have married someone like . . . Rumpelstiltskin! That's the jumping-off place for Diane Stanley's highly amusing reworking of the old fairy tale. Sixteen years later, Rumpelstiltskin's daughter finds herself in just the same predicament her mother was in—locked away by that greedy king who's on the lookout for easy gold. This cunning young woman shrewdly sizes up her situation and decides she can foil her tormentor, set the kingdom to rights, and get a great job in the process. Our kind of fairy tale!

The Samurai's Daughter: A Japanese Legend
Written by Robert D. San Souci/Illustrated by Steven T.
    Johnson
Copyright 1992
Cloth: Dial Books for Young Readers
Paper: Puffin

⌒ Iridescent pastels illuminate this admirable Japanese medieval folktale. Tokoyo has been schooled "in the samurai virtues of courage, discipline, and endurance." When her father is banished unjustly to a remote island by the emperor, Tokoyo decides to follow him into his exile. Disguised as a peasant, she undertakes the difficult journey. Along the way she must battle ghostly warriors and an enormous sea serpent. Unexpectedly, her victory over the serpent releases the emperor from the demons that have been clouding his mind, and Tokoyo's father is thus restored to favor. Tokoyo is a vigorous heroine whose story is enhanced by especially exquisite artwork.

Sarah, Plain and Tall
Written by Patricia MacLachlan
Copyright 1985
Cloth: HarperCollins

Paper: HarperTrophy
Newbery Medal
Christopher Award
Golden Kite Award
ALA Notable Book

~ There aren't many adult novels as finely written as this.

On the prairie, Anna struggles to run a home. Her father is quiet—too quiet—and her younger brother, Caleb, pesters her with questions about their mother who died in childbirth. They are a sad little family, just barely holding together, when Papa announces he has advertised for a new wife. Immediately the atmosphere is charged with a new poignant anticipation. Will Sarah like them? Will she stay?

When Sarah arrives from Maine, she pitches right in, plowing, fixing the roof, driving the wagon. But it is her gift for making the grind of daily life sweet again that captures Anna's heart, that saves them all.

This slim book, with its simple plot and spare prose, reverberates with profound emotion. It is a memorable story of a family healing itself. The film version, though broader in scope, still manages to capture the very real yearnings of these characters.

Savitri: A Tale of Ancient India

Written by Aaron Shepard/Illustrated by Vera
    Rosenberry
Copyright 1992
Cloth: Albert Whitman & Co.

~ A beautiful, intelligent princess usually has her pick of suitors, but not the splendid Princess Savitri. Her father tells her, "Weak men turn away from radiance like yours. Go out and find a man worthy of you. Then I will arrange the marriage." Savitri falls in love with the virtuous Prince Satyavan and is not deterred from marrying him even after a seer tells her that the prince has only one year to live. When Yama, the god of death, comes to claim Satyavan, Savitri will not leave her husband's side. She pursues Yama, and the compassionate god is so impressed with her loyalty that he stops three times to grant a favor upon Savitri—anything but the life of her husband. On the third wish, clever Savitri backs Yama into a corner. Yama releases Satyavan from death, saying, "Princess, your wit is as strong as your will."

This famous Indian story comes from an ancient Hindu epic, *The Mahabharata*. It is adorned here with exquisitely detailed watercolors.

The School Mouse
Written by Dick King-Smith/Illustrated by Cynthia
      Fisher
Copyright 1995
Cloth: Hyperion
Paper: Hyperion

⌒ Precocious, curious Flora wants to know *why* small children come five days a week to the building where she lives, *why* a big person makes noises at them, and *why* they make black marks on sheets of paper. One day she leans out of her mouse hole and sees a picture of herself with the word *mouse* underneath. The earth-shattering connection is made, and Flora is soon reading books like mad. Her practical mother takes a dim view of her erudite accomplishment—what is reading, and why would any respectable mouse need it? When the exterminator arrives and Flora's new skill saves her from the poison, Flora not only rises in her mother's estimation but also becomes the first schoolteacher mouse ever! King-Smith, the brilliant author of *Babe* and the Sophie books (see Index), scores again!

Secret Soldier: The Story of Deborah Sampson
Written by Ann McGovern/Illustrated by Harold
      Goodwin

Copyright 1975
Paper: Scholastic

⟶ On May 20, 1782, Deborah Sampson joined the Continental Army disguised as Robert Shurtliff. For a year and a half she fought the Tories, bravely taking a bullet in her leg and digging it out by herself so that no one would discover her secret. In fact, her deception remained safe until Deborah caught a fever and sank into a coma.

After a rough childhood—her mother had to give her away because she was too ill to care for her and Deborah ended up an indentured servant until she was eighteen—Deborah longed for adventure. She taught for awhile but it wasn't enough. When the war came, Deborah was ready to go. In her later years, Deborah became the first woman to travel alone giving talks for money. Her recollections of her days in the Army were enormously popular. Young readers are intrigued by the story of the "secret" soldier.

Seven Kisses in a Row

Written by Patricia MacLachlan/Illustrated by Maria Pia
     Marrella
Copyright 1983
Cloth: HarperCollins
Paper: HarperTrophy

⟶ Emma is definitely not thrilled at the prospect of having her aunt and uncle come stay with her and her brother Zachary when her parents go off to a conference. Aunt Evelyn and Uncle Elliot don't know that she needs seven kisses in a row when she wakes up and that she eats divided grapefruit with a cherry in it for breakfast. On top of that, they have lots of rules that Emma doesn't think are worth following. How is she going to last through five whole days of this?

Written with her trademark gentle humor and understated charm, this is another MacLachlan jewel. By the end, Emma has

taken the edges off Aunt Evelyn and Uncle Elliot and given herself
two new people to love.

The Seven Ravens
Retold by Laura Geringer/Illustrated by Edward S. Gazsi
Copyright 1994
Cloth: HarperCollins
⌒ There's not much for us to choose from among the Brothers
Grimm canon of fairy tales—too many passive princesses! Geringer
has adapted one of their familiar stories, sometimes called "The
Seven Swans" or "The Twelve Brothers," emphasizing the heroic
actions of the little girl who rescues her brothers. She must journey
great distances, to the sun, the moon, and the stars, to reunite her
family. The striking, vividly colored illustrations accentuate her
enchanted travels.

Shark Lady: True Adventures of Eugenie Clark
Written by Ann McGovern/Illustrated by Ruth Chew
Copyright 1978
Paper: Apple
⌒ One visit to the aquarium when she was nine, and Eugenie
Clark knew what she wanted. "Someday I'll swim with sharks," she
thought. Eugenie was lucky. She had a dream and an understanding mother who supported it. Eugenie grew up to be one of the
world's foremost ichthyologists. She has her own marine laboratory
in Florida, has written bestselling books, and has made many
important discoveries about shark behavior. Her message to children is timeless and valuable: "I love my work and I never stop
learning about the sea and its creatures."

She's Wearing a Dead Bird on Her Head!
Written by Kathryn Lasky/Illustrated by David Catrow
Copyright 1995
Cloth: Hyperion

Paper: Hyperion
New York Times Best Illustrated Children's Book of the Year
⌢ First it was feathers. Then, wings. Finally, Harriet Hemenway could scarcely credit it, there were dead birds decorating ladies' hats. The whole thing was revolting. And who could take seriously a woman with an egret on her head? Harriet called her cousin Minna Hall, and these two proper Bostonians hatched a scheme to halt this trend in its tracks. Together these two real-life heroines formed the Massachusetts Audubon Society and worked to have laws enacted to protect birds from being killed for fashion.

Our children just could not believe the fads of the 1890s. The illustrations are absolutely outrageous. This book is definitely something to crow about!

The Sign on Rosie's Door

Written and Illustrated by Maurice Sendak
Copyright 1960
Cloth: HarperCollins
⌢ What a diva! Alinda, the lovely lady singer, is the talk of the neighborhood children. She is sometimes known as Rosie but always known as the instigator of endless amusement for the stoop-sitting urchins on her Brooklyn block. They'd be bored silly without her; even just hanging out and waiting for something to happen is more fun with Rosie around. When Rosie is thwarted in her desire for a real firecracker on the Fourth of July, she just wraps herself in a red blanket and declares herself "the biggest red firecracker in the whole world . . . BOOMM! BOOMM-BOOMM-aWHISHHHH!" Sendak captures the way real kids play and pass the time—it's perfectly obvious why grown-ups and children clamor for this author/illustrator.

Silver

Written by Gloria Whelan/Illustrated by Stephen Marchesi
Copyright 1988

Paper: Random House

⟶ Rachel is ecstatic when she finally is given a huskie puppy of her own to raise. Silver is the runt of the litter, but Rachel is determined to turn him into a real sled dog racer. Her father has forty-eight dogs, and this winter he is competing in Alaska's famous Iditarod. While he's away for the grueling three-week race, Rachel feeds and cares for her tiny puppy. One night, though, she discovers Silver is missing from the dog shed. She finds prints in the snow and bravely tracks them to a wolf's cave. Silver is there: the wolf mother has taken Silver to replace a pup of her own that died. Entering the cave, Rachel scoops Silver up and runs home through the cold, dark night. Lots of drama and excitement in a book that children can easily read on their own.

Sleeping Ugly
Written by Jane Yolen/Illustrated by Diane Stanley
Copyright 1981
Paper: PaperStar

⟶ Here's a fractured fairy tale that's wise and witty. In a tiny cottage in the dark woods, Plain Jane meets the beautiful Princess Miserella. The princess is as nasty as can be; Jane is as nice as they come. When a fairy offers Jane three wishes, Miserella flies into fits, but it is deserving Jane who gets the happy ending. This is a terrific read-aloud with a great moral about not trusting appearances. At our houses there were many cheers for Jane and much laughter at the fate of the crummy princess!

Sophie's Tom
Written by Dick King-Smith/Illustrated by David Parkins
Copyright 1991
Cloth: Candlewick Press
Paper: Candlewick Press

⟶ There is a lovely series of Sophie books, of which this is the second. All are special; we chose this one just because it turned out to be the favorite title of one of our daughters. Because of Sophie, she wants to grow up to be a farmer, too.

Sophie is so desperate to have a farm she will turn anything into a pet—a snail, even wood lice. This plot spins on Sophie's war with her parents to keep a stray cat. Her scrapes are uproarious, and her no-nonsense ways are engaging. Other marvelous Sophie titles include *Sophie's Snail, Sophie Hits Six,* and *Sophie in the Saddle.*

The Story of Holly & Ivy
Written by Rumer Godden/Illustrated by Barbara Cooney
Copyright 1957, 1985
Cloth: Viking

～ You could make a tradition of reading this beautiful book aloud each Christmas. It begins with a doll in a toy shop wishing for a little girl. Then we meet a little girl in an orphanage - wishing for a home, a family, a doll. We follow the parallel stories of the doll, Holly, and the girl, Ivy, and hope that, through all the Dickensian twists and turns that beset them, they will find each other.

Christmas stories can be so treacly. This book sidesteps cloying sentimentality because Ivy is such a determined, brave little girl. When you combine such a terrific character with Rumer Godden's always elegant writing, you have something extraordinary. This is a Christmas story that is both suspenseful and magical. A gem!

The Story of Ruby Bridges
Written by Robert Coles/Illustrated by George Ford
Copyright 1995
Cloth: Scholastic

～ Pulitzer Prize–winning author and child psychiatrist Robert Coles has written an eloquent tribute to the little, six-year-old, African-American girl who, in 1960, integrated the William Frantz Elementary School in New Orleans. Every day for months Ruby

Bridges walked through a mob of angry, yelling people, a solitary child surrounded by U.S. marshals. Her faith and her family sustained her. This is a powerful and upsetting story, yet Coles has made it understandable for young readers. We think this is a terrific accomplishment.

The Story of Stagecoach Mary Fields
Written by Robert H. Miller/Illustrated by Cheryl Hanna
Copyright 1992
Cloth: Silver Press
Paper: Silver Press

⌐ Born a slave in 1832, the legendary Mary Fields jumped at the opportunity to move to Montana and become boss of a construction crew. She wore western clothes, smoked cigars, and toted a six-shooter. "Faster than you can say giddyap," she was subsequently the first African-American woman rider ever hired to carry the United States mail. True to the post office motto, she delivered letters on time—neither sleet nor snow, bandits nor wolves deterred her. After eight years, Mary retired from her stagecoach to open a laundry business and sometimes brandished her gun to collect what was owed her. This true story is exciting enough to stand on its own, but children will also enjoy the illustrations, which convey the feisty spirit of the Wild West.

Swamp Angel
Written by Anne Isaacs/Illustrated by Paul O. Zelinsky
Copyright 1994
Cloth: E. P. Dutton
Paper: Penguin
Caldecott Honor Book
New York Times Best Illustrated Children's Book

⌐ You've heard of Pecos Bill? Step right up and meet Angelica Longrider, alias Swamp Angel. At two she built her first log cabin. At twelve she lifted an entire wagon train mired in the mud. And

RUBY BRIDGES

~

Civil Rights Activist
President, Ruby Bridges Foundation

In 1960, when I integrated the school system, I got fan mail from all over the country that supported what my parents were doing, who believed it was the right thing to do. I even got lots of presents—clothing, toys, and books. And some of those books were Dr. Seuss books and became my favorites: *Green Eggs and Ham, The Cat in the Hat.* I loved them and read them over and over again because my parents could never really afford to buy us books. So those are the ones that stick in my mind. To those people, if they are still around, who sent me those great Dr. Seuss books—I want them to know they made a great impact on me as a child. Even today I make sure I buy Dr. Seuss books for my children.

when she grew up, she fought Thundering Tarnation, the fastest, wiliest, most "low-down pile of pelts" bear in Tennessee. Their legendary battle lasted for days and days as Swamp Angel threw that varmint into the sky, lassoed him with a tornado, and wrestled him to the bottom of the lake. Over-the-top, exaggerated illustrations broaden this knee-slapping tall tale.

Sweet Clara and the Freedom Quilt
Written by Deborah Hopkinson/Illustrated by James Ransome

Copyright 1993
Cloth: Alfred A. Knopf
Paper: Random House
A Reading Rainbow Book

⟶ Distinguished by James Ransome's luminous illustrations, this is an affecting story of quiet, serious determination.

Sold away from her family before she's even twelve years old to be a slave on a different plantation, Clara longs to find her way back to her momma. A friendly woman takes the lonely girl under her wing and teaches Sweet Clara to sew. With this new skill, Clara begins to work in the Big House, where she overhears whispered stories about the Underground Railroad. She's inspired to incorporate these scraps of knowledge into an original quilt design. There are blue pieces for creeks and rivers, green for fields, and white for the roads. Soon people are dropping by with bits of information they've gleaned about crossing to freedom. When her quilt is done, Clara escapes, rescues her mother, and flees north to Canada. She generously leaves her quilt behind as a map for others to follow.

Sybil Rides for Independence

Written by Drollene P. Brown/Illustrated by Margot Apple
Copyright 1985
Cloth: Albert Whitman & Co.

⟶ "Listen, my children, and you shall hear / of the midnight ride of . . ." Sybil Ludington? Two years after the better-known ride of Paul Revere, sixteen-year-old Sybil was asked by her father, Colonel Ludington, to saddle her horse and gallop through the countryside to sound the warning that the British were on the march. While her father stayed to draw up the battle plans, Sybil rode from house to house, not wasting even a minute to dismount but shouting her message, "Danbury's burning! Gather at Ludingtons'!" She covered more than thirty miles in the dark and pouring rain. By dawn, four hundred men were ready to fight and the British were forced to retreat to their ships. General Washington himself came to thank Sybil for her courage. The pencil drawings portraying this nearly forgotten heroine of the American Revolution are also very nicely done.

Tam Lin

Written by Jane Yolen/Illustrated by Charles Mikolaycak
Copyright 1990
Cloth: Harcourt Brace
Paper: Voyager/Harcourt Brace

∽ An old Scottish ballad was the inspiration for this dramatic tale of Jennet MacKenzie, a brave and bonny young lass bent on reclaiming her ancestral home, stolen by the Fairy Folk. When she arrives at Carterhaugh, she meets Tam Lin, a young man imprisoned for centuries by the Queen of the Fey. Jennet decides to rescue Tam Lin even as she takes back her castle, and she stands her ground despite all the artful trickery of the Fairy Queen. Jennet is a swashbuckling heroine, and this is a grand, romantic story.

Tatterhood and the Hobgoblins: A Norwegian Folktale

Written and Illustrated by Lauren Mills
Copyright 1993
Cloth: Little Brown & Co.
Paper: Little Brown & Co.

∽ With its magical full-page illustrations, this book resembles an old-fashioned volume of fairy tales, yet the story soon swerves off into something unpredictable.

A queen so longs for children that she makes a bad bargain with some demonish hobgoblins, promising to give them one of her children. In due time she gives birth to twin daughters who are devoted to each other. One child, the fair Isabella, is a proper

princess, meek, tame, and bland, but it is her wild and unkempt
twin, Tatterhood, who turns into the tale's true heroine. When the
hobgoblins steal Isabella, Tatterhood boldly sails off to rescue her.
Confident, steadfast, and capable, Tatterhood is a resolute nonconformist. Wrapped in her ragged cloak, heedless of her mop of
unruly hair, she gives no credence to people who trust only in
appearances. This spirited retelling of an old Norwegian folktale
exults in Tatterhood's stout individualism.

Thee, Hannah
Written and Illustrated by Marguerite de Angeli
Copyright 1940
Cloth: Doubleday

⌐ Though the author's Newbery Medal–winning *The Door in
the Wall* is still available, this book, alas, is out of print. We share
the sentiments of a friend who called us in an outrage because she
was having such a hard time locating de Angeli's books in stores and
hope you find this and other de Angeli titles on your library shelf.

Nobody likes to be different. Very few of us want to wear
plain clothes if everyone else is attired in fancy dresses. This is the
plight, and then the temptation, of nine-year-old Hannah, a
Quaker girl living in Philadelphia at the time of the Civil War.
Time and time again in this quaint story Hannah compares herself
unfavorably to her friends and risks Mother's punishment by adding
ribbons to her bonnet and fashionable pantalettes under her skirt.
But when she is able to assist a runaway slave and her child because
they recognize her Quaker bonnet as a sign of a Friend, she is
proud at last of being different.

They Led the Way: 14 American Women
Written by Johanna Johnston/Illustrated by Deanne
        Hollinger
Copyright 1973
Paper: Scholastic

⌒ These pithy, nicely written vignettes of fourteen outstanding women are terrific. The author has expertly highlighted the contributions these women have made and has made each story so vivid that it is our bet children will want to learn more.

From Anne Bradstreet, the first poet in colonial America, to Emma Willard, who started the first college for women; from Victoria Woodhull, the first woman to run for president, to Carrie Chapman Catt, who fought for the Nineteenth Amendment to the Constitution, these are famous women every child should know. Highly recommended.

This Time, Tempe Wick?
Written by Patricia Lee Gauch/Illustrated by Margot Tomes
Copyright 1974
Cloth: Putnam

⌒ For Patricia Lee Gauch, " 'Tempe Wick' was merely the name of a winding New Jersey road until [I] discovered the lively experiences of this real Revolutionary heroine."

Temperance Wick was certainly unusual. She could stay at the plow as long as her father, and she could toss her friend David across the kitchen when they wrestled. When General Washington brought 10,000 soldiers to spend the winter in her village, Tempe was unfazed. She pitched right in, knitting and cooking. But on New Year's Eve in 1781, the soldiers, tired of being cold and hungry, started a mutiny and decided to steal her horse. Where could Tempe hide a horse? In her bedroom, of course! For days she outwitted the soldiers at every turn. Humorous, detailed illustrations accompany this little-known slice of history that fulfills the author's desire to write "books that hold a mirror of possibility up to a young person."

The Three Little Pigs and the Fox:
An Appalachian Tale
Written by William H. Hooks/Illustrated by S. D. Schindler

Copyright 1989
Cloth: Simon & Schuster
Paper: Aladdin

⌒ In this amusing Appalachian version of the traditional tale, three hillbilly piglets, Rooter, Oinky, and their baby sister, Hamlet, are firmly warned by Mama Pig to beware of that "mean, tricky old drooly-mouth fox." When Mama decides that her pigs are big enough to leave the holler to find sturdy stone homes of their own, her advice flies right out of the boys' heads as the first pangs of hunger hit. Oblivious to all but their snacks, Rooter and then Oinky are easily snatched up by that drooly-mouth critter. Not so their self-sufficient little sister! Hamlet's got more on her mind than just eating and wallowing in mud. Thanks to her sharp thinking, she outfoxes that fox and rescues her silly brothers. The down-home twang of this story makes for great - read-aloud fun.

Tye May and the Magic Brush
Written and Illustrated by Molly Garrett Bang
Copyright 1981
Paper: Mulberry Books

⌒ Little Tye May is only a beggar girl, but she wants to paint. She draws in the dirt but longs for a real brush. One morning she awakens to find that her wish has been mysteriously granted. Even stranger, she finds that the things she paints come alive. Soon she begins to use her brush to help the poor of her village. For a weaver she paints a loom. For a farmer she paints a hoe. When the evil emperor hears of this magic, his greed knows no bounds. But clever Tye May is ready. She shrewdly paints him into a corner from which there is no escape!

Very Last First Time
Written by Jan Andrews/Illustrated by Ian Wallace

Copyright 1985
Cloth: Atheneum
Paper: Aladdin
A Reading Rainbow Book

~ "Today, for the very first time in her life, Eva would walk on the bottom of the sea alone."

With these mysterious words we're pulled into an adventure story like no other we've read. Eva is an Inuit girl who is now old enough to hunt for mussels on the ocean floor under the ice. When the tide goes out, she and her mother chisel a hole through the ice and Eva lowers herself down to the sea bed. Lighting her candles, she begins to collect mussels, but she wanders too far. When her candles go out and she hears the tide returning, she wonders if she'll survive.

We wish we could adequately describe the artwork. The colors are mostly deep purples and greens—eerie, bewitching, and altogether otherworldly. They glow with a strange light that accentuates the peril Eva is in. You'll sigh with relief when Eva finds her way back to the ice hole and dances in the moonlight to celebrate her narrow escape. Terrific.

The Warrior Maiden: A Hopi Legend
Written by Ellen Schecter/Illustrated by Laura Kelley
Copyright 1992
Paper: Bantam Doubleday Dell

~ Every year at harvest time, the Hopi commemorate Huh-ay-ay, the "brave and clever Warrior Maiden." Legend has it that one day, long ago, when the men and boys left the pueblos to plant corn, an Apache war party appeared on the horizon. Levelheaded Huh-ay-ay instructs the women and children to "get drums and beat them. Get rattles and shake them. Make them think our pueblo is full of warriors. It will give me time to run for help." She races across the desert and returns with the men in time to save the tribe. This good first chapter book is part of the Bank Street College of Education Ready-to-Read series.

The Widow's Broom
Written and Illustrated by Chris Van Allsburg
Copyright 1992
Cloth: Houghton Mifflin

⁓ The sly solution to a widow's dilemma sneaks up on the reader—catching most girls unaware until the very last page of Van Allsburg's phantasmal tale.

Minna Shaw's broom can sweep by itself; it can play the piano, chop wood, feed the chickens, and bring the cow in from the pasture. When the neighbors hear about this unusual broom, they growl with suspicion. Mr. Spivey is especially vehement: he rants that the broom must be possessed of an evil force and should be burned. The widow, with a clever trick, not only rids herself of her menacing neighbor, but keeps her happy, hardworking broom by her side.

Widely acclaimed for his powerful children's books, here Van Allsburg's shadowy pencil illustrations lend just the right shivery touch.

Wilma Mankiller
Written by Linda Lowery/Illustrated by Janice Lee Porter
Copyright 1996
Cloth: Carolrhoda Books
Paper: Carolrhoda Books

⁓ In 1956, ten-year-old Wilma Mankiller and her family, in search of better jobs and schools, moved from their Oklahoma home to San Francisco. But Wilma never forgot her Native American heritage. As soon as she was able, she moved back with her two young daughters to rejoin her Cherokee Nation. She took a job helping to improve the living conditions of the Cherokee. The chief was so impressed, he asked her to be his assistant and run for deputy chief. It was a tough battle, for Wilma found unexpected resistance to the idea of a woman holding such a powerful position. The tires on her car were slashed and threats were made against her life, but Wilma practiced the Cherokee Way: "You do not think about the bad things. You think about the good. Even if you feel

KATHLEEN KRULL

⁓

Children's Book Author

eekly visits to the library with my mom were the highlight of childhood—a way to escape from, among other things, three brothers, I read *a lot*. Favorites included historical fiction (Laura Ingalls Wilder; Elizabeth Speare's *Calico Captive* or *The Witch of Blackbird Pond*), biography (the Landmark Book series on people like Helen Keller, Elizabeth Blackwell, Susan B. Anthony; anything on queens), mysteries (the Famous Five series by Enid Blyton was thrilling), fantasy (the resourceful girls in Edward Eager's magical books), romance (Mary Stolz, Betty Cavanna), adventure (Scott O'Dell's *Island of the Blue Dolphins*), fun books like Louise Fitzhugh's *Harriet the Spy* and Astrid Lindgren's *Pippi Longstocking*. I will always be grateful to the all-women library staff—and my mom—for keeping me afloat.

you will never make it, you move ahead." Not only did she win that
election, but this accomplished leader went on to become an influential chief of the Cherokee Nation.

Wilma Unlimited: How Wilma Rudolph Became the World's Fastest Woman
Written by Kathleen Krull/Illustrated by David Diaz
Copyright 1996
Cloth: Harcourt Brace
ALA Notable Book

⌒ Crippled by polio at the age of five, Wilma Rudolph faced
insurmountable odds. It was a fifty-mile trip to the nearest hospital that would treat African-American patients. She couldn't attend
school because she couldn't walk. But a strong mother, a warm and
supportive family, and, most of all, her own indomitable will led
Wilma to walk, run, and eventually triumph in the 1960 Olympics.
She was the first American woman to win three gold medals at a
single Olympics. This dramatic story is told beautifully and brought
us both to tears.

INDEPENDENT
READERS

AGES EIGHT THROUGH ELEVEN

irls are now reading actively on their own. They read about school, friends, history, and fantasy. Though their literary adventures are far-flung, they recognize themselves in all the disparate heroines they encounter. In fact they seem to step into the lives of these characters. Suddenly the phrase "lost in a book" takes on true significance.

Perhaps more than in our other categories, you'll find a wide range of reading levels. The books are as diverse as *Charlotte's Web* and *A Wrinkle in Time*. What links these books is their complex character development, their multilayered plots, and their broad themes. The gripping drama of a heroine confronting a bewildering decision yet ultimately making the correct choice is what sustains readers at this age.

An Actor's Life for Me!

Written by Lillian Gish as told to Selma G. Lanes/Illustrated
     by Patricia Henderson Lincoln

Copyright 1987

Cloth: Viking

⌒ For girls who dream of going on the stage, here is a slice of
theater from the turn of the century.

When their father abandons the family, Lillian and Dorothy's
enterprising mother finds work for them, and soon they are child
stars, playing in small theaters across the country. Often they are
apart, with Lillian by herself touring with one company (at age six!)
and her mother and Dorothy with another. Gish is upbeat, choosing to view her life as blessed and special, despite the long separa-
tions, the endless train trips, the often dingy, cold quarters. She
remembers the funny moments and the kindness of her fellow
actors.

Her unconventional childhood seems to us like the very stuff
of the melodramas she acted in and makes for grand reading.

Adventurous Spirit: A Story About
Ellen Swallow Richards

Written by Ethlie Ann Vare/Illustrated by Jennifer Hagerman

Copyright 1992

Cloth: Carolrhoda Books

⌒ Just having been, in 1873, the first woman to graduate from
MIT would have been enough to earn her a footnote in history, but
Ellen Swallow Richards was not one to just frame her degree and
watch it gather dust. She put her hard-won knowledge to work.
Richards was interested in "applied science," and as the nation's first
woman chemist, she set about finding ways for science to be useful and practical to women. When the Massachusetts Board of
Health wanted to know if bacteria in water could really be making people ill, Richards devised the first way to analyze water chem-

ically. Because she believed "you are what you eat," she established the country's first hot lunch program for the Boston schools. Richards was "determined to bring modern science into old-fashioned homes."

The friendly tone of this biography makes it exceptionally easy to read. Richards comes across as a brisk, bright individual whom girls should know about.

BROOKE ASTOR

⌒

Philanthropist
Honorary Chairwoman, New York Public Library
Trustee Emeritus, Metropolitan Museum of Art
and Pierpont Morgan Library

 remember so many wonderful books from my childhood that it is hard to choose just one. But Sir Walter Scott's *Ivanhoe* was a particular favorite, for it was so full of adventure and romance!

Alanna: The First Adventure
Written by Tamora Pierce
Copyright 1983
Paper: Random House

⌒ Armor? Sword fighting? Wrestling? Traditionally not the stuff of girls' books!

Alanna is so certain of her true calling to become a knight that she passes herself off as Alan so that she may learn the arts of warfare and chivalry. Keenly aware that she is smaller and slighter than the boys, she takes on harder and harder tasks to prove her mettle. The culminating triumph comes when Alanna finally can admit to herself that she has done all she has set out to do—and more. She knows without question that her gender does not matter. It is *she* who should be the prince's squire.

Note: This book is usually found in the Young Adult section of the library because it contains a few references to Alanna's developing body as she tries to keep up her disguise. However, the language and plot are easily understood and enjoyed by younger readers. The Lioness Quartet, of which *Alanna* is the first book, is also a big hit with boys. The other titles are *In the Hand of the Goddess, The Woman Who Rides Like a Man,* and *The Lioness Rampant.*

Alice's Adventures in Wonderland
Written by Lewis Carroll/Illustrated by John Tenniel
Published 1865; numerous editions available
⟶ Alice exerts an undeniable fascination for many readers. Her eccentric adventures are not sweet, preachy, predictable, or even comfortable—and there lies their appeal. While encountering the oddest, most baffling cast of characters in children's literature, Alice retains her courage and her poise. She moves with a kind of calm through the surreal landscape, shifting her perspective as required. Although Wonderland gets "curiouser and curiouser," Alice is unfazed. With its wealth of inventive characters and its sophisticated language, this rewarding, though difficult, masterpiece (and *Through the Looking-Glass*) is well worth the effort. You'll enjoy rediscovering it yourself.

Alien Secrets
Written by Annette Curtis Klause
Copyright 1993
Cloth: Delacorte

NATALIE BABBITT

~

Children's Book Author, Tuck Everlasting

hen I was growing up, in the thirties and forties, books were very much a part of my life, but I didn't like them all. Some that my mother read aloud from her list of children's classics, like *Pinocchio*, seemed tiresome, and others, like *The Water-Babies*, were downright annoying. Any story that preached, had a feeble heroine, or used uninteresting language was put aside as quickly as possible. So of course the book I loved best was *Alice in Wonderland*. It had no lessons to teach, except a corroborative one that grown-ups often do strange and silly things. Its heroine was utterly fearless, with a strong sense of self. It had wonderful, uncondescending pictures. And its use of the language was so fine and funny that I soon knew much of it by heart. My copy was given to me when I was nine years old. It was responsible for my firm decision to work in the field of children's books when I grew up. So it gave me a goal, and in many ways it gave me a philosophy: "Why is a raven like a writing desk?" Nobody at the mad tea party knows, and best of all, nobody cares.

Paper: Yearling

~ Hurtling through space on the freighter *Cat's Cradle*, Puck is a passenger bound for the planet Aurora. Poor grades have just gotten her expelled from boarding school, and she is traveling to rejoin her brilliant scientist parents, who are researching alien life on that distant planet. Although Puck is understandably anxious about confessing her expulsion, nothing can really dampen her boundless curiosity and good intentions. When she's introduced to her first alien, a lonely Shoowa named Hush, she learns the sad story of the Shoowa people. Most of the Shoowa were captured and carried off by the evil Grakks centuries ago. During their enslavement, the Shoowa kept a sacred symbol of their freedom, a statue they call the Soo. Hush was appointed to carry this statue back to Aurora and return it to his newly liberated people. But the Soo has been stolen from him, and Puck immediately vows to help Hush find it. It is hidden somewhere on the *Cat's Cradle*, and Puck finds herself in numerous spine-tingling predicaments as she doggedly searches for it. Puck's determination never flags, nor does the excitement. In addition to bringing about a happy resolution for Hush, Puck surprises herself by discovering her own innate scientific talents. Her journey through hyperspace has given her a real goal to work for. Plenty of zing in this sci-fi thriller!

Always Dream: The Story of Kristi Yamaguchi
Written by Kristi Yamaguchi with Greg Brown
Copyright 1998
Cloth: Taylor Publishing
⌒ "I've written this book to encourage you, no matter what happens, always dream."

When world-famous figure skater Kristi Yamaguchi was born in 1971, it was immediately apparent that her feet were deformed. For the first two years of her life, Kristi wore casts and braces. At age four, the little girl saw her first ice show and began to badger her parents for lessons. She wanted to skate and her ambition never wavered. In this personable autobiography, Kristi confides her fears of scary movies, her frustration at never conquering the triple axel, her funny opinions of hockey players, and the sacrifices both she and her parents made to support her dream. She also shares her pride in her Japanese heritage, without hiding the prejudice her family has encountered, especially during World War II.

An open, airy layout with enough photographs to satisfy Kristi's many avid fans makes this a very attractive book about a determined, dedicated athlete.

Anna Is Still Here
Written by Ida Vos
Copyright 1986
Cloth: Houghton Mifflin
Paper: Puffin

⌒ This is a believable novel about the lingering effects of the Holocaust on a young girl.

Anna spent the war years all alone in Mr. De Bree's attic. Now Holland has been liberated, and thirteen-year-old Anna lives once again with her parents. But she acts as though she is still in hiding. Anna is convinced her parents are keeping secrets. She's afraid to make noise. She's certain a Nazi is living in the white house she must pass on her way to school, waiting to grab her and take her to Germany. Anna's thoughts are not simple paranoia. Her parents do have trouble confiding the horrible details of their war years. Her father does have to take her to the beach to practice shouting. And there is someone living in the white house, but it is a Jewish woman who is waiting, waiting for her little girl to come home. The friendship that Anna is able to give this woman finally heals Anna, and it is Anna who brings about the reunion of her new friend with her lost daughter.

Anne of Green Gables
Written by L. M. Montgomery
Published 1908; numerous editions available

Some old-fashioned books have characters that never go out of fashion. Anne, with her impetuous nature, romantic notions, and unflagging optimism, transcends her era. Girls read her as fervently today as their great grandmothers did. They still enjoy the humorous troubles she gets in and out of, her passionate emotions, and her stubborn independence. Die-hard fans will read all seven other Anne books. Anne, we hope, will always be a most cherished kindred spirit.

The Ballad of Lucy Whipple
Written by Karen Cushman
Copyright 1996
Cloth: Houghton Mifflin

California Morning Whipple makes no bones about being "sad, mad, and feeling bad" upon arriving in Lucky Diggins, California. Her recently widowed mama just refused to stay put in Massachusetts but up and sold the house and then packed the family on a steamer headed west. Plus, she's got this awful name to reckon with. Back home it didn't seem so bad, but in California it's an embarrassment.

California changes her name to Lucy, but it's harder to change her fate. Her mama is running a boardinghouse—a boarding *tent*, actually—for miners hoping to strike it rich. The work is hard and the comforts are few. Lucy is indignant about what she's missing in Massachusetts, especially her books. Happily, even though she's pretty much stuck in Lucky Diggins, her good humor and industrious temperament help keep her going. She sets up a -pie-selling business on the side, hoping to earn enough extra gold dust to pay her way home. She amasses a tidy sum, but troubles and tragedies keep hitting, and the gold keeps disappearing. When Mama falls in love again, Lucy balks at the move Mama proposes. She finagles a job as a nursemaid for a family headed east—

While we were researching *Once Upon a Heroine*, we couldn't resist the opportunity to ask our own mothers about their favorite childhood books. Here's what Alison's mother had to say; Jennifer's mother's recollections can be found next to *Emily of New Moon* (see Index).

GLORIA COOPER

Alison's Mother
Managing Editor,
Columbia Journalism Review

rom the moment of my first encounter with *Anne of Green Gables*, I hoped to be one of Anne's kindred spirits, and no matter how many trips I took to Avonlea—and they were countless!— she never failed to inspire and delight. I loved her adventurousness, her imagination, and the intensity with which she experienced everything that came her way. I recognized her small vanities, was moved by her generous impulses. I understood her enchantment with words. And I admired enormously her inquiring, wide-ranging, independent mind. "Anne-with-an-E" was the embodiment of all the qualities of character and personality that I could wish to find in a friend—and, more important, in myself.

home!—but at the last minute discovers her heart's desire right there in Lucky Diggins: "I am Miss Whipple, town librarian. . . . I am doing fine on my own." Outspoken fun from a spunky young spirit.

Ballerina: My Story
Written by Darci Kistler with Alicia Kistler
Copyright 1993
Paper: Minstrel Books

~ Watching her four older brothers rack up their wrestling trophies, little Darci learned "that you had to be tough and you had to work hard to get what you wanted. You also had to be unafraid to fail." What Darci wanted was to be a ballerina. From the time she put on her first tutu at age five, all she wanted to do was dance. At thirteen, she left her California home to study with George Balanchine at the School of American Ballet. At seventeen she became the youngest principal dancer in the history of the New York City Ballet. The demanding hours and grueling practices meant nothing beside the joy that ballet gave her.

This engaging autobiography is full of snapshots and funny anecdotes—Darci loved a dare, and her family nickname was "Crash Kistler" for her exploits on her motorcycle. She's unafraid to tell a story on herself: on an opening night at the Kennedy Center, an eager Darci ran onstage too early, upsetting the staging of *Swan Lake*. This is a motivating book, by a captivating ballerina who believes "dreams do come true. . . . You just have to find yours, then believe in it enough to make it happen."

Ballet Shoes
Written by Noel Streatfeild/Illustrated by Diane Goode
Copyright 1937
Cloth: Random House
Paper: Bullseye Books

MERRILL ASHLEY

~

Principal Dancer, New York City Ballet

s a young girl, books were my constant companions. But as I try to think back on a specific book, the one that comes to mind is the autobiography of Sammy Davis, Jr., *Yes, I Can.*

What I identified with the most was his great love of song and dance—of performing. That love helped him overcome the many enormous obstacles in his life. I think reading about his experiences helped me learn that through perseverance, dedication, single-mindedness, and a positive "Yes, I can" attitude, you can make your dreams come true.

~ This is one of the best old-fashioned books still around. Three unrelated orphans are found by the adventurous fossil collector, Great-Uncle Matthew, on his far-flung voyages. Sent back to his house in London to be brought up by his great-niece Sylvia, they are: Pauline, who becomes a charming actress; Petrova, who falls in love with airplanes; and Posy, who seems destined to be a great dancer. The book follows them from their decision early on to take the last name of Fossil and their vow to try to put their name in history books because "it's our own and nobody can say it's because of our grandfathers." Nearly always out of money, these very believable children cheerfully contrive ways to educate themselves, clothe themselves, and help the wonderful Sylvia through every crisis. At our houses this one is continually pulled off the shelf for rereading. We wish you the same good fortune.

Other Shoe books include *Dancing Shoes* and *Theater Shoes*. They involve different characters but are similarly enchanting.

Barbara McClintock: Alone in Her Field
Written by Deborah Heiligman/Illustrated by Janet Hamlin
Copyright 1994
Cloth: Scientific American Books for Young Readers/W. H. Freeman & Co.
Paper: Scientific American Books for Young Readers/W. H. Freeman & Co.

⌐ Not many people know the many challenges Barbara McClintock faced before winning the Nobel Prize for Physiology and Medicine in 1983. Born in 1902, McClintock's references were markedly unconventional for the day. She loved machines, tools, insects, football, science, and math. In college she became fascinated by genetics but was not allowed to enroll in the plant-breeding department because she was a woman. She circumvented this obstacle by studying cytology in the botany department, where she began her pathbreaking experiments on corn. When she discovered that genes could jump, thereby creating new, unexpected patterns, the scientific community completely ignored her. For thirty years McClintock just kept on working. As she herself said, she never doubted herself: "I was an oddball. . . . What you have to understand about people is that. . . . [t]hey don't always fit the mold." With her unswerving dedication to her research, McClintock was a woman way ahead of her time.

The BFG
Written by Roald Dahl/Illustrated by Quentin Blake
Copyright 1982
Cloth: Farrar Straus & Giroux
Paper: Viking

⌐ Here is a grand book filled with astonishingly funny word play, a wildly inventive plot, and a spiffy orphan heroine.

One night Sophie is snatched out of her bed by an awesomely huge giant while he's on his rounds blowing dreams into the sleeping minds of children. Once back in Giant Country, though, he reveals himself to be the BFG, or Big Friendly Giant, and gallantly protects her from the Fleshlumpeater and the Bone-cruncher and the other ghastly giants who habitually guzzle children for dinner. When Sophie learns about the fate of these hapless children, she is righteously indignant. She concocts a splendid scheme to stop the bogthumping creatures once and for all, a scheme that even involves the queen of England! All the resources of Great Britain—plus, of course, the BFG himself—are called on to eradicate the giants, and when things almost go awry, Sophie wields the queen's brooch as a mighty weapon.

Kids (adults too) fall off the couch laughing when they read this book. Quentin Blake's amusing line drawings are the perfect partner to the text.

Birds in the Bushes: A Story About Margaret Morse Nice

Written by Julie Dunlap/Illustrated by Ralph L. Ramstad
Copyright 1996
Cloth: Carolrhoda Books

～ Easy to read and enjoyable, this well-written biography makes the point that playing in your backyard can start you on a lifelong avocation!

No matter what her parents thought might be proper and suitable for a young girl growing up in the 1890s, Margaret Morse was *not* going to stop climbing trees and crawling through bushes to observe the bird life around her Massachusetts home. At that time ornithologists and zoologists conducted their studies using only dead specimens in stuffy laboratories. Margaret was repelled by this, and when she grew up, she became part of a new movement to study bird life in the wild. She and her husband took their four daughters camping throughout Oklahoma to observe and record the habits of 361 species of birds. When they moved to a house in Ohio and fieldwork became impossible, Margaret simply turned her attention to her backyard. Her reputation was secured when, after an eight-year investigation of the birds there, she published her remarkable book on the life of the song sparrow. She became an active conservationist, helping to preserve the Wichita Wildlife Mountain Refuge and the Dinosaur National Monument. We've said many times that there isn't enough information available on women scientists—this book is a real find.

Black Star, Bright Dawn
Written by Scott O'Dell
Copyright 1988
Cloth: Houghton Mifflin
Paper: Ballantine
⁓ O'Dell's forte is delineating the struggle of an individual pitted against the elements.

In this fine novel, O'Dell writes about a young Eskimo woman, Bright Dawn, who hunts with her father, even though tradition holds that a woman belongs at home. Her father's passion is dog-sled racing and when he is injured, he turns to his daughter to win the famous Iditarod race for him. With her favorite husky, Black Star, in the lead, Bright Dawn unhesitatingly embarks on the hazardous thousand-mile race through Alaska's frozen wilderness.

Bright Dawn's adventure leads her into dangerous territory; she confronts unexpected storms, aggressive animals, and a frightening whiteout that leaves her stranded on an ice floe heading out to sea. Even though she knows it will cost her valuable time, Bright Dawn repeatedly stops along the way to help floundering competitors and their dogs. These selfless acts of heroism earn her the Iditarod's Sportsmanship medal and respect of her village. Throughout, O'Dell gives us authentic details of the race and of Bright Dawn's way of life. A bracing story.

JORJA FLEEZANIS

⌒

Concertmaster, Minnesota Orchestra

y dad was an avid reader of Greek history and general politics, but I spent more of my childhood around my mother and her mother, who lived down the street. Since *Yiayia* only spoke Greek, my earliest literary memories are in the form of spoken myth and island lore from her isle of Samos.

When I turned ten, this rich story-telling segued into my first contact with *The Odyssey*, read and studied in a class held at a neighborhood high school in Detroit, taught by schoolteachers direct from Greece, stern and clad in black. This often terrifying education of cramming Greek grammar on top of my "American" homework, the slow, painstaking translation of Greek into English through the eyes of Odysseus, forever marked me with the yearning to wander and the thirst to imagine.

The Book of Goddesses
Written and Illustrated by Kris Waldherr
Copyright 1995
Cloth: Beyond Words Publishing

⌒ Artist and author Waldherr has culled stories from around the world about twenty-six powerful goddesses. She shares her extensive research about each, setting forth the myths surrounding their origins and their powers. Diana, the Roman goddess of the hunt and the moon, was renowned for her strength and athletic prowess. Kuan Yin is still worshiped in China as a deity of mercy who freely chose to remain on earth after her death to help suffering human beings. In India, Sarasvati is the dazzling goddess of all knowledge whose influence extends in every direction. The Greeks held Athena in the highest esteem for her wisdom, her skill as a great warrior, and her sagacious gift to the Athenians of the olive tree. Each fascinating description is accompanied by a graceful full-page painting of the goddess in the costume and jewelry of her culture.

Bounce Back

Written by Sheryl Swoopes with Greg Brown/Illustrated by
    Doug Keith
Copyright 1996
Cloth: Taylor Publishing

⟶ Open the book and look at the picture of sweet, bespectacled seven-year-old Sheryl Swoopes. Then turn the page. Is this one of the coolest ladies around or what? Swoopes writes that "I've written this book to share with you one great lesson I've learned . . . no matter how much you hurt, you can always bounce back." Growing up in a small town in Texas, at times on public assistance, Swoopes learned to play basketball with her brothers. She kept at it (it took her thirteen years to beat her brothers) and was a thrilling college player where she set NCAA records. She then began preparing for the Olympic tryouts; a highlight of that time was playing one-on-one with Michael Jordan. In 1996 Swoopes and the undefeated American Olympic basketball team captured the gold. Lots of photographs enliven this upbeat, entertaining autobiography.

Caddie Woodlawn

Written by Carol Ryrie Brink/Illustrated by Trina Schart
    Hyman
Copyright 1935

RUTH BADER GINSBURG

⌐

Associate Justice,
Supreme Court of the United States

mong my earliest memories were poems read aloud by my mother at bedtime, rhymes from *When We Were Very Young*. I repeated those rhymes to my children and now recite them to my grandchildren. We are all fond of our dear Mary Jane, who could not abide rice pudding again. In my growing-up years, my mother read aloud, and I reread when old enough to manage on my own, such treasures as *Nobody's Girl* and *Nobody's Boy, The Secret Garden, Little Women,* and *Jo's Boys*. On weekly trips to the library my mother would leave me to browse alone and at leisure in the children's section while she attended to errands. Mythology, especially Greek mythology, captivated my imagination. My first role model, long before I knew that term, was the wondrous Pallas Athena, surely a woman who made things happen.

Paper: Aladdin
Newbery Medal
⌐ Based on stories told by the author's grandmother, this is a rollicking tale of a redheaded tomboy in Wisconsin in the 1860s. Caddie's father prevails on her mother to let Caddie run with her brothers rather than be confined to the domestic skills that her older sister is busy acquiring. Caddie is full of funny pranks that leave the reader giggling, but she also shines as a girl of great

courage and independent thinking, particularly in the chapters where she warns the Indians of an attack by her own people. This is a beloved classic that every child will treasure. The sequel, *Magical Melons*, is just as good a read.

The Cat Ate My Gymsuit

Written by Paula Danziger
Copyright 1974
Cloth: Delacorte
Paper: Bantam Doubleday Dell

⌒ Marcy has an incredible array of excuses designed to keep her out of gym class and a laundry list of problems. She's self-conscious about her weight and despairs of ever being thin. She hates her father and, in fact, pretty much hates her life at Dwight D. Eisenhower Junior High. When Ms. Finney arrives as her new English teacher, life becomes a lot more interesting. Ms. Finney has a knack for involving and motivating her students. Marcy's a smart girl, and for the first time she's enjoying school. She and her friends are dumbfounded when Ms. Finney is suspended for her unorthodox teaching methods and her refusal to say the Pledge of Allegiance. Galvanized into action, Marcy organizes a protest movement to reinstate Ms. Finney. In doing so, she goes against her father's express wishes. Not all of Marcy's problems get solved, but it's clear she's on the right track. Kids love Marcy's real-life dilemmas and her wisecracking attitude. Even nonreaders find this book irresistible.

Catherine, Called Birdy

Written by Karen Cushman
Copyright 1994
Cloth: Clarion Books
Paper: HarperTrophy
Newbery Honor Book
ALA Notable Children's Book
Golden Kite Award

PAULA DANZIGER

⁓

Children's Book Author,
The Cat Ate My Gymsuit

t is impossible to pick just one book, so I'm going . . . to make a list. *The Little Engine That Could,* the Nancy Drew books (and the Cherry Ames and Sue Barton ones too), *Little Women* (yes, I wanted to be Jo), *A Tree Grows in Brooklyn, Pride and Prejudice* (which I believe is the first young adult novel), and the book most important to me, *Catcher in the Rye.*

OK . . . so *Catcher in the Rye* has no heroine. I don't care. The best books for girls are the best books for people. I hate saying about any novel, "It's a boy book," "It's a girl book." Hopefully, the "best books for girls" can also be the best books for boys and vice versa.

⁓ The year 1290 was a difficult one for fourteen-year-old Catherine, nicknamed Birdy. Because Birdy kept her promise to her brother to keep a journal, we get to read over Birdy's shoulder as she chronicles her life in medieval England.

A girl's life was her father's, and Birdy's father has plans to marry her off for a good price. Birdy successfully (sometimes hilariously) evades suitor after suitor, but in the end she is cornered. She finally consents to a wedding and barters her consent so as to free a caged bear from a traveling show. She recognizes how she and the bear are both trapped: "We can neither of us live alone and free and survive in this world, but we might wish for a cage less painful and confining."

KAREN CUSHMAN

⌐

Children's Book Author, The Ballad of Lucy Whipple *and* Catherine, Called Birdy
1996 Newbery Medalist

 o be honest, my favorite book was usually the one I was reading at the moment. Some titles stand out: *Little Women, Strawberry Girl, The Diary of Anne Frank, Seventeenth Summer.* But the book that made the greatest impression on me was *Anna Karenina.* Even as a twelve-year-old, I could not *believe* Anna, could not imagine such hysteria, such abject slavery to a man so obviously unworthy, such inability to be a person without a man. I resolved never to be as dithery and wimpy as that. And I never have. Well, hardly ever.

Only a stroke of luck could save Birdy, and fortunately for the reader, the author gives her just that by sending her unsavory suitor to a quick end. Thus the reader gets to imagine that this outspoken, quick-witted, and observant young woman might have a chance at a life she deserves. A terrific historical novel.

Note: Cushman explores medieval times again in *The Midwife's Apprentice.*

Charlotte's Web
Written by E. B. White/Illustrated by Garth
    Williams
Copyright 1952
Cloth: HarperCollins

Paper: HarperTrophy
Newbery Honor Book
～ Who doesn't love this book? It has everything: White's masterful prose, delightful characters, a fine moral sensibility, and an ingenious plot that gently introduces children to the cycle of life. From the first page, when eight-year-old Fern rescues Wilbur, the runt of the new litter of pigs, to the last, when Wilbur meets Charlotte's children, this is in a stratosphere of its own.

Charlotte A. Cavatica, a beautiful gray spider who lives in the barn with Wilbur, undertakes to save him from becoming the Christmas ham. She is able to do so by writing words in her web—what seems a miracle to the farmers is really just the power of a few good descriptive words. Nobody ever looks at Wilbur the same way after that. Charlotte is a "true friend and a good writer," and this is an incomparable book.

The Clay Marble
Written by Minfong Ho
Copyright 1991
Cloth: Farrar Straus & Giroux
Paper: Sunburst/Farrar Straus & Giroux
～ Twelve-year-old Dara, her mother, and her brother, Sarun, flee their bombed-out Cambodian village for the Thailand border, hoping for rice and safety. In the refugee camp Dara is befriended by a slightly older girl, the bolder, more confident Jantu. She not only teaches Dara the ins and outs of camp life but shows her how to hold on to her spirit as well. It is Jantu who creates a play world for them out of clay, and the simple marble Jantu makes for Dara becomes her talisman of magic and good luck. When fighting erupts again, Dara is separated from her family. Her faith in the clay marble's magic feeds her growing bravery as she struggles to find her mother again.

The strong characterization and gripping plot lift this book above the ordinary. The author has also written about political upheavals in her native Thailand in another fine book, *Rice Without Rain.*

Coast to Coast with Alice
Written by Patricia Rusch Hyatt
Copyright 1995
Cloth: Carolrhoda Books
Paper: Carolrhoda Books

⌐ On June 9, 1909, twenty-one-year-old Alice Ramsey set out to drive across the country in her bright green Maxwell touring car. She was the first woman to attempt such a daring feat. For company, she took along her two sisters-in-law and a young sixteen-year-old neighbor, Minna Jahns. This book is Minna's fictionalized diary of that trip. Alice is undaunted by the task before her: there are few roads, no maps, no gas stations with helpful mechanics. With great aplomb, Alice handles every situation. Broken axles, flat tires, gigantic mudholes, steep hills, pigs, and wild barking dogs have nothing on Alice. They reach San Francisco in fifty-nine days, breaking the record. But after all, they could drive forty miles per hour and even drive at night, thanks to those newfangled headlamps! Photographs from the actual journey enliven the fun.

Crown Duel
Written by Sherwood Smith
Copyright 1997
Cloth: Jane Yolen Books/Harcourt Brace

⌐ Fantasy and its sister genre, science fiction, can give us enviable worlds to wander through.

Crown Duel, by the author of the successful *Wren to the Rescue* (see Index), portrays a culture completely free of gender bias. There is never even a hint that the young Countess Meliara, brave and headstrong, can't lead her country into war alongside her brother. Although her tiny kingdom of Tlanth is ill suited to overthrow the evil king Galdran, Mel's canny maneuverings keep, at least for the short term, Galdran's ambitions contained. When Mel impetuously tries to spy on the enemy army, she is captured and sentenced to a grisly death. Her narrow escape and breathless flight through the countryside are full of heart-pounding peril. Mel's stamina is sorely tested, but she uses everything, even her emotions, to her advantage: "I got angry. There is nothing like good, honest, righteous anger to infuse a person with energy." Her valiant efforts on behalf of Tlanth make her a legend among her people. The countess is an exciting heroine in an exemplary society.

Note: Don't miss *Court Duel*, the exciting sequel.

Daphne's Book
Written by Mary Downing Hahn
Copyright 1983
Cloth: Houghton Mifflin

⌒ This is a believable, recognizable story about the slippery slopes of seventh-grade friendship.

Mr. O'Brien is Jessica's favorite teacher—until the awful day he assigns partners for the Write-a-Book contest. Mr. O'Brien pairs her with Daphne Woodleigh, the weirdest, most bizarre, and most ridiculed kid in the entire school. How could he? Jessica isn't popular, but she's tolerated by the girls who are, and she's positive that any association with Daphne will mean ending up without a single friend in the world. But Jessica makes some surprising discoveries about Daphne. Just as Jessica loves to write, Daphne loves to draw. The two are, in fact, a great team, and Jessica begins to look forward to Daphne's company. It dawns on Jessica that there are compelling, even tragic, reasons for Daphne's slovenly clothes and erratic behavior. But the social forces dominating the seventh grade don't want to understand Daphne. In scenes that will be painfully familiar to middle-school readers, Jessica guiltily betrays her new friendship again and again, bowing before the peer pressure of the popular girls, before she finally takes a stand.

Dealing with Dragons
Written by Patricia C. Wrede
Copyright 1990
Cloth: Harcourt Brace
Paper: Point/Scholastic

⁓ The picture-perfect enchanted land of Linderwall has only one blemish: the princess Cimorene. She hates it. Life in Linderwall is nothing but a dead end. To every new thing she wants to try, to every new thing she wants to learn, she's always told, "But that's not done." Cimorene has absolutely no intention of putting up with this. When a talking frog gives her some helpful advice on running away, she slips out of her kingdom and finds herself employment as a dragon's princess.

This witty send-up of the conventions of fairy tales (the first in a series of four called The Enchanted Forest Chronicles) is well on its way to becoming a classic. It punctures all the traditional balloons of proper princesses, handsome princes, fire-breathing dragons, and happily-ever-after marriages. The eminently satisfying story line gives Cimorene all the excitement she was craving and gives the reader a new, improved fairy-tale ending: ". . . life with the dragons would be interesting and busy, and in Cimorene's opinion that would go a long way toward making her happy."

The Egypt Game
Written by Zilpha Keatley Snyder/Illustrated by Alton Raible
Copyright 1967
Cloth: Atheneum
Paper: Yearling/Dell
Newbery Honor Book

⁓ April Hall is shunted off by her careless mother to live with her grandmother, a move not to April's liking. She fancies her mother to be a great actress and dreams of the day her mother will sweep her off to a swanky Hollywood life. Meanwhile, in the humdrum Casa Rosada apartments, April meets Melanie, and the two form a prickly friendship that picks up speed when they concoct "The Egypt Game." This is a grand, increasingly elaborate game of pretend that takes place in a vacant lot behind a mysterious antique shop.

There are several things we really liked about this book. The rituals of the pretend game are exactly as we remember from our childhoods. The plot that lurks beyond the children's game has the right amount of suspense and danger. The multiracial friendships aren't contrived or heavy-handed. Neither are the friendships that develop with the boys who join the game. In fact, this book works beautifully like a great piece of ensemble acting.

April comes to terms about her flighty mother and sheds the fake eyelashes and upswept hairdo of her false dreams. She and Melanie become the very best of friends. This is a favorite with every fifth-grader we know.

Ella Enchanted
Written by Gail Carson Levine
Copyright 1997
Cloth: HarperCollins
Newbery Honor Book

⌒ Erase Cinderella's syrupy demeanor and unaccountably docile subservience, and you'll happily latch on to this hilarious version of that tired fairy tale. Ella's discovery that she need be nobody's servant puts this book at the top of our charts.

A dim-witted fairy's foolish gift to Ella was to make her obedient. Now Ella *must* do as she's told. She tries to undermine the horrible spell by complying as little as possible: she throws the slippers she was ordered to pick up into the pig slops. This rebellious sense of humor keeps her sane even after she's been enslaved by her ugly stepsisters. The worst thing of all, though, is that Ella is in love with the worthy prince of her kingdom. How can she possibly marry while under this cursed enchantment? Trapped in a most precarious situation, Ella hunts everywhere for a way out. Ultimately Ella rescues herself and delightedly finds that she is at last her own mistress.

Emily of New Moon
Written by L. M. Montgomery
Published 1923; numerous editions available

~ Couldn't get enough of Anne of Green Gables? If you're longing to return to Prince Edward Island, you'd do well to read Montgomery's three Emily novels. Well-worn editions of these were given to us as young girls by our mothers, who treasured them as much as they treasured Anne.

Emily is orphaned at the beginning of this story and is raffled off to live with her stiff New Moon cousins. She scribbles furiously in her journal, describing all the ups and downs of her new, sometimes difficult life. Her intense passions and emotions lead to some rather purplish prose, but she is a determined girl whose artistic sensibilities and independent opinions sustain her. Old-fashioned fun.

A Family Apart
Written by Joan Lowery Nixon
Copyright 1987
Cloth: Bantam
Paper: Bantam

~ "It's always easier to place boys, because boys can help with the outdoor farm chores. Some families will even take two children from a family if they're boys." Quick-thinking Frances Mary overhears the people in the Children's Aid Society discussing the Kelly children's chances for adoption and immediately disappears into the bathroom to chop off her hair and disguise herself. She will do everything she can to stay with her littlest brother, Petey.

Since her father's death, Frances Mary and her mother have been cleaning offices in New York City, but six hungry children

CAROLYN T. MARMADUKE

∼

Jennifer's Mother, Author, Art and Library Docent, Community Activist

I don't remember the book's name, but its cover was gray with a picture of two rabbits seated on a rocking horse slowly rocking out over the windowsill into the starry night sky. I became aware that there was something beyond my small world and from that time forward, books became the pathway for me to speculate, to emulate, to dream.

I remember Polly of *The Five Little Peppers* baking and burning Mamsie's birthday cake and thinking, "Could I take care of four siblings?" I was an only child. Of course, I remember Anne with her flaming red hair (mine was non-descript brown) and Nancy, who had a convertible and solved REAL problems, but most of all I remember the world of *Emily of New Moon*, with the Wind Woman and Lofty John's Bush—all beyond her window sill and certainly beyond mine. But how eagerly I went there with her.

I know of all our scientific explorations, but I am still certain that the starry night holds for the curious a myriad of images. Some of mine came from the past; others are in the present and future. My childhood book friends have told me so!

couldn't live on those meager wages. Desperate, Mrs. Kelly makes a heartbreaking sacrifice: she sends her children out west to be adopted.

Her new family has no idea that Frankie is really Frances, and so they ask her to undertake a dangerous job they would never ask a girl to do—helping escaped slaves travel on the Underground Railroad. In several nail-biting scenes, Frances completes her perilous mission but is then captured by the marshal. It's a wonderfully ironic moment when her gender is revealed. The marshal lets her go because he can't believe that a little thirteen-year-old girl is actually capable of such daring action!

This is the first book in the popular Orphan Train Quartet series. *In the Face of Danger* follows the exciting adventures of Megan, another sister.

JOAN LOWERY NIXON

～

Children's Book Author, A Family Apart *and* The Name of the Game Was Murder

hen I was young, I gobbled books, taking home from the library as many as the librarian would allow. With excitement I dove into them and came up for air only so I could race back to the library for another armful of books. But there was one book I read more than once—my all-time favorite: Louisa May Alcott's *Little Women.* I closely identified with Jo, who wrote stories in her attic. Jealous because our California bungalow didn't have an attic, I still wanted to be like Jo because I knew that someday I was going to be a published writer.

The Farthest-Away Mountain
Written by Lynne Reid Banks/Illustrated by Dave Henderson
Copyright 1976
Cloth: Doubleday
Paper: Avon

~ Dakin has some untraditional and traditional wishes for herself: "to visit the farthest-away mountain, and see a gargoyle, and find a prince to be my husband." Her family is not at all pleased, but when Dakin wakes up early one morning and feels the mountain calling her—indeed, it nods to her—she sets off on a quest to fulfill her wishes.

Banks, best known for her Indian in the Cupboard series, knows how to write a page-turner. Dakin foils one enemy after another, deftly handling the many dangers she faces. She discovers "It wasn't enough to be good. One had to be wise and brave as well." Her third wish never does come true, but Dakin is wiser now and happy to cast it aside. Nifty adventure tale.

The First Woman Doctor
Written by Rachel Baker/Illustrated by Evelyn Copelman
Copyright 1944, 1971
Paper: Scholastic

~ This in-depth biography delves into the reasons Elizabeth Blackwell decided to become our nation's first woman doctor. She was no stranger to hardship. Her father died when she was eighteen, leaving Elizabeth's mother and seven brothers and sisters penniless. To make ends meet, they established a school, but Elizabeth remained restless. An ill friend suggested that Elizabeth study medicine, and Elizabeth took up the challenge. She was admitted to Geneva Medical School as a joke but graduated at the top of her class in 1849. Even so, no hospital would hire her. She struggled on, working in London and Paris before returning to New York. Because no one would rent office space to a female doctor, she bought her own house and set up her own hospital and medical college. She was one of the first—if not *the* first—proponents of preventive medicine. Self-reliant and tireless, Elizabeth Blackwell accomplished the unthinkable.

Note: Give younger children a copy of Carol Greene's *Elizabeth Blackwell* (see Index).

Fog Magic
Written by Julia L. Sauer
Copyright 1943
Paper: Puffin
Newbery Honor Book

⁓ A fourth-grade teacher we know urged us to read this book, although it came with a warning that some of her students found it too slow. It is true that this book is short on action and long on atmosphere, but for the right child, one who can shorten her stride to match the leisurely pace of this story, the quaint charms of this fantasy are delightful.

The Nova Scotia fog always seems to beckon to eleven-year-old Greta Addington, hinting of magic, until one day Greta finds the secret the fog has been hiding: through it, she can step back in time. She's welcomed as a friend by the townspeople of long-ago Blue Cove and shares three stories about women of the day, absorbing their lessons (two are painful and one is valiantly heroic) along the way. When Greta turns twelve, Blue Cove, like Neverland, is closed to her, but unlike Peter Pan, Greta looks forward to the years ahead, knowing that "none of the things you think you've lost on the way are *really* lost. Every one of them is folded around you—close."

The Forestwife
Written by Theresa Tomlinson
Copyright 1993

BERNADINE HEALY, M.D.

～

Dean, College of Medicine and Public Health,
The Ohio State University
First woman director, National Institutes of Health

o this day I clearly remember the book *The Nun's Story* by Katheryn Hulme. The heroine was Sister Luke, a Belgian nun. In the process of becoming a perpetually-vowed nun, she underwent an enormous physical, emotional, and spiritual discipline that developed in her a very strong character. Sister Luke worked with the sickest of psychiatric patients in a locked ward, witnessing the murder of one of her sister nuns by a deranged patient. She was sent to the Belgian Congo. Tuberculosis forced her to return to Belgium, amidst the horrors of Nazi aggression in Europe.

It was then that her strongest principles came into direct conflict with the admonition of the Church that its nuns remain neutral toward both the Allies and Germany in the war. When she accidentally discovered a news report that her father had been murdered by Nazi soldiers, she left the Order to join the Belgian underground as a nurse.

This was a vivid book for me as a young teen, and it remains vivid. It captured the mysteries of science in study and research, the humanism of medicine, and the ability of one person devoted to high principles to better the lives of many and be true to herself.

Cloth: Orchard Books

Paper: Random House

⌐○ We loved this book for many reasons: fast-paced plot, great characters, wonderful medieval setting, rich language. And we especially loved seeing Maid Marian as the central figure in the Robin Hood legend.

The author, in the book's afterword, says it best: "From an early age . . . Robin Hood was my favorite. . . . He was a hero I could *almost* identify with. The only problem was that it was natural as a girl to see myself more as Maid Marian; and I sometimes found that rather irritating. Marian was usually locked up in a castle and needing to be rescued—being terribly brave about it, of course. What I really wanted was to imagine myself running through the forest, along with the men. I wanted to be the one doing the rescuing."

Author Tomlinson has written the book she wanted to read as a young girl. Your children will love it as ours do.

From Anna

Written by Jean Little/Illustrated by Joan Sandin

Copyright 1972

Paper: HarperCollins

⌐○ As we learned in Jean Little's wonderful autobiography, *Little by Little* (see Index), one of her missions as an author was to write books that realistically portrayed children learning to live with handicaps.

Here Little writes about Anna, the youngest child of a German family in the 1930s. Her older sisters and brothers are all happy, well-adjusted children who excel in school. And then there's Anna, nicknamed Awkward Anna for her clumsiness and avoided for her grumpy disposition. The teacher picks on Anna, asking constantly why she can't shine at her studies like her siblings. Even her mother finds herself exasperated by Anna's prickly behavior. Only her papa

RUTH WHITNEY

⁓

Editor-in-Chief, Glamour *Magazine*

 had a mile to walk home from school in Oshkosh, Wisconsin, when I was in sixth and seventh grade. My friend Anna Mae walked with me until she got to her house on Cherry Street. We argued often along the way about the book *Little Women.* She adored it, read it again and again, and wanted to discuss it again and again. I read it once. A good read, yes, but it never gave me the kind of soaring inspiration I found in *Robin Hood*, which I read until the covers fell off. It wasn't the economic message of "take from the rich, give to the poor" that enthralled me; it was the action, the adventure, the derring-do, the camaraderie that kept me spellbound.

Decades later, *Glamour*'s executive editor and I bonded when we learned that, for each of us, *Robin Hood* was the big book of our childhood.

loves her unreservedly. Papa's decision to emigrate to Canada causes upheaval for the whole family but provides an unexpected boon for Anna: a sympathetic doctor examines her and discovers that she can barely see. Anna needs glasses and needs to attend a special school for the visually impaired. Finally, Anna can read the letters on the blackboard. The nurturing teaching style relaxes Anna and she gains confidence in her skills and intelligence. When the children decide they must save money by making Christmas presents for Mama and Papa, no one expects that Anna will be able to contribute anything. Written off by her siblings, Anna works in secret on a special gift that stuns them all and makes them really look at her for the very first time. No longer Awkward Anna to her family, Anna is instead their "dearest, dearest child."

From the Mixed-Up Files of Mrs. Basil E. Frankweiler

Written and Illustrated by E. L. Konigsburg
Copyright 1967
Cloth: Atheneum
Paper: Aladdin
Newbery Medal

⁀ Teachers often say this is the most popular book they teach in the fourth or fifth grade. The daring escape from home, the clever survival techniques in the Metropolitan Museum of Art, and the intriguing art mystery surrounding a Renaissance sculpture hold children spellbound. Eleven-year-old Claudia is the brainy mastermind behind the extraordinary adventure she takes with her younger brother, Jamie. Kids come back to this one again and again for the intricately detailed plot, the familiar sibling give-and-take, and the chance to follow a complex heroine in search of herself.

Gentle Annie: The True Story of a Civil War Nurse

Written by Mary Francis Shura
Copyright 1991
Paper: Apple

⁀ Anna Etheridge was a real woman who was a nurse in the front line of nearly every major battle fought by the Army of the Potomac during the Civil War. She enlisted at sixteen and made her mark at the very first engagement, Blackburn's Run, when she stayed to tend the wounded while others fled. The anecdotal details (she's friends with Sarah Emma Edmonds, the famous Union spy) and the military history are neatly handled. Annie's grace under fire, her valor, and her winning manner are movingly brought to light in this fine fictionalized biography.

A Girl of the Limberlost
Written by Gene Stratton-Porter
Published 1909; numerous editions available
⌒ This is an old chestnut indeed! We (and our mothers) loved this as children and we've found that the dramatic story line keeps our daughters reading.

Elnora is the much-neglected daughter who prevails against all odds. Ignored, indeed thwarted, by her mother, she fights for an education, which she pays for by collecting moths in the Limberlost, the swamp and woods near her home. Elnora's affinity for the natural world is unusual and delineated in excellent scientific detail. That and the mother-daughter struggle are the better parts of the book; the overwrought romance at the end is not as interesting. A sentimental favorite.

The Girl-Son
Written by Anne E. Neuberger
Copyright 1995
Cloth: Carolrhoda Books
Paper: Carolrhoda Books
⌒ We couldn't put this biography down.

In Korea in 1896 a little girl, Induk Pahk, was born. "Well . . . a girl is better than nothing" was her father's reaction. Little better than nothing, really, for a girl in those days had no opportunities for education, no life other than submission and marriage. But Induk had the most remarkable mother. After her husband's death, she disguised Induk as a boy so that she could attend school. Induk's year as a boy was liberating and exhilarating. Not only did she thrive academically, but she could play—sled, climb trees, fly kites—as she would never have been allowed to as a girl.

Induk and her mother found a missionary school for girls so that Induk could continue her education. She finished high school, then college, and was teaching when she was thrown into jail for supporting Korean independence from Japan. After she was freed from prison, she devoted her life to educating Korea's poor.

An exceptional woman whose unusual life story holds lessons for us all.

Go Free or Die: A Story About Harriet Tubman

Written by Jeri Ferris/Illustrated by Karen Ritz
Copyright 1988
Paper: Carolrhoda Books

⌐ The story of Harriet Tubman is so astounding that the best thing to do is get out of the way and let it "tell itself." Six-year-old Harriet is literally torn from her mother's arms by a plantation owner so that Harriet can be rented out to another farm. Thus begins the awakening of Harriet's brave and indomitable spirit. As Harriet grows up and hears about slave revolts and the Underground Railroad, hope stirs within her. Even a debilitating injury from a white overseer that has left her prone to sudden sleeping spells doesn't stop her. In fact it makes the account of her own escape and her lifelong effort to free more slaves all the more amazing. As the book states, "Harriet made 19 trips to the South. She led over 300 slaves to freedom and never lost one." Ritz's drawings are a fine accompaniment to the story of a woman who was a beacon to her people.

Good Queen Bess: The Story of Elizabeth I of England

Written by Diane Stanley and Peter Vennema/Illustrated by Diane Stanley

DIANE STANLEY

～

Children's Book Author, Good Queen Bess *and* Rumpelstiltskin's Daughter

rowing up as an only child, reading became my best friend. I had many, many books I loved, but there are two that touched me particularly. Partly, I'm sure, it's because the heroines of both books had to go it alone and did so splendidly. The first is *Anne of Green Gables* by Lucy Maud Montgomery. Imaginative, adventuresome, and full of the doubts and fears all children know, Anne ("with an E") is one of the best characters in children's literature. I adored her. The second, *The Secret Garden* by Frances Hodgson Burnett, tells of hopelessness and tragedy overcome by the resilience of children. The mysterious locked garden and the miracle of healing it symbolized thrilled me. It is a magical story. It's hard to stop—I haven't even mentioned *Charlotte's Web* yet!

Copyright 1990
Cloth: Simon & Schuster
～ "It would not be Henry VIII or Philip II or any of the kings of France who would give their name to the age they lived in. It would be called the Elizabethan Age after the remarkable queen who loved her people so dearly and ruled them so well."

Although this is a picture book, an especially beautiful and historically accurate picture book, we've saved it for this category because of the complex rendering of Elizabeth's remarkable forty-five-year reign. Elizabeth's shrewd and savvy instincts were honed out of necessity when, as a young princess, her life was always in danger. After she finally ascended to the throne, Elizabeth was able to gain her ends by her adroit political manipulations. With the defeat of the Spanish Armada, Elizabeth brought security and peace to her country. Under her sage leadership, England saw a cultural flowering such as it had never seen before. The authors do a superb job of portraying this magnificent, glorious queen.

Goodbye, Vietnam
Written by Gloria Whelan
Copyright 1992
Cloth: Alfred A. Knopf
Paper: Random House

～ This nicely written novel takes a very real plight from recent headlines and telescopes in on a young girl and the strong women around her.

A girl's life in a tiny Vietnamese village is strictly proscribed: "Children must sit where their parents place them." But when Mai's family flees from the soldiers who have threatened her grandmother and embarks on a rickety boat for Hong Kong, Mai finds that the customary rules no longer apply. The journey brings together refugees from all walks of life. Mai's grandmother, the village medicine woman clinging to her traditional beliefs, is juxtaposed against a modern female doctor. Before now, Mai could never have imagined a woman being a trained physician. The bridge between the old way and the new is slow in forming, but the two doctors come to respect each other's healing practices. The dangerous voyage on an overcrowded boat, with no charts, no sanitation, meager food and water, nevertheless opens a window on another world for Mai.

Grace Hopper: Programming Pioneer
Written by Nancy Whitelaw/Illustrated by Janet Hamlin
Copyright 1995

Cloth: Scientific American Books for Young Readers/W. H. Freeman & Co.

Paper: Scientific American Books for Young Readers/W. H. Freeman & Co.

⁓ Peppered with entertaining quotes and anecdotes from her childhood through her incredible career, this lively biography explains in clear language Rear Admiral Grace Hopper's exceptional contributions to the operations of computers. She began her work in 1944 on a huge, cumbersome Mark I machine and saw the computer develop through the microchip. Her pioneering computer programs for the Navy and private business were, quite simply, the stuff of legend. She was a woman who never took no for an answer and who believed the worst thing you could say was "We've always done it this way." She didn't leave the Navy until she had to—at age seventy-nine!

When Grace Hopper died in 1992, the list of her awards and honorary degrees filled eight single-spaced pages. When you've finished this book, you'll appreciate why she was so aptly nicknamed "Amazing Grace."

(We were interested to learn about Rear Admiral Hopper's favorite childhood books: *Little Women* and a series called The Boy's Own Library by G. A. Henley, about which Whitelaw notes, "In these books, the heroes—all boys—traveled to faraway places seeking adventure. Grace wanted adventure too.")

Harriet the Spy
Written by Louise Fitzhugh
Copyright 1964
Cloth: HarperCollins
Paper: HarperTrophy

⁓ Although she is only eleven, Harriet has already chosen to think of herself as a writer. To write, she needs material. Spying is how she gets it. She has a regular neighborhood route covering an eccentric assortment of people, and she faithfully records her original observations in a secret notebook. Her journal also contains honest but highly unflattering portrayals of her classmates. Unfortunately for her, her journal lands in the wrong hands and her classmates turn against her. For the first time, Harriet must consider the implications of being a writer and come up with a way out of this excruciating mess.

This is a sophisticated book with an extremely precocious, singular heroine. Harriet's fresh and funny comments are believable, and the pain she suffers is all too recognizable. Many have called this a modern-day classic.

Heart of Gold
Written by Kerri Strug with Greg Brown/Illustrations by
    Doug Keith
Copyright 1996
Cloth: Taylor Publishing

⌐ Few who saw it can forget the amazing vault Kerri Strug performed on an injured ankle at the 1996 Centennial Olympic Games. Her brave action to help clinch the first-ever gold for the American gymnastic team won her friends around the world. In this honest, forthright autobiography Kerri describes the events that led up to that dramatic moment. She tells about her years of intense training, first near home and then with Bela Karolyi, the famous coach of Nadia Comaneci and Mary Lou Retton. Kerri reveals that being a gymnast is far from being a glamorous life: she was often homesick, jealousy sometimes surfaced, and she endured two nearly completely debilitating injuries. She conquered her fears by thinking about her successes rather than dwelling on her mistakes. There's lots of fascinating detail about Kerri's demanding sport, and every page is packed with photographs. The biggest appeal here is Kerri herself—a winner with a "heart of gold."

Heartlight

Written by Thomas A. Barron
Copyright 1990
Cloth: Philomel Books
Paper: Forge

⌒ Seventh grade is definitely no fun for Kate. She's just moved, she has new braces, her parents are always busy, and, incredibly enough, although she spends every free moment with her famous astrophysicist grandfather, she's flunking science. But one day her grandfather lets her in on his most precious secret: he has discovered that when Pure Condensed Light reacts with a person's inner light—heartlight—that person can travel anywhere in the universe at a speed faster than light. When evil spirits from a distant galaxy try to steal the PCL he has made in his lab, Grandfather and Kate find themselves on a perilous journey to alien planets.

Time after time in this Star Wars–like fantasy, Kate must rise above her insecurities to avert the cosmic destruction threatening them all. Her heroic deeds ultimately lead to nothing less than the salvation of mankind. This is a book that positively vibrates with provocative mystical ideas and a thrilling sci-fi plot.

The Hidden Life of Fanny Mendelssohn

Written by Gloria Kamen
Copyright 1996
Cloth: Atheneum

⌒ In Virginia Woolf's famous essay *A Room of One's Own*, she speculates that if Shakespeare had had a sister, her genius would have been ignored and she would have died without having written a word. Felix Mendelssohn *did* have a sister, as gifted and brilliant as he. Born to a wealthy Jewish family in the early 1800s, Fanny and Felix studied the piano together from childhood. With his father's grudging approval, Felix launched a dazzling career as a pianist and composer, but this approval never extended to Fanny. Her father believed that for a woman music was to be "only an ornament." Within the strict confines of her upper-class existence, Fanny contrived to practice, perform, and compose. Her brother never bothered to champion the sister who loved him so well, and Fanny's reputation has languished—most of her works have still never been published. (The modern reader will find much of this book infuriating, but it is gratifying to learn that she is finally being discovered.) This is a smoothly written biography that does justice to Fanny's genius as well as describing the unwelcoming world around her.

His Majesty, Queen Hatshepsut

Written by Dorothy Sharp Carter/Illustrated by Michele
     Chessare
Copyright 1987
Cloth: Lippincott-Raven

⌐ Girls will relish the rare opportunity to read about an unabashedly ambitious woman. Formidable, regal, divine, Hatshepsut has nerves of steel. The daughter of a great pharaoh who becomes the wife of the next pharaoh, she is now the widowed queen regent, governing only until the pharaoh's male heir comes of age. Hatshepsut sees no logic to stepping aside for him. She reasons "In Egypt the line of dynastic succession runs not through men but through women. *My* blood is the most royal blood in all of Upper and Lower Egypt. *No* one has more right to rule than I. For the bar to one's destiny to be an accident of sex—what injustice! . . . Very well. I will rule as a king . . . with the full powers of a king."

So Hatshepsut seizes the throne from her young stepson, sweeping aside any objections from the powerful priests, and is crowned His Majesty, Queen Hatshepsut. She rules Egypt for twenty-one years, probably around 1503 to 1482 B.C., and we're

ELLEN TAAFFE ZWILICH

~

1983 Pulitzer Prize for Music
Carnegie Hall Composer's Chair

y male colleagues remember reading many biographies of musicians. I didn't, perhaps because there weren't any biographies of women musicians for me to read about.

treated to vivid portrayals of what Egyptian court life might have been like. There is pageantry and ceremony, but there are also treacherous palace intrigues.

A first-rate historical drama.

Homesick: My Own Story
Written by Jean Fritz/Illustrated by Margot Tomes
Copyright 1982
Cloth: Putnam
Paper: Dell
Newbery Honor Book
Christopher Award
American Book Award
~ This is a thoroughly engrossing autobiography by a top-notch writer.

In 1925, Jean Fritz didn't know where she fit in. She lived in Hankow, China, with her parents. She had a grandmother in Pennsylvania she'd never met. She went to a British school, where a bully tormented her for refusing to sing "God Save the King." ("It is not my national anthem," she explained to the teacher.) She was torn. She spoke Chinese fluently, loved her Chinese *amah* (nanny), and visited the Great Wall every summer. But her feelings for China became complicated with the rise of the Communists and the taunts of "foreign devil" in her ear.

When at last her family flees China for America, Jean believes she is going home. Meeting her grandmother is everything she'd hoped it would be, but Jean learns that a homecoming is not as simple as she believed. Will she ever belong anywhere? Her grandmother looks her straight in the eye and says, "I thought you were going to be a writer. . . . Writers do more than just fit in. Sometimes they don't fit in at all."

Maybe this outsider's perspective is what made Jean Fritz a great historian. At any rate, don't miss this or its fine sequel, *China Homecoming*.

I Am Lavina Cumming

Written by Susan Lowell/Illustrated by Paul Mirocha
Copyright 1993
Cloth: Milkweed Editions
Paper: Milkweed Editions

⌒ The Cumming family motto is "Courage" and courage is what Lavina needs when, after her mother's death, Father sends her away from her beloved Arizona ranch to live with starchy Aunt Agnes in Santa Cruz, California. She had run free with her brothers for years, riding her horse, climbing the mountains. Now Father feels she must learn to be a lady.

Lavina is crushingly homesick, and matters are not helped by her spoiled cousin, who insists on treating her like a poor relation. She faces a host of bewildering new experiences: a bathtub, a three-story house, Christmas with a real tree, a beautiful porcelain dolly, the ocean, wearing shoes all the time. . . . It would overwhelm smaller spirits, but Lavina holds fast to the Cumming motto.

Based on the author's own grandmother's stories, this superbly written historical novel (Lavina lived through the great San Francisco earthquake of 1906!) dramatizes the dilemma of growing up: how much of your freewheeling girlhood can you take with you as you become an adult? We've bought this book for countless birthday presents.

The Illyrian Adventure
Written by Lloyd Alexander
Copyright 1986
Paper: Yearling

~ Grab a bag of popcorn and munch your way through this high-flying tale and its many sequels. They're better than a Saturday afternoon at the movies!

In 1872, Vesper Holly sets off for the mysterious land of Illyria to restore her father's tarnished academic reputation. She takes along her guardian, Brinnie, who chronicles the story and acts as an admiring Dr. Watson to Vesper's Holmes. Vesper is flamboyant, erudite, witty, intrepid, and clever. The devilish twists and turns in the plot keep the reader hopping. Featuring dastardly villains, hair-raising adventures, and a fearless heroine, all of these books pack quite a punch.

In the Year of the Boar and Jackie Robinson
Written by Bette Bao Lord
Copyright 1984
Cloth: HarperCollins
Paper: HarperTrophy

~ Sixth Cousin moves from China to Brooklyn in 1947 and becomes Shirley Temple Wong. America is an amazing place, but Shirley has a hard time fitting in. When Mabel, the strongest and scariest girl in her grade, befriends Shirley and chooses her for the stickball team, Shirley is hooked on playing ball. The Brooklyn

Dodgers become her introduction to America. At the end of her memorable, often funny first year, the spunky Shirley presents the key to P.S. 8 to the great Jackie Robinson. An adventure that began with trepidation ends as a "year when dreams came true. The year of double happiness."

Note: Older readers will appreciate another story of a childhood tied to the fortunes of the Brooklyn Dodgers, *Wait Till Next Year* by Doris Kearns Goodwin (see Index).

Indian Captive: The Story of Mary Jemison
Written and Illustrated by Lois Lenski
Copyright 1941, 1969
Cloth: HarperCollins
Paper: HarperTrophy
Newbery Honor

⌒ Based on a true story, this is a fascinating tale of one girl's fortitude as she struggles between two cultures.

In 1758, Mary Jemison was captured by the Seneca Indians and taken away to live in the wilderness. She is left with only her mother's words to comfort her: "No matter where you are, Mary, my child, have courage, be brave! *It don't matter what happens, if you're only strong and have great courage.*"

Nicknamed Corn Tassel because of her blond hair, Mary slowly becomes accustomed to, then comfortable with, and finally happy with the Seneca way of life. Lenski does a fine job of making Mary's thoughts and actions real as she grapples to understand her captors. The sympathetic portrayal of the Senecas is detailed and excellent. In a tense climactic scene she must choose whether to stay with the Senecas or return to the world of her people. Mary's courage is staggering and will impress every girl.

Inspirations: Stories About Women Artists
Written by Leslie Sills
Copyright 1989

Cloth: Albert Whitman & Co.

ALA Notable Book

⁓ What could be more encouraging to a young, maturing girl of independent mind than the four life stories of Georgia O'Keeffe, Frieda Kahlo, Alice Neel, and Faith Ringgold? Each of these outstanding painters persevered despite the odds against them and the often sad events in their lives. *Inspirations* is beautifully laid out with many color reproductions, making it a pleasure to look at. A second volume, *Visions,* discusses Mary Cassatt, Leonora Carrington, Betye Saar, and Mary Frank. Both are highly worthwhile.

Note: Younger readers should take a look at Mike Venezia's *Georgia O'Keeffe* (see Index). *Talking to Faith Ringgold* (found in this section) is a fun way to further explore this artist and her work.

Into the Land of the Unicorns
Written by Bruce Coville

Copyright 1994

Cloth: Scholastic

Paper: Apple

⁓ The first chapter of this fantasy novel will have your pulse racing! Cara and her grandmother are being stalked by a mysterious man who chases them up the winding stairs of a church bell tower. Her grandmother hands her a special amulet and instructs Cara to jump before the bell chimes twelve. She tells her that when she lands she must "Find the Old One. Tell her, 'The Wanderer is weary.'" Confused and scared, Cara nonetheless trusts her and leaps into the Land of Luster, the land of unicorns. Cara is helped on her quest by the Dimblethum, a man-bear; the Squijum, a talking squirrel; and Lightfoot, a spirited young unicorn. At stake is the very survival of all the unicorns. Cara never falters—even when she uncovers the shocking identity of the villain.

Filled with wild magic and exciting adventures, this has been popular in both our houses.

Beatrice Wood

⌒

Ceramist and Painter

he first books I read and loved were Louisa May Alcott's *Little Women* and a wonderful book about mythology. So the first years of my life went into nice relationships and an interest in the unseen world around us. Fortunately I was spared the violence that now overwhelms us with our technical genius accomplishments.

I wish on television we could find more on romance and the compensation of building fine character.

Island of the Blue Dolphins
Written by Scott O'Dell
Copyright 1960
Cloth: Houghton Mifflin
Paper: Yearling/Dell
Newbery Medal

⌒ Scott O'Dell is noted for his many distinguished novels about remarkable young women. This is one of his finest.

As he describes it himself, "The girl Robinson Crusoe whose story I have attempted to re-create actually lived alone upon this island from 1835 to 1853, and is known to history as 'The Lost Woman of San Nicolas.'" Karana's story is indeed unforgettable. Left behind on the island when her tribe moves away, twelve-year-old Karana must struggle for survival and against horrible loneliness. O'Dell has convincingly detailed what her life must have been like:

she makes weapons with sea elephant tusks, crafts a skirt from cormorant feathers, gathers abalone, builds a fence from whalebones, and makes a pet of a murderous wild dog. Absorbing, enthralling reading.

A Jar of Dreams
Written by Yoshiko Uchida
Copyright 1981
Cloth: Atheneum
Paper: Aladdin

⌒ In this novel, set in 1935, Rinko Tsujimara and her family are living in Berkeley, California. Because of the repeated discrimination they are subjected to, they have all reined in their dreams of success in America. Papa and Mama are pinning their hopes on their children: Cal, who is debating whether to continue his engineering studies, and Rinko, who is unhappy with, and sometimes embarrassed by, her Japanese heritage, especially in school.

Everything changes one summer when Aunt Waka comes from Japan to visit. Aunt Waka is entirely comfortable with herself, and her subtle example inspires a shift in attitude. Papa stands up to the menacing bigot who has been bullying his family and trying to destroy Mama's new laundry business. Cal decides to pursue his education. And Rinko learns to be proud of her double heritage. Rinko resolves to have *two* jars of dreams, one for college in America and one for a visit with Aunt Waka in Japan. You can meet Rinko again in *The Best Bad Thing* and *The Happiest Ending*.

Jean Craighead George
Written by Alice Cary
Copyright 1996
Paper: Learning Works

⌒ Oh, to have had a childhood like that of author Jean Craighead George! Her family canoed, fished, and camped out every possible weekend. Her entomologist parents schooled their children in the lore of the wild; turkey vultures and falcons were their pets. When she married in 1944, she and her husband lived for four years in a tent in the Michigan woods. This Newbery Medal winner has written sixty-five books for children, explored the Arctic, raised 173 different kinds of pets, and is still going strong. We dare you not to be charmed by the biography of this most intelligent, fascinating woman!

Jennifer Murdley's Toad
Written by Bruce Coville/Illustrated by Gary A.
    Lippincott
Copyright 1982
Cloth: Harcourt Brace
Paper: Minstrel Books

∽ Jennifer Murdley has an impossible desire: to be beautiful. Impossible because she is a very ordinary, plain, slightly pudgy fifth-grader. Her father brings her a geode and explains about appearances and inner beauty, and together she and her father bury a "Barbie doll in the backyard, under a tombstone that said Beauty Victim." Despite these lofty sentiments, she still longs to be as gorgeous as her classmate and number-one enemy, Sharra Moncreiffe.

When Jennifer buys a talking toad from a magic shop, she embarks on a wild adventure. Snappy, funny writing, a roller-coaster plot, and important lessons about appearances make this story irresistible.

Jenny of the Tetons
Written by Kristiana Gregory
Copyright 1989
Cloth: Harcourt Brace
Paper: Harcourt Brace

Golden Kite Award

∼ At the base of the Tetons lies a beautiful lake—clear, cold, blue. It was named, in 1872, for the real Shoshone Indian woman who, with her English husband, acted as a guide for a survey team. Her name was Jenny, and this is her fictionalized story.

To structure her book, the author has imagined a narrator, Carrie Hill, a fifteen-year-old white girl whose family has just been killed by Indians. With no place to go, it is suggested that she live with Beaver Dick and help his wife with their large family. Carrie's eyes are wide with horror when she meets his wife, Jenny, and finds her to be an Indian.

Carrie has several "journeys" to make. She must mourn her family without losing her hold on life; she must give up her hatred of Indians; she must move out of childhood into womanhood. (There is one brief, nonexplicit sexual scene.) Like another famous Shoshone, Sacagawea, Jenny is an excellent guide, and it is Jenny who mothers and points the way for Carrie. A beautifully written story that is a lovely paean to Jenny.

Julie of the Wolves
Written by Jean Craighead George/Illustrated by
    John Schoenherr
Copyright 1972
Cloth: HarperCollins
Paper: HarperTrophy
Newbery Medal

∼ Miyax is thirteen, a modern Eskimo girl schooled in the ancient ways of her people by her father, Kapugen, a legendary hunter. When a traditional marriage arranged by her father turns threatening, Miyax escapes to the tundra, heading for San Francisco and the pen pal who knows her as Julie.

The core of this book is an incredible story of endurance in one of the most forbidding places on earth. Miyax, desperate for food, seeks to become adopted by a wolf pack. The author's astonishing knowledge of wolf behavior and the "old ways" of Eskimo living are honored through George's meticulously detailed writing.

The love Miyax comes to feel for her wolf pack and the strength she gains from knowing that she can live as her ancestors lived are cruelly betrayed in the book's final pages. This is a haunting saga for fifth- and sixth-grade readers.

Keeping the Good Light
Written by Katherine Kirkpatrick
Copyright 1995
Cloth: Delacorte
Paper: Laurel Leaf

∽ Rebellious Eliza Charity Brown is chafing at the bit. She has grown up on a tiny lighthouse island in New York Harbor. Her turn-of-the-century world is one of confining rules, from the strict lighthouse regulations her family must follow to society's tyrannical expectations of ladylike behavior. It is a lonely existence. Even at sixteen, Eliza is allowed to leave the island only to row to school. But when her older, married sister becomes pregnant, Eliza is sent to live with her on City Island and teach in the local school. Here, despite the trouble she swiftly gets into, Eliza begins to see that she really does have choices.

Rich in impeccable historical details—the list of guidelines Eliza must obey as a female teacher is seriously daunting—this is a finely nuanced portrait of a headstrong girl who learns to value her individuality and independence.

Letters from Rifka
Written by Karen Hesse
Copyright 1992
Cloth: Henry Holt

Paper: Puffin
National Jewish Book Award
Christopher Award
Sydney Taylor Book Award

⌒ Based on the real-life story of the author's aunt, this is a harrowing immigrant's tale, told with unsparing honesty.

Rifka is only twelve, but it is her job to distract the Russian soldiers so her family can flee the country. That is only the beginning of the trials that await her. In Poland the family is stricken by disease and then separated when Rifka is denied passage to America. Her family leaves without her, and Rifka arrives months later on a boat that barely survives a brutal storm. Rifka meets all of her difficulties unflinchingly and recounts them poignantly in her letters to her cousin Tovah.

Listening to Crickets: A Story About Rachel Carson

Written by Candice F. Ransom/Illustrated by Shelly O. Haas
Copyright 1993
Cloth: Carolrhoda Books
Paper: Carolrhoda Books

⌒ As this biography clearly shows, Rachel Carson left us an admirable legacy. Carson's original goal was to study literature and become a writer, but midway through college she switched her major to biology, a move considered highly unsuitable for women in the 1920s. Carson didn't rest there: She went on to earn a master's degree in marine zoology from Johns Hopkins University. She was then hired by the U.S. Bureau of Fisheries, the first woman to be employed as a scientist at that agency. At forty-four, Carson wrote *The Sea Around Us* and became instantly famous. In 1962 *Silent Spring* was published, documenting for the first time the horrible ramifications of pesticide use. It caused such a furor that President Kennedy set up a committee to study environmental hazards.

Despite a bombardment of ridicule from chemical companies, her controversial conclusions were ultimately accepted. There's no question that the debt we owe Rachel Carson for her prophetic, groundbreaking work is enormous.

Note: *A Clean Sea* (see Index) will appeal to younger readers.

A Little Princess
Written by Frances Hodgson Burnett
Published 1905; numerous editions available
⌐ This uplifting classic turns on the liberating power of a child's imagination, where the possible becomes real.

Sara Crewe, as you doubtless know, is the indulged, adored daughter of Captain Crewe, sent from India to board in high style at Miss Minchin's Select Seminary for Young Ladies in London. When her father dies and her fortune disappears, the duplicitous Miss Minchin relegates Sara to the attic and a life of servitude. Sara gamely fights this lonely and impoverished existence with the best, and only, weapon she has: her genius for storytelling and "playing pretend." Ultimately Sara's soaring vision finally vanquishes the sorrows around her and brings about a true fairy-tale ending. One of the quintessential books of childhood.

Little Women
Written by Louisa May Alcott
Published 1868; numerous editions available
⌐ What makes a book with a sentimental story line, often mawkish prose, and a contrived ending still worth reading? Jo! Alcott drew her so convincingly as an independent, ambitious young woman filled with recognizable longings that one can't help turning the pages. The vividness of her personality has made this book a classic. Certain scenes, such as when Jo sells her hair so Marmee can travel to their sick father, are part of our literary heritage. Once your girls read it, they, too, will know most of it by heart.

The lovely movie adaptation by Gillian Armstrong is not to be missed. It highlights Jo's wonderful, memorable character while sidestepping the unfortunate stereotypes of the nineteenth century.

Lyn St. James: Driven to Be First
Written by Ross R. Olney
Copyright 1996
Cloth: Lerner
Paper: Lerner

～ If your child hankers to be a grease monkey, she'll get a kick out of this biography of the "fastest woman on wheels."

Born in 1947, St. James was a painfully shy girl raised with traditional expectations and with dreams of being a concert pianist. When her mother took her to an Indy 500 race, St. James discovered that she loved cars, engines, and racing. She struggled for many years to get sponsorships—what came easily for so many

GLORIA STEINEM

～

Consulting Editor, Ms. *Magazine*

 ouisa May Alcott was my friend. I read all her adult novels as well as her young ones, and used to fantasize endlessly that she would come back to life and I could show her all the new things in the world. *Little Women* was my favorite book, and Jo was my favorite heroine. She represented the search for freedom and honesty to me. Among her adult novels, *Work* captured both personal and suffragist struggles.

SUSAN STAMBERG

~

Special Correspondent,
National Public Radio

f course Jo was my favorite character, with her long beautiful hair and the skirt that caught fire. She had daring and flair, tremendous bravery and kindness. And she wrote. As an only child, I envied that March family. So many sisters growing up together, taking care of one another. But of them all, Jo was my hero, the one I kept coming back and back and back to, until the edges of the pages were frayed. I reread Louisa May Alcott's book not too long ago, when the latest film version of *Little Women* came out. You return to beloved books as you do to friends you haven't seen in a long time. With some trepidation that they'll be different and you won't enjoy the differences—they've changed, or you have. But *Little Women* was as marvelous as I'd remembered it from those long-ago Manhattan afternoons when I'd stretch out with it propped open on my nonexistent chest, on the pink upholstered love seat in my parents' living room. Lying horizontal, at that age, all of me *fit* end to end on that loveseat. Today, the couch has moved to Washington with my ninety-year-old mother. And the very copy of *Little Women* that was so important to my childhood sits on the shelf of one of my bookcases, poised for reading aloud to a longed-for grandchild.

male drivers was doubly difficult for her. Eventually, though, after *Autoweek* magazine named her Rookie of the Year in 1984, St. James captured a sponsorship from Ford and her career really took off. In 1992, she entered the Indy 500 and did so well she was honored as the best new driver in the race. When asked if it was difficult being a woman and a race driver, St. James replied, "The car doesn't know the difference and no one can even see that it's a woman driving. No one judges me by my smile or personality, but by my results." Lots of action-packed color photographs round out this biography of an intense competitor.

Lyrico
Written by Elizabeth Vincent Foster/Illustrated by Joy Buba
Copyright 1991
Paper: Parabola Books
~ Who says they don't write books the way they used to? This utterly enjoyable novel involves a winged horse, Lyrico, whose arrival completely transforms the lives of Phillipa and her parents. Because of Lyrico, Phillipa is able to have the Wild West adventures she's always dreamed of. There are several suspenseful scenes where Phillipa deftly handles danger, but for the most part this is a gentle, humorous tale and growing-up story, with plenty of magic sprinkled about. It is a treasure for any girl longing for open spaces and a horse of her own.

Madeleine L'Engle: Author of **A Wrinkle in Time**
Written by Doreen Gonzales
Copyright 1991
Cloth: Dillon Press
~ It should come as no surprise that Madeleine L'Engle's favorite childhood book was *Emily of New Moon*. Like Emily, Madeleine wanted to be a writer from the time she could hold a pencil. This

CHRISTINE TODD WHITMAN

⮑

Governor of New Jersey

 loved mysteries and read all the Hardy Boys and Nancy Drew books. I also enjoyed the series of "Cherry Ames, Nurse" books. My favorites, however, were the books in the The Black Stallion series, which combined my love of mysteries with my love of horses. I wrote a letter to the author, Walter Farley, to thank him for his wonderful stories. To my delight, he wrote back! I remember his letter started, "Black is out to pasture right now, so I have a few minutes to write this note to you. . . . "

biography delves deeply into L'Engle's stiff, proper upbringing, her painful time spent at boarding school, her insecurities, and the roots of her beautiful writing. *A Wrinkle in Time* was rejected by more than thirty publishers but, as every young reader knows, when finally released, the book received almost every literary prize awarded. L'Engle has legions of adult fans as well. We particularly admire her stance on children's literature: "If it's not good enough for adults, it's not good enough for children."

Marie Curie and the Discovery of Radium
Written by Ann E. Steinke/Illustrated by Roger Xavier
Copyright 1987
Paper: Barron's
⮑ As a young woman, Marie Curie wrote, "We must believe that we are gifted for something, and that this thing, at *whatever cost,*

must be attained." Anyone reading her dramatic life story will be struck by her passionate commitment to her work.

Marie Sklodowska was born in Poland in 1867. The little girl's genius blossomed early, but there were many tragedies and hardships that could have prevented a less hardy soul from prevailing. An older sister died of typhus, her beloved mother died of tuberculosis, and financial problems stalked the family, threatening Marie's ambitious dreams of higher education. But Marie refused to be beaten down. In 1891 she realized her goal of studying at the Sorbonne in Paris. She married another dedicated scientist, Pierre Curie, in 1895. The research for her doctorate led her to the discovery of two hitherto unknown elements: polonium and radium. Working for over four years, in a deplorably ramshackle, drafty shed, she and Pierre isolated one-tenth of a gram of pure radium, enough to calculate its atomic weight so that it could be listed on the Periodic Table of Elements.

Burning with a single-minded zeal for research and pure science, Marie Curie won the Nobel Prize—once, in 1903 (shared with her husband), for physics and again, in 1911, for chemistry, becoming the first person ever to win this coveted honor twice.

Mariel of Redwall
Written by Brian Jacques
Copyright 1991
Cloth: Philomel Books
Paper: Avon

⌐ For every fifth- and sixth-grade reader, this is a swashbuckling adventure story (part of a hugely popular series) about a group of valiant mice and their woodlander friends. It is rife with nefarious villains who are finally defeated by the heroic actions of a courageous mousemaid.

An eleven-year-old friend of ours has read every single Redwall book. We asked her why she loved them so much. "The secret," she said, "is that there is always a really, really bad guy and he wants to destroy Redwall Abbey and do these awful things. The neat part is the changing point of view. In every chapter, you get inside different characters' heads and see what they're seeing. Of course, I liked *Mariel* best because this one is about an incredibly brave girl. *She's* the one who saves the day, and that's fun to read about." The spine-tingling clash of good and evil makes this book grand as a read-aloud, too.

Note: Jacques's newest title is *Pearls of Lutra*, also with a staunch heroine at its center.

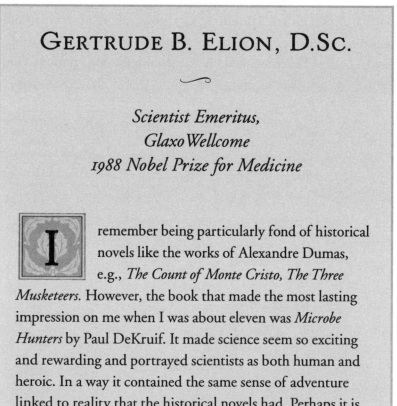

GERTRUDE B. ELION, D.SC.

⁓

Scientist Emeritus,
GlaxoWellcome
1988 Nobel Prize for Medicine

I remember being particularly fond of historical novels like the works of Alexandre Dumas, e.g., *The Count of Monte Cristo, The Three Musketeers.* However, the book that made the most lasting impression on me when I was about eleven was *Microbe Hunters* by Paul DeKruif. It made science seem so exciting and rewarding and portrayed scientists as both human and heroic. In a way it contained the same sense of adventure linked to reality that the historical novels had. Perhaps it is not so surprising that, four years later, I decided to become a scientist.

Mary Leakey: In Search of Human Beginnings
Written by Deborah Heiligman/Illustrated by Janet Hamlin
Copyright 1995
Cloth: Scientific American Books for Young Readers/W. H.
   Freeman & Co.
Paper: Scientific American Books for Young Readers/W. H.
   Freeman & Co.

⌒ How did human beings evolve? What can we find out about people who lived in prehistoric times? This biography shows that, from the time she was a child, these are questions that Mary Nicol Leakey wanted to answer.

Born in London in 1913, her parents gave her an unfettered and unconventional childhood, always fostering her lively curiosity. She never attended a formal school until she was thirteen. She traveled widely, visiting the cave paintings in France as well as Stonehenge. By the time she was seventeen, she was working on digs with Dorothy Liddell. When she attended a lecture at the Royal Anthropological Institute, she met Louis Leakey, already a well-known palcoanthropologist. The two shared a passion for archaeology, and soon Mary found herself in Africa. It was she who introduced a systematic method of excavating that is followed everywhere today. It was fascinating to read that many of the Leakeys' most famous finds are really attributable to Mary and it is because of her exacting labors that we know as much as we do about life twenty million years ago.

Mary Poppins
Written by P. L. Travers/Illustrated by Mary Shepherd
Revised and reissued in 1962
Cloth: Harcourt Brace
Paper: Harcourt Brace

⌒ Her tongue is sharp and her manner is brisk. She can freeze you in your tracks with her chilly glare of disapproval. She's stern, cross, and never wastes time being nice. Yet for Jane and Michael Banks, Mary Poppins is the most exciting nanny in the world and the magical adventures they share with her are the stuff of dreams. For children to know that wonderful mysteries can lurk behind a grown-up's crusty exterior is thrilling indeed. Mary Poppins, the least likely "fairy godmother" imaginable, sweeps Jane and Michael into lands of enchantment. She hasn't stopped bewitching young readers since she first appeared on the doorstep of Number Seventeen Cherry Tree Lane.

Math Curse
Written by Jon Scieszka and Lane Smith
Copyright 1995
Cloth: Viking

⌐ Your daughter + this book = a dizzying, original, hilarious experience!

Forget math anxiety. This girl needs to get free of a math *curse*. From the moment she awakes, everything looms as a math problem. "I have 1 white shirt, 3 blue shirts, 3 striped shirts, and that 1 ugly plaid shirt my Uncle Zeno sent me. How many shirts is that all together? How many shirts would I have if I threw away that awful plaid shirt? When will Uncle Zeno quit sending me such ugly shirts?" She's panicking! Math is all around her! Breakfast is a lesson in measurements, the bus ride an education in addition, lunch an exercise in fractions. We'll leave you to discover how she figures out the ingenious solution to her problem. Kudos to the authors for offering a visually spectacular, riotous look at a topic not usually known for its humor.

Matilda
Written by Roald Dahl
Copyright 1988
Cloth: Viking Penguin

SANDRA DAY O'CONNOR

~

Associate Justice,
Supreme Court of the United States

grew up on a ranch. There were no other
children with whom to play. For a good part of
my early years books were among my closest
and dearest companions. When I was very young, I loved
Mary Poppins and *Winnie the Pooh*. In later years I particularly enjoyed *The Book of Knowledge*. Whenever I wanted
to know something about anything, I would turn with
confidence to it.

Reading is the key that opens the door to knowledge.
Knowledge is what enables us to function as individuals and
as nations. If I could bestow one gift on a friend or child
of mine, it would probably be the ability to read well,
because this is the foundation on which so much of our lives
is built.

Paper: Puffin
~ This is a contemporary comic book of a fairy tale.

At four years Matilda is reading *Great Expectations*. But no one
in her low-life, TV-obsessed family cares. In fact, she is constantly
belittled and told she is ignorant and silly. Resentment against her
beastly parents finally stings Matilda into devising elaborate practical jokes to torture them. But those turn out to be mere target
practice. At school she faces an even more formidable foe in her
headmistress, Miss Trunchbull, who is a terrifying, tyrannical men-

ace. Luckily, Matilda discovers that she has superhuman powers enabling her to take sweet revenge in a way that every child finds outrageously entertaining. Kids love to see brilliant Matilda get the upper hand.

May Chinn: The Best Medicine
Written by Ellen R. Butts and Joyce R. Schwartz/Illustrated
    by Janet Hamlin
Copyright 1995
Cloth: Scientific American Books for Young Readers/W. H.
    Freeman & Co.
Paper: Scientific American Books for Young Readers/W. H.
    Freeman & Co.

⌒ Here is a fine biography of a dignified, courageous woman.

In the 1920s, out of 150,000 doctors in the United States, only sixty-five were African-American women. Thirty-year-old May Chinn was one of them. When she was younger, however, May Chinn had dreamed of a career in music, not medicine. Her mother made immense sacrifices to give May the lessons she needed. Although she did perform with the great Paul Robeson, a prejudiced music professor at Columbia ridiculed her so mercilessly that the pragmatic May looked elsewhere to fulfill her course requirements. Fortunately, she stumbled across a sympathetic professor who encouraged her in science. After graduation this ambitious young woman took the extraordinary step of going on to medical school. Because she was barred from hospital work on account of her race, she opened her own practice in Harlem, helping those who could not get treatment elsewhere. She went on to specialize in cancer research for women at the famous Strang clinic.

Minnie
Written by Annie M. G. Schmidt/Illustrated by Kay Sather
Copyright 1970

AUDREY F. MANLEY, M.D., M.P.H.

～

President, Spelman College

 ithout question, the book that had the most profound impact on me as a child was *Gone with the Wind*. I was in the fifth grade when I first read Margaret Mitchell's classic story about the antebellum South and the Civil War. Since I grew up in a segregated town in Mississippi, *Gone with the Wind* provided me with a great deal of insight about the history of my region of the country, about race relations, about the impact of war on society, and about determination under adversity. I was also greatly inspired by the fact that the book, which is so beautifully written, had been authored by a woman. That fact helped me realize that girls, too, could aspire to great accomplishments.

Cloth: Milkweed Editions
Paper: Milkweed Editions
Netherlands Silver Pencil Prize as one of the Best Books of
      the Year

～ Stay with us while we describe a most unusual, thoroughly enjoyable novel.

Minnie is a ginger cat who has eaten something that has turned her into a human. She is extremely embarrassed about this; she is a cat disgrace. Kicked out of the house by her sister, Minnie wends her way to the home of Mr. Tibbs. Mr. Tibbs adores cats to the point of being unable to write about anything else in his newspaper column. In fact, his editor has threatened to fire him unless he comes up with some real investigative reporting. Because Minnie has felicitously retained her ability to communicate with cats, she is able to pick up all the news and relay it to Mr. Tibbs. Their most sensational scoop comes when they are able to expose Mr. Elbow, the town's most renowned citizen, as an animal hater.

The charm of this fantasy is its original premise and the skillful way the author follows through on it. The cat press hot line that feeds Minnie and Mr. Tibbs the gossip is thoroughly entertaining. And the author makes sure that Minnie never loses her feline ways—she climbs trees to escape barking dogs, she rubs her head against the fishmonger's sleeve, she sleeps in a cardboard box, she has trouble controlling her instincts when she's near goldfish or mice. At the end Minnie must choose whether she will change back to being a cat or stay human. She's a different kind of heroine, but she's an always honest, always helpful one. We think you'll like her.

The Missing 'Gator of Gumbo Limbo: An Ecological Mystery

Written by Jean Craighead George
Copyright 1992
Cloth: HarperCollins
Paper: HarperTrophy

⌒ Here's a different kind of mystery altogether.

To escape Liza's abusive father, Liza's mother has moved them deep into the Everglades, to an unspoiled corner called Gumbo Limbo Hammock. Liza still goes to school and does her homework, but all her free time is spent at the lake, fishing and keeping Dajun, a twelve-foot-long alligator, company. When a government official declares that Dajun is dangerous and must be killed, Liza determines to save him. But Dajun has suddenly vanished, and Liza is baffled. She thought she knew all of Dajun's habits. Where could he have gone? The clues to the alligator's disappearance lie in Liza's dissection of her own substantial knowledge of the natural world. The fascinating combination of informative observations on the environment and full-fledged mystery makes for original, engrossing reading.

The Moorchild
Written by Eloise McGraw
Copyright 1996
Cloth: Margaret K. McElderry Books
Newbery Honor Book
ALA Notable Book
Boston Globe–Horn Book Honor Book

～ The author dedicates this book "To all children who have ever felt *different*." Since that sentiment has probably, at one time or another, included all of us, it is hard to imagine someone not taking to *The Moorchild*.

Saaski is a changeling, half human and half Folk, who's abruptly turned out of the amoral fairy world when it's discovered she cannot make herself invisible at will. The fairies exchange Saaski for a charming, pretty human baby whom they plan to enslave. Saaski baffles both herself and her new parents by the extent to which she cannot fit in. Everything about her screams her differences: her eyes, which change color, the strange melodies she instinctively plays on her bagpipes, her aversion to iron and salt. The villagers become suspicious and begin to make her the scapegoat for all their ills. There will be no comfortable place for Saaski. Recognizing this, she resolves to strike out on her own, but not before she can bestow on her human parents—at great risk to herself—the one gift they really want.

This is such a deeply absorbing story that readers will be sorry when they get to the last page.

Mrs. Frisby and the Rats of NIMH
Written by Robert C. O'Brien
Copyright 1971
Cloth: Atheneum
Paper: Aladdin
Newbery Medal

⌐ There are only a few novels, such as *Wind in the Willows* and *Watership Down*, with perfectly imagined animal worlds. This is one of them.

Mrs. Frisby, a widowed mouse, lives during the winter in a cinder block in the vegetable garden of a farmer named Mr. Fitzgibbon. But moving day is coming, the day when Mr. Fitzgibbon plows up the garden for spring planting. Normally, Mrs. Frisby would just pack up her four children and take them to her summer house. But this year her son Timothy is extremely ill with pneumonia, and she cannot risk his breathing cold air for even a short time. To save Timothy, Mrs. Frisby must venture into dangerous parts of the garden to ask for help from creatures she barely knows. Her quest leads her first on a flying journey to a mysterious owl, then into the elaborate underground kingdom of the rats. There she discovers the frightening secret of her husband's death and the reason the rats will help her. In turn, Mrs. Frisby is able to help keep them from almost certain extinction.

Full of suspenseful scenes, thought-provoking dialogue, and intriguing characters, this is a well-written and well-conceived novel that is just impossible to put down!

My Life with the Chimpanzees
Written by Jane Goodall
Copyright 1988, 1996
Paper: Minstrel Books

⌐ In this autobiography, Jane Goodall remembers her favorite childhood books were *The Story of Dr. Dolittle, The Jungle Book,* and *Tarzan*; she claims that they led her to her life's work as a naturalist.

When Goodall was just twenty-three, she journeyed to Africa, where she met the great anthropologist and paleontologist Louis Leakey. He arranged for her to travel to the remote Gombe National Park and begin her pioneering study of chimpanzees. It took a year before the chimps would let her come close to them, but her patient work was rewarded when she became the first to recognize that chimpanzees use objects as tools. Goodall's contributions to this field are legendary.

She is as fine a writer as she is a naturalist. Her tone is totally forthright and engaging, and there are terrific photographs throughout the book. She includes all kinds of fascinating details about her daily life in the jungle that kids find intriguing: her encounters with leopards, how she had to protect her son from wild animals, how the chimps make pillows at night.

Maybe this book will change your daughter's life the way Dr. Dolittle changed Jane Goodall's!

The Name of the Game Was Murder

Written by Joan Lowery Nixon
Copyright 1993
Cloth: Doubleday
Paper: Laurel Leaf
Edgar Allan Poe Award

⌐ In the tradition of *Murder on the Orient Express* comes this contemporary crime thriller by the author of The Orphan Train Quartet (see Index). Fifteen-year-old Samantha wants to learn the craft of writing so badly that she wangles an invitation to spend two weeks at the baronial island mansion of her great uncle Augustus Trevor, a famous novelist. He turns out to be an imperious, appalling man with a vicious streak who is horrified at her presence, but his kind wife insists that she stay. Augustus has asked five egomaniacal celebrities to come to the island to play a nasty game: they must decipher mysterious clues, or he will reveal their terrible secrets in his forthcoming novel. Samantha finds herself appointed chief detective when Augustus is found bludgeoned at his desk, a raging storm cuts communication from the mainland, and the lights go out. A fun, page-turning read.

Nightbirds on Nantucket
Written by Joan Aiken/Illustrated by Robin
　　Jacques
Copyright 1966
Cloth: Doubleday

⌒ Adventures abound in this delightfully implausible, suspense-ful yarn. After being plucked from the ocean following a ship-wreck, scrappy young Dido Twite uncovers a nefarious plot by wicked English Hanoverians to shoot a cannon all the way from Nantucket to England to kill King James. Of course Dido must stop them, and you can rest assured that, after several close calls and narrow escapes, stop them she does. By far the nicest touch, how-ever, is Dido's relationship with the sea captain's daughter, dutiful Penitence Casket, who is a study in overwrought timidity. How Dido's stalwart example brings poor Pen out of her shell and how the admiring Pen finally gets the gumption to prove her worth are what set this jolly read apart from others in this genre.

Sadly, this book and a companion title, *Black Hearts in Bat-tersea,* are out of print. However, they're easily found in libraries. Aiken is also well known for her Gothic tale *The Wolves of Willoughby Chase,* still in print, wherein two girls triumph over a malicious guardian.

Number the Stars
Written by Lois Lowry
Copyright 1989
Cloth: Houghton Mifflin

Paper: Dell
Newbery Medal
~ In this novel Lowry has told the moving story of the integrity of the Danish people during World War II.

Annemarie Johansen and Ellen Rosen are two ten-year-old friends living in Copenhagen during the Nazi occupation. The Johansens are a traditional family. They don't seem to be made of the stuff of heroes, yet they don't hesitate to help their neighbors, the Rosens, evade the Nazi deportation of Jews. Annemarie and her family play a dangerous game: they take Ellen in as a daughter and spirit her out of the country on a fishing boat. Annemarie risks her life protecting her friend from the German soldiers and delivering the secret that ensures Ellen's getaway to Sweden.

Annemarie says that she is "glad to be an ordinary person who would never be called upon for courage." But, in fact, she, her family, and her country showed extraordinary valor and decency in the face of evil.

On the Bus with Joanna Cole:
A Creative Autobiography

Written by Joanna Cole with Wendy Saul
Copyright 1996
Cloth: Heinemann
~ The Magic School Bus and the dauntless Ms. Frizzle have taken millions of schoolchildren to explore the waterworks, the solar system, the human body, the ocean floor. . . . In this engaging book, acclaimed children's writer Joanna Cole takes readers on an exploration of her entire writing process. We are treated to inside information on the inspiration for her ideas, the real people on whom her characters are based, and how she conducts her scientific research. Children will enjoy browsing through this—there are many photographs, sketches, and rough drafts that show a gloriously imaginative mind hard at work.

The Ordinary Princess
Written by M. M. Kaye
Copyright 1984
Paper: Dell

⌒ Instead of the traditionally useful christening gifts of "Unfailing Charm and Unfading Beauty," Amethyst's fairy godmother has a better idea. "My child, I am going to give you something that will probably bring you more happiness. . . . You shall be Ordinary!" Just like that, Amethyst turns into a real person, and no one at the palace knows what to do with her. When Amy realizes how desperate her parents are to marry her off, she climbs out the window and down the wisteria vine to freedom. She lives in blissful simplicity in the woods until she has to face facts: she needs a job. At the neighboring castle, she hires on as a kitchen maid. It won't surprise you to learn that ultimately the king of this castle turns out to be Amy's true soul mate. Her charming adventures, laced with amusing dialogue, make this a sunny tale about a not-so-ordinary heroine.

Our Golda: The Story of Golda Meir
Written by David A. Adler/Illustrated by Donna Ruff
Copyright 1984
Paper: Viking

⌒ Informative and easy to read, this short biography chronicles the life of a most amazing woman, who so many people looked on with such great affection that they called her "*Nasha Golda*"— "Our Golda."

When Golda Meir was just eleven years old, she organized the American Sisters Society, dedicated to raising money for poor children in Milwaukee. She sent out invitations, rented a room, and, without notes, made her first speech. This story is characteristic of Golda, a girl of energy, drive, and commitment to social and political justice. Born in Kiev, Russia, in 1898, Golda and her family struggled to survive under its cruel anti-Semitic regime and were finally able to emigrate to America in 1906. When Golda's parents wanted her to drop out of school at fourteen and marry an older man of their choosing, Golda flatly refused and ran away to her sister in Colorado. Her passion to establish a homeland for the Jewish people led her to emigrate again. She moved to Palestine in 1921 and began the long, hard work toward fulfilling her dream of a Jewish state. She served as Israel's ambassador to Russia, then minister of labor and foreign minister, and finally prime minister.

Out of Many Waters
Written by Jacqueline Dembar Greene
Copyright 1988
Paper: Walker & Co.

~ Dramatically told, this fictionalized history of Isobel Ben Lazar and the twenty-two other immigrants who, in 1654, founded the first Jewish settlement in America will have you glued to your chair.

Isobel and her sister, Maria, were taken forcibly from their parents by the Inquisition and sent from Portugal to Brazil to work as slaves in a monastery. Twelve and sixteen when the story opens, they are determined to escape from Brazil and find their way back to their parents. Convinced that it will be easier to hide if they are not together, they stow away on separate ships. Isobel is now completely on her own and confronting staggeringly significant decisions. Should she tell someone of a plan she overhears to divert the ship's course? Should she trust the groups of Jewish refugees who seem to want to befriend her? Should she disguise herself when Spanish privateers commandeer the ship? Should she publicly admit to being Jewish? Should she, when safe on land at last, claim America as her new home?

Isobel's conflicts of conscience, the overriding threat of danger, and the well-researched historical setting make a heady brew. The well-chosen title comes from Psalm 18.

One Foot Ashore is a companion book that follows Maria's journey, which leads her back to Europe and a friendship with Rembrandt.

Peppermints in the Parlor
Written by Barbara Brooks Wallace
Copyright 1980
Paper: Aladdin

⌒ Something is very, very wrong at Sugar Hill Hall. Newly orphaned Emily Luccock doesn't recognize her aunt and uncle Twice's mansion. Once elegant and grand, it is now dark, musty, and dangerous. Uncle Twice has unaccountably disappeared, and Aunt Twice is a helpless prisoner in her own home. Emily is almost frightened out of her wits. But Emily's papa had always described her as "thin as a thread, strong as wire," and Emily means to prove Papa right. With the help of the fishmonger's son, Kip, Emily uncovers the source of the villainy shadowing Sugar Hill Hall and restores it to the sunlit home it had always been. Even reluctant readers will gobble up this delicious mystery!

The Perilous Gard
Written by Elizabeth Marie Pope
Copyright 1974
Paper: Puffin
Newbery Honor Book

⌒ By the middle of this swiftly paced book, Kate Sutton, former lady-in-waiting to the Princess Elizabeth, is enslaved by the pagan fairy folk in their dark underground world. How will she free herself? How can she stop the fairies from cruelly sacrificing her friend, Christopher Heron, on All Hallows' Eve? Kate's curiosity may have led her into trouble, but not to worry, her common sense and matter-of-fact practicality will lead her out to safety.

Every necessary ingredient for a galloping read is here. To the wonderful Elizabethan setting the author has added a mysterious castle (the "Perilous Gard" of the title), wary townsfolk, unscrupulous servants, mystical creatures, an enchanted well, a tormented hero, and best of all, a tart-tongued, no-nonsense, brainy heroine with a good heart and an upright conscience.

Philip Hall Likes Me. I Reckon Maybe.
Written by Bette Greene/Illustrated by Charles Lilly
Copyright 1974
Cloth: Dial Books for Young Readers
Paper: Bantam Doubleday Dell
Newbery Honor Book

⌐ When you're done with this warmhearted, funny novel about a young, competitive girl, you'll have trouble choosing your favorite part.

Beth Lambert is an African-American sixth-grader growing up in rural Arkansas. She is the smartest girl in her class and crazy in love with Philip Hall, the smartest boy. Philip always edges her out until an insidious thought dawns on Beth: could it be that Philip is number one only because she's *letting* him beat her? In one entertaining episode after another, Beth finds that her naturally ambitious spirit will no longer allow her to hold back. Beth's uninhibited vitality is contagious—every girl should catch it.

Pippi Longstocking
Written by Astrid Lindgren/Illustrated by Louis S.
    Glanzman
Copyright 1950
Cloth: Viking
Paper: Puffin

⟿ Pippi, for many girls, is the ultimate fantasy: no grown-ups, no rules, boundless energy, strength, and imagination! Here is a girl who lives by herself with her horse and her monkey, enjoying endless escapades. Pippi's antics are outrageously amusing to children. She constantly defies authority based on her own peculiar logic, but she has a fine sense of justice, which is extremely satisfying, and she is as generous as they come. We can't think of any child who wouldn't like to live at Villa Villekulla!

Poppy
Written by Avi/Illustrated by Brian Floca
Copyright 1995
Cloth: Orchard
Paper: Avon/Camelot
Boston Globe–Horn Book Award

⟿ Poppy's family of deer mice have made a deal with the devil. They've completely bought into the specious argument of the evil owl, Mr. Ocax, that their true enemy is the porcupine. Mr. Ocax has sworn to protect them from porcupines *if* the mice will obey each and every one of his strict rules. . . . Of course, obeying these rules really means that Mr. Ocax is continuously supplied with his favorite delicacy: mice. When Poppy sees her boyfriend killed by the owl, Poppy begins to question the rules for the first time in her life. This independent thinking leads Poppy to undertake a dangerous quest to find a new home—against the express orders of Mr. Ocax—for her burgeoning family.

Avi easily combines adventure and humor in this enjoyable novel about the cost of blind obedience.

Profiles of Women Past and Present: Women's History Monologues for Group Presentations
Thousand Oaks California Branch Inc. of the American Association of University Women/Illustrated by Ann Mathews

GUN DENHART

～

Founder and Chairwoman,
Hanna Andersson Corporation

y absolute favorite author growing up was Astrid Lindgren, who wrote the books about Pippi Longstocking. Imagine a nine-year-old girl who lived on her own, who slept with her feet on the pillow, who broke all the rules! Pippi cleaned her floor by skating around on brushes, which sounded much more fun than the way we did it in my house.

But she was also a girl who was kind and generous, and never ever boring. Pippi was my hero!

Copyright 1996
Paper: AAUW

～ This unusual approach to making women's history come alive is irresistible.

The book is designed so that teachers, parents, librarians, or students can present a brief first-person monologue (with suggestions for costumes and props) that condenses a famous woman's life. For instance, the one on Elizabeth Blackwell begins "I was born in England in 1821. I had nine brothers and sisters and my family believed we were all equal." Amelia Earhart's starts out "When I was a little girl, instead of playing house or making doll clothes like other girls, my sister and cousins and I built a roller coaster." This volume contains scripts as well from Grace Murray Hopper, Barbara Jordan, Emma Lazarus, Annie Oakley, Sandra Day O'Connor, Georgia O'Keeffe, Beatrix Potter, Sally

Ride, Eleanor Roosevelt, Sacagawea, Elizabeth Cady Stanton, Sojourner Truth, and Babe Didrikson Zaharias. A second volume is also available.

Clearly an invaluable resource for Women's History Month, this is also great fun to pull out on a rainy day.

Purely Rosie Pearl
Written by Patricia A. Cochrane
Copyright 1996
Cloth: Delacorte
Paper: Bantam Books

⟶ A+ historical fiction with lots of details of the Dust Bowl days.

"Grit" should have been Rosie Pearl's middle name. In 1936, she is twelve years old and has spent most of her childhood picking crops with the rest of her large migrant family. When they arrive in the Sacramento Valley camp, the nasty foreman tells her she will never amount to anything, that she had better think about having babies right away, and intimates that those babies should be his. Never one to back off, Rosie Pearl tells him she'd rather touch a dead skunk. But inside, she is so shaken by the idea that she might always be a migrant that she determines to prove him wrong. With the help of her new friend Margaret, Rosie Pearl works on her vocabulary (it takes her two weeks to rid herself of 'ain't') and, by the end of the book, is looking for a college scholarship.

Cochrane has done a wonderful job creating a character who has a fierce sense of pride and a quick sense of humor. The family scenes are warm and touching, and the Depression backdrop is convincingly conveyed.

Quake!
Written by Joe Cottonwood
Copyright 1995
Cloth: Scholastic

Paper: Apple

~ "People change, I told myself. Lives change. . . . Nothing is permanent. Maybe that was why . . . I was . . . drawn to science, where the laws don't change. Earth is earth. Rock is rock." But the earth *did* change on October 17, 1989, as a massive earthquake struck northern California. In this novel set amid that real disaster, fourteen-year-old Franny, her erstwhile best friend, Jennie, and her bratty little brother, Sidney, are at home alone in a small mountain community. At 5:04 P.M. the earth roars and the land moves like "waves on the ocean." Levelheaded Franny remembers that once a quake is over, the first thing to do is shut off the gas and electricity. She then leads the others off to look for help, but they give as much help as they get—rescuing a neighbor trapped under his car, turning off the power at other homes, sending assistance to where it's needed most. The author wisely does not make Franny a grandiose, larger-than-life character. She's sensible and practical, with typical teenage concerns, and keeps her wits about her. Her neighbor tells her she's "the best kind of hero. . . . Unrehearsed. Fumbling. An everyday sort. A small hero." Franny does all you would hope for.

Queen Eleanor: Independent Spirit of the Medieval World
Written by Polly Schoyer Brooks
Copyright 1983
Cloth: Lippincott-Raven

~ This is a colorful biography of a liberated woman who lived centuries before that expression was coined.

Eleanor was born in 1122, at a time when "women had no equal rights and little or no power . . . [yet] she ruled like a king herself and dealt with emperors and popes. More important, she won respect for women and made gentlemen of crude warrior knights." The only daughter of the wealthy Duke of Aquitaine, fifteen-year-old Eleanor wed Louis VII and became Queen of France. A flamboyant, exciting ruler, she traveled with the Crusades to Constantinople, governed beside the king, and brought the poetry and music of troubadours to Paris. Eleanor flouted convention when it suited her: she obtained a divorce, then married the future King of England. She brought her restless energy to the English court, importing her "new ideas of chivalry and romance" along with her belief in codified law and justice. She lived to be eighty-two and was a prime political player until her death.

Queenie Peavy
Written by Robert Burch
Copyright 1966
Cloth: Live Oak Media
Paper: Viking
Jane Addams Children's Book Award
Phoenix Award

⁀ Tough. That's Queenie's cover. Her pa is in jail for robbery, and her schoolmates torment her with the fact. She's got a reckless, defiant, tobacco-spitting, rock-throwing, "I don't care" suit of armor to protect her from the hurt she feels so deeply. Convinced that the school wants to send her off to a reformatory, she hopes that Pa's unexpected return home will change her life around. But Pa brings nothing but disappointment. Facing up to the fact that Pa is no good finally frees Queenie from wasting her days in loyalty to a man who doesn't deserve it. She can follow her own dreams at last.

Queenie is a well-drawn heroine. Perhaps because this book, set in the rural South during the Depression, was written before the women's movement had really gathered momentum, she doesn't quite apply her unblinking honesty and blunt assessments to her potential romance as much as we'd like. On the other hand, we feel that we can trust Queenie's fighting spirit; she'll stick to her ambition of becoming a doctor no matter what.

Quest for a Maid
Written by Frances Mary Hendry
Copyright 1988
Paper: Sunburst (Farrar Straus & Giroux)

⌒ The theme of two widely divergent sisters is as old as a fairy tale. Hendry has spun this classic rivalry into a colorful, splendid drama set in Scotland's thirteenth century. She has also woven in penetrating questions about rank and class as Meg, a shipbuilder's younger daughter, is sent to Norway with a delegation to bring home a princess, the Maid of Norway, for marriage to the English prince. Meg is only too well aware who began this chain of events: her beautiful, beloved older sister, Inge, killed the king of Scotland with her sorcery, igniting a struggle for the throne. Inge's lust for power and prominence set her down a path that she could not seem to resist. Meg courageously strikes off on a different road. She allies herself with her fiancé, a well-born lad with a disfiguring harelip, and her manservant, a youth of no background, to rescue the Maid from a shipwreck and the scheming ambitions of those anxious to claim the Scottish crown. The heart-pounding action never falters, right through the climactic final encounter between the two sisters. A great read for a long winter's day!

Red-Dirt Jessie
Written by Anna Myers
Copyright 1992
Cloth: Walker & Co.
Paper: Walker & Co.

⌒ This looks like a little book, but there is lots in it. It is a "teachable" book with wonderful character development, big themes, an interesting historical setting, and a heart-stopping climax.

The first line is one of the most lonesome we've come across: "My little sister Patsy is dead." From there it's Jessie's perceptive narration that ties this book together. The story is set on a failing

Oklahoma farm during the Depression. Patsy's death completely undoes Jessie's papa. He can't do anything but sit and stare. The burden of Papa's chores falls more and more on Jessie's shoulders. But she keeps on believing that "Papa will come back to us just when we need him most."

When Ring, a half-wild mangy dog, enters her life, Jessie becomes obsessed with taming him. She patiently works to bring him into the family. Somehow she senses that "Ring and Papa are an awful lot alike. They been hurt, down deep. But they're both good. And they will both heal." Because of Jessie, this becomes an unforgettable story of faith and redemption.

Remember the Ladies:
The First Women's Rights Convention
Written by Norma Johnson
Copyright 1995
Paper: Apple

⌐ If you're searching for an expert account of the 1848 Women's Rights Convention in Seneca Falls, this is it. The personalities of the key figures are portrayed vividly, and the historical milieu is fascinating. The individual accomplishments of these women are remarkable, but this book focuses on their collective authoring of the radical Declaration of Sentiments and its accompanying Resolutions. In its most controversial clauses the declaration called for women's equality and right to vote, thus setting in motion the ongoing struggle for women's rights. A good reference tool, nicely illustrated with photos and a useful chronology.

Return to Bitter Creek
Written by Doris Buchanan Smith
Copyright 1986
Cloth: Viking
Paper: Viking

ALA Notable Book

～ Lacey and her liberated, fiercely independent-minded mother, Campbell, left Bitter Creek for Colorado when Lacey was just a baby. She doesn't know her father or her grandparents, and she's never met her cousins. They are returning to the Appalachians in North Carolina because Campbell's boyfriend, David, has found work there as a blacksmith. Lacey is unsure about this move. She doesn't know how she will ever fit into this rural community, how welcome she will be. Lacey's doubts increase when her grandmother turns out to be a quintessentially difficult matriarch. Unhappy, unfinished business surfaces between her mother and her grandmother, and Lacey finds herself a pawn in their war. She realizes it is up to her to stop the family from disintegrating.

Smith has a guilelessly straightforward way of writing. Her characters are rendered in depth, and she handles the morass of misunderstanding between these contemporary mothers and daughters with empathy and tenderness.

The Root Cellar
Written by Janet Lunn
Copyright 1981
Cloth: Atheneum
Paper: Puffin

～ Orphaned twelve-year-old Rose doesn't feel at home anywhere, least of all with her quirky relatives on a remote island on the north shore of Lake Ontario. Their house is a shambles, her cousins seem rude, her aunt and uncle appear preoccupied. Left to herself, she discovers an old root cellar, and when she enters she "shifts" back in time to the 1860s. Immediately she is swept up in the lives of Susan, a servant girl, and her friend Will, who, out of conscience, crosses the Canadian border to join the Union Army.

When the Civil War is over and Will still hasn't returned, Rose uses her twentieth-century sensibilities to convince Susan they should travel to Washington by themselves to get him. Thus begins their difficult, adventurous journey, the journey Rose must take to realize where she really belongs. Lunn has crafted a touching historical novel; she is an effective writer who has a gift for investing both the past and the present with vitality.

Rosa Bonheur

Written by Robyn Montana Turner
Copyright 1991
Cloth: Little Brown & Co.
Paper: Little Brown & Co.

⁓ In France in the mid-1800s, women were barred from the finest art schools. Yet this unfriendly climate did not deter Rosa Bonheur from fulfilling her dream. After several unsuccessful stints at traditional schooling, Rosa was finally enrolled by her father as one of his own students. He kept various animals in his studio so that Rosa's sculptures and paintings would be realistic. Rosa flourished under her father's tutelage, winning, when she was just twenty-three, the Gold Medal from the prestigious Salon of 1848. Suddenly she was sought after as a painter, and her new earnings brought her unexpected freedom. She purchased a château, which she stocked with a menagerie of beasts—monkeys, yaks, Icelandic ponies, even a lion.

This is a fun-to-read biography of a gifted artist, the first woman to be awarded the French Legion of Honor medal.

Running Girl: The Diary of Ebonee Rose

Written by Sharon Bell Mathis
Copyright 1997
Cloth: Browndeer Press/Harcourt Brace

⁓ In this fictional diary of a dedicated, competitive field and track star we are introduced to eleven-year-old Ebonee Rose (E.R.). She is entered in four events in the All-City Track Meet. For the two weeks leading up to it, she confides all her fears and hopes to her diary. There is acute tension on the team between E.R. and another girl, she is certain she can't manage the long jump, and she twists her ankle. E.R. tells her mother, "Suppose we don't win." "Suppose you don't lose," her mother retorts.

To clinch first place, E.R. is relying on her long hours of practice and her conviction that the runners that have gone before her are cheering her on. Evelyn Ashford, Gail Devers, Florence Griffith Joyner, Jackie Joyner-Kersee, Wilma Rudulph, and Gwen Torrence are just a few of her heroines. E.R. is a fanatic about runner lore and includes many statistics and stories about these champions to boost her morale. The book itself is dotted with inspirational quotes from and photos of these glorious African-American athletes.

Running Out of Time
Written by Margaret Peterson Haddix
Copyright 1995
Cloth: Simon & Schuster
Paper: Aladdin

⌒ Alfred Hitchcock would have loved this book where things are not as they seem. Jessie lives the life of a pioneer girl in Clifton, Indiana, in 1840. Her father is a blacksmith; her mother tends the sick with herbs. But children are starting to die of diphtheria, and Jessie's mother is desperate to stop the disease. She has to confide the shocking truth to her daughter: *it is not 1840 at all, but 1996!* Their village is a historic reconstruction, like Williamsburg, where tourists can view them at work through special cameras. The sinister scientists who started the village have sealed it off so they can perform macabre experiments—they have allowed the diphtheria to spread so they can develop a strong gene pool. A stunned Jessie, who knows nothing of the world outside, must escape and bring back the modern medicine they need.

Jessie's flight is fraught with ominous episodes. Each time she manages to keep her wits and go on. A very suspenseful story, with a well-drawn, self-sufficient heroine and a most original plot.

Sally Ride: Shooting for the Stars
Written by Jane Hurwitz and Sue Hurwitz
Copyright 1989
Paper: Ballantine

⌒ It never occurred to Sally Ride that there was anything she couldn't do. She excelled at sports (she was the eighteenth-ranked junior tennis player in the United States) and science (she got her doctorate degree in astrophysics). In 1978 she was selected as one of six women in NASA's astronaut class. And on June 18, 1983, she became the first American woman in space as a crew member of the shuttle *Challenger*.

The descriptions in this biography of the training involved, the experiments done aboard the shuttle, and Dr. Ride's expertise with the robotic arm are top-notch. Although she's accomplished much more than just that historic flight, that achievement "firmly established an equal role for women in the space exploration program."

P.S. Reading this, we learned that Dr. Ride's favorite girlhood books were Nancy Drew and Superman!

Sarah and Me and the Lady from the Sea
Written by Patricia Beatty
Copyright 1989
Cloth: William Morrow
Paper: Beech Tree Books

⌒ Lots of historical details add to the pleasure of reading this novel.

Marcella Abbott's 1890s world has flipped upside down. She won't be able to return to Portland, Oregon, after the summer because her father's business has failed. Instead she, her upper-crust mother, and brother will have to tighten their belts and remain in their drafty vacation house on the Olympic peninsula. No more rides in her pony carriage, no more fancy teas. She will have to learn to get along with the locals and absorb their peninsula ways, a prospect that frankly appalls her. Little by little, though, Marcella's attitude thaws and she comes to respect and love the people whose kindness and fortitude help her family over their rough moments. At the end Marcella has helped solve the enigma of a mysterious shipwrecked woman and made fast friends with those she hadn't considered her social equal. Even her helpless mother has gained enough confidence to open a business.

Scholastic Encyclopedia of Women in the United States
Written by Sheila Keenan
Copyright 1996
Cloth: Scholastic

⌐ It's funny how our kids keep picking up this book. Our copies are well thumbed through, no doubt because of the 260 entries, hundreds of photographs, useful sidebars, an appealing layout, and a great index. Starting from the colonial women of the 1600s and continuing through the present, Keenan presents concise, snappy biographies of important American women. Anne Bradstreet, Margaret Sanger, Bessie Smith, Ida Tarbell, Wilma Mankiller, Billie Jean King, Toni Morrison—every influential woman receives her due. In short, a well-thought-out and well-researched reference tool. It is a perfect book to leave lying around.

Scooter
Written and Illustrated by Vera B. Williams
Copyright 1993
Cloth: Greenwillow

⁓ Elana Rose Rosen embodies the exuberant, perpetual-motion spirit of her hometown, New York City, in this snappy story of a girl, her scooter, and her mom.

When Elana moves into the Melon Hill apartment houses, she's momentarily unsure how to go about making new friends. Her practical mom simply pushes Elana out the door with her scooter in tow, and Elana pretty much takes over from there. She can ride that scooter like nobody's business, and soon she's off and running with the scooter and a ton of kids in tow. Her adventures with the neighborhood gang have a genuine slice-of-life feel to them that's hard to duplicate. Elana has illustrated "her" book with lots of acrostic poems and drawings that are integral to the story. Along with the terrific art go great characterizations, capable women, and a lively heroine, making this ode to the sidewalks of New York a smash hit.

A Season of Comebacks
Written by Kathy Mackel
Copyright 1997
Cloth: Putnam

⁓ Loaded with action and humor, this is that rare occurrence: a grand slam sports book for girls.

"Nobody knows me. I'm Molly Burrows, the ten-year-old shadow of the great Allie. I'm expected to worship my sister as much as the rest of her world does." Allie is twelve and so famous for her fastball pitching that TV cameras and reporters follow her around like mosquitoes. Their dad is her softball coach and so completely wrapped up in Allie's stardom that he forgets his youngest daughter plays too. When Allie's dad finds his team short a crucial player, he reluctantly drafts Molly up from the minors. That doesn't fix either the lineup or the relationship among the three of them. Things come to a head when Dad pressures Allie to switch leagues—both girls turn on him for working harder at being a coach than a father. Caught off base, he admits his error. Once he relaxes, everyone starts to have fun, and by the end Molly surprises herself by becoming the ace catcher for Allie's phenomenal pitching.

The Secret Garden
Written by Frances Hodgson Burnett
Published 1911; numerous editions available

⁓ Sour and sallow Mary Lennox is sent from India to live at forbidding Misselthwaite Manor with her reclusive uncle Archibald. She's so imperious and disagreeable that everyone gives her a wide berth. Alone for most of her days, Mary discovers a mysterious, neglected garden. For the first time not only is her imagination piqued but she's found something she's willing to work for. Restoring the abandoned garden to its former beauty awakens her parched soul.

Misselthwaite Manor holds other secrets as well. A sickly cousin, as petulant and ill tempered as Mary, has been kept hidden

LINDA ALLARD

⁓

Director of Design, Ellen Tracy

When I was growing up, my all-time favorite book was *The Secret Garden*. I read it seven times! I loved the magical quality of the book; it made me feel as if anything in life was possible. And who knows, it may be a coincidence, but now I love to garden!

from sight. Their friendship blossoms as Mary heals his unhappy spirit, mirroring the magic that is taking place within the garden. In the pantheon of children's classics, the rejuvenating power of nature has never been expressed better.

The Secret of the Old Clock:
A Nancy Drew Mystery
Written by Carolyn Keene
Copyright 1959; first published 1930
Cloth: Putnam

⟶ This is the first title in the perennially popular Nancy Drew series. Nancy's attraction is easy to understand. As America's girl detective, she led an independent life, drove a cool car, and solved thrilling mysteries that stumped the police. We remember reading these books under the covers late at night—the excitement was almost too much to bear! Nancy is studied now by feminist scholars; there are conferences and books devoted to her. (Adults might be interested in Bobbie Ann Mason's *The Girl Sleuth: On the Trail of Nancy Drew, Judy Bolton, and Cherry Ames*.) Nancy's star seems in little danger of fading, and that's fine with us.

As you will see when you read the following quotations, the outpouring of affection for Nancy Drew by so many of the women who responded to us is very telling. Nancy is a significant heroine and cherished role model.

LILLIAN VERNON

⌒

Founder and CEO, Lillian Vernon Corporation

ancy Drew mysteries were always my favorites. They embodied the excitement and adventure most young girls could only dream of. For me she represented a female role model who wasn't the traditional homemaker. . . . She was an independent, bright young lady who wasn't afraid to think for herself and she put those thoughts into action. In retrospect, perhaps I was playing the role of Nancy Drew as I explored the mysteries of business and the mail-order industry.

FAYE WATTLETON

⌒

President, Center for Gender Equality

side from my schoolwork and the Bible, I was a voracious consumer of Nancy Drew books. Given the social context of the 1950s, she was a liberated woman. She was independent, spunky, and took on the world on her own terms. Her life was an adventure of solving mysteries. She wore white gloves and hats, and she spent a great deal of time changing clothes and "freshening up"—all a reflection of that era and consistent with my upbringing, in which great importance was placed on appearance and grooming. Immersing myself in Nancy Drew's world was my escape from an existence dictated by fundamentalist religious rigidity. Even though I did not identify with her blond hair and blue eyes, I absorbed the strength of her power as a woman, her ability to solve problems, and her sense of justice.

ANN REESE

*Executive Vice President and
Chief Financial Officer, ITT Corporation*

he first books I remember loving as a child were Nancy Drew mystery stories by Carolyn Keene. I read and reread the stories, fascinated by Nancy's analytical logic and the perseverance she brought to tracking down every answer. The rest of her life seemed ordinary, but she earned respect in an adult world as well as among her peers by the work she did. I never thought about emulating her life in a literal sense, but I wanted to train myself to think the way I perceived she thought. I admired her lack of shyness and her willingness to keep asking questions until she understood something.

Later I was exposed to the more classic girls' books like *Little Women*, but I can trace some of my personality traits to Nancy. On a humorous note, I was convinced to buy the house we now live in, despite the fact it was a several-year renovation project, because it is on Larkspur Lane, site of one of Nancy's mysteries.

NINA TOTENBERG

⟍⟋

Correspondent, National Public Radio

 confess that my favorite and most formative books during my growing-up years were the Nancy Drew mystery books. It may be a commentary on the times that back then there were so few female heroines. So when I discovered Nancy, I was hooked.

She was ideal. She was smart, pretty, popular, had a boyfriend (and a car), and anything she tried she did well, perhaps even perfectly. She didn't lord her superiority over other mere mortals, because she was also nice. And I must confess that if I had thought women could become police detectives, I might have tried that instead of becoming a reporter. All because of Nancy.

The other books I remember loving were a series of biographies in my grammar school library, some of which were about women, from Marie Curie to Dolley Madison. I loved those books because they were about real people, real women, and women who had done something.

Today there are many more books like these for young women, though not nearly enough, and I am always on the lookout for them for my nieces and granddaughters. Through these books girls come to think they too can do anything, maybe even be president.

SHERRY LANSING

~

Chairman and CEO, *Paramount Pictures*

s a young girl I was a great fan of the Nancy Drew mysteries by Carolyn Keene. Nancy Drew was a very modern young woman— smart, independent, interested in pursuing a career, but equally committed to her family and friends. As I avidly followed her adventures, I realized that a woman could work outside the home, lead a really interesting life, and love what she does. I also saw that a woman could be successful in her chosen career without sacrificing her feminine side; she doesn't have to become "one of the guys" to reach her goals. These are qualities that I've tried to emulate in my own life.

WILMA MANKILLER

~

Chief of the Cherokee Nation

ntil I was ten years old we had no indoor plumbing or electricity. We entertained ourselves by reading and playing board games. I read a lot of Nancy Drew, but I also read whatever my parents read, ranging from biographies to western novels and mysteries.

Dianne Feinstein

⁓

U.S. Senator, State of California

 I remember reading the Nancy Drew mysteries when I was a girl. To me Nancy Drew was just the kind of girl I wanted to be. She was smart, she was brave, and she didn't let anything get in the way of solving her latest caper. I don't remember how many of those books I bought; I think there were eleven. But every week, without fail, I'd save my allowance to have enough to buy the latest edition. Back then the books were only sixty cents, but I'd still have to save up to buy one.

JUDITH L. LICHTMAN

～

President, Women's Legal Defense Fund

ith great pleasure I want to tell you about the books that absorbed all my attention as a young reader.

There were classics like *Little Women* and *Rebecca* that I read more than once—thrilled by women who conquered adversity.

As well, I was hooked on the Nancy Drew detective and Cherry Ames student nurse series. In both instances these were stories where women were the protagonists; strong leaders who were making a difference in people's lives. They were all terrific role models for me whether leading traditional or nontraditional lives.

CATHLEEN P. BLACK

～

President, Hearst Magazines

 I loved reading as a child, and now as a mother, reading to my two kids (a son, age nine and a half, and daughter, five and a half) is something we all treasure very much. Books that I remember liking a lot were the Nancy Drew mystery stories and the Bobbsey twins because of the adventures in the plot. I also loved *Black Beauty* because, like many young girls, I was in love with horses. *Little Women* will always be a favorite, too.

A Separate Battle: Women and the Civil War
Written by Ina Chang
Copyright 1991
Cloth: Lodestar Books
Paper: Puffin
ALA Notable Book

～ When children see the real people behind the dates, the documents, the troop movements, history comes alive. Here is an admirable book that quotes letters and diaries, illustrates with period photographs and engravings, and effectively highlights with sidebars to pull together the myriad voices of the women (both famous and obscure) who were so important during the Civil War

JoAnn Falletta

∼

Orchestra Conductor
Virginia and Long Beach Symphonies

or as long as I can remember I have been a voracious reader—gobbling up books of all kinds with an insatiable appetite and extraordinary pleasure. As a young girl, I read everything within reach, but my two great passions were the Nancy Drew series and anthologies of poetry.

After concert performances, I can never sleep, so I spend many nights curled up with a mystery—a lifelong love fostered by Nancy Drew. In the last few years writing my own poetry about music has become very important to me. After music, books remain the great delight of my life.

years. From Harriet Beecher Stowe's incendiary novel *Uncle Tom's Cabin* to Harriet Tubman's travels on the Underground Railroad, this illuminating book captures the imagination. Louisa May Alcott served as a nurse, Sojourner Truth's rallying speeches stirred the abolitionist movement, and Sarah Edmonds disguised herself as a man so she could fight. The intellect, the drive, the commitment that these strong women exhibited influenced the outcome of the war and makes for wonderful reading.

Shoeshine Girl

Written by Clyde Robert Bulla/Illustrated by Leigh Grant
Copyright 1975

Cloth: HarperCrest

Paper: HarperTrophy

⌒ Short and easy to read, but with an older sensibility, this is a great contemporary story of Sarah Ida, a ten-year-old who has been flirting with delinquency. Sullen and uncooperative, she's sent to spend the summer with Aunt Claudia because her mother is very ill. Sarah Ida has such a chip on her shoulder that she bristles at any overture of friendship. What she does value is money, and when, in a gutsy move, she finds herself a job with Al, the shoeshine man, some of her rough edges begin to wear off. Al's example teaches her to respect hard, honest work. After Al is injured in an accident, Sarah Ida garners a lot of attention for unhesitatingly stepping in to keep his shoeshine stand open. When the local paper calls her a heroine, it rings true. Excellent.

Sky Pioneer: A Photobiography of Amelia Earhart

Written by Corinne Szabo

Copyright 1997

Cloth: National Geographic Society

⌒ In 1920, at the age of twenty-three, Amelia Earhart took her first ride in an airplane. "As soon as we left the ground, I knew I myself had to fly." With her characteristic determination, she took flying lessons and by her twenty-fifth birthday had bought her first plane. Flying became the center of her life, and she became America's heroine for her exploits in the air. She set speed records and made history by flying solo across the Atlantic, across the Pacific, across the country.

You'll cherish this absolutely gorgeous book, lavishly laid out with sixty photographs, maps of her routes, and quotations from her writings. Daring, visionary, capable, clear-sighted, and articulate, Amelia Earhart pioneered the way for women in aviation, saying "Women should do for themselves what men have already done—and occasionally what men have not done—thereby establishing themselves as persons, and perhaps encouraging other women toward greater independence of thought and action."

Note: *Amelia Earhart: Courage in the Sky* (see Index) is perfect for younger readers.

So Young to Die: The Story of Hannah Senesh

Written by Candice F. Ransom
Copyright 1993
Paper: Scholastic

⌒ "Hannah Senesh is a folk heroine in Israel. Monuments have been dedicated to her memory. Several streets, a ship, farming settlements, a forest, and a species of flower have been named after her. Every schoolchild in Israel can recite [her] 'Blessed Is the Match' poem." What did she do in her brief life to inspire so many honors?

Hannah was an extremely bright, talented girl who grew up in Budapest during the years when the Nazis came to power. When she was eighteen, she left to go to Israel to help build a Jewish homeland. But working on kibbutzim didn't make Hannah feel she was contributing enough. She trained to become a member of a top-secret British air force mission. Her goal was to parachute back into enemy territory in Hungary and rescue downed Allied pilots and Jews.

Paramount in her courageous decision was her hope that she could save her mother. The mission went awry, though, and Hannah was captured, tortured repeatedly, and thrown into solitary confinement. Her mother was captured as well, and the two were kept far apart. But even under the harsh prison rule, Hannah looked for opportunities to help. Out of scraps she made paper dolls for the young incarcerated children, she devised ways to communicate with her mother, and she sustained the other prisoners with her confidence that victory would ultimately be theirs. Just a few months before the war ended, Hannah was executed. This moving biography is a fitting memorial to a valiant young woman.

The Star Fisher

Written by Laurence Yep
Copyright 1991
Cloth: William Morrow
Paper: Puffin
Christopher Award

⟀ Negotiating the shoals of behavior, tradition, and custom in a small West Virginia town in 1927 might be difficult for any newcomer. But for fifteen-year-old Joan Lee and her family it is excruciating. Although Joan was born in America, her parents immigrated from China. They've moved to Clarksburg to start a laundry business. No one will patronize their store, and nasty slogans appear on their fence. The Lees have almost no money: Joan has only crackers and lettuce for lunch at school, something she hides by eating by herself every day. On top of everything else, Joan is the appointed translator for the family, a role she finds both burdensome and humiliating.

The Lees have no place else to go. Joan and her family must make this life work. With considerable tenacity Joan hangs on, finds a friend, and opens the door for her parents to become part of the community. This is a truly excellent book about race and family. Among Lawrence Yep's other fine titles, be sure to find *Child of the Owl* and *Ribbons*.

Stateswoman to the World: A Story About Eleanor Roosevelt

Written by Maryann N. Weidt/Illustrated by Lydia M. Anderson
Copyright 1991
Cloth: Carolrhoda Books
Paper: Lerner

⟀ From her lonely childhood, this unlikely heroine went on to a lifetime of public service. Eleanor Roosevelt worked tirelessly to further the cause of women, minorities, and the poor. She was FDR's eyes and ears, advising him about conditions around the country, but she was also much more—an influential, powerful woman who left her mark on national policy. Her daily column reached millions; she was as famous as her husband. After FDR's death, she never let up. She headed the United Nations Commission on Human Rights and the National Commission on the Status of Women. Eleanor Roosevelt is revered for her ideals and sense of duty, and this is a fine beginning biography.

Note: In our Young Adult section, we recommend *Eleanor Roosevelt: A Life of Discovery* by Russell Freedman.

Stop the Presses, Nellie's Got a Scoop! A Story of Nellie Bly
Written by Robert Quackenbush
Copyright 1992
Paper: Aladdin

〜 In 1885, Elizabeth Cochran was twenty years old. After an article poking fun at women who wanted to work in "male professions" appeared in the *Pittsburgh Dispatch*, she wrote a furious letter to the editor about what it was like to be a young woman unable to find meaningful work. Impressed, the editor hired her as a reporter, and her career as "Nellie Bly," America's first newspaperwoman, began.

Her outspoken articles, globe-trotting adventures, and investigative reporting led to debate and reform. Her scoops were so sensational that she became a celebrity. She'd be a remarkable woman today, but in the late 1800s she was absolutely astounding. Written in a breezy style, with lively illustrations, this is an entertaining biography.

Stranded
Written by Ben Mikaelsen

Copyright 1995
Cloth: Hyperion
Paper: Hyperion

⌒ Twelve-year-old Koby's life has run aground. Ever since the accident that took part of her leg four years ago, nothing's been right. Her parents testily argue about how to handle her new disability. Koby's dad is all for pushing Koby on to test her limits; Koby's mother is nearly smothering her with panicky overprotectiveness. Koby herself is awkward and horribly self-conscious around her schoolmates. In fact she's really only comfortable alone, out on the ocean sailing her little dinghy. When she rescues a pilot whale caught in a net, she has finally found something *she* can help. As Koby fights for the survival of the pilot whale and its calf, she forgets to worry about her amputated leg and her mother begins to respect Koby's capabilities. All the characters in this book—human and animal—have been stranded in one way or another. It is Koby's gutsy actions that begin the rescue process. Kid appeal is very high in this dramatic, exciting adventure.

The Summer of the Swans

Written by Betsy Byars
Copyright 1970
Cloth: Viking
Paper: Viking
Newbery Medal

⌒ When you're fourteen, sometimes nothing seems right. Discontent has turned Sara's summer upside down. Her aunt Willie seems bossier than usual; her sister seems more perfect; even her *feet* seem bigger than ever. The one constant is her little brother, Charlie. Brain-damaged from a fever when he was still a toddler, Charlie loves Sara unreservedly.

One evening Sara takes Charlie to look at the swans on the lake. Charlie is entranced by them and irritates Sara by refusing to leave. She drags her reluctant brother home. But the next morning, Charlie is gone. The search for Charlie takes on almost mythic proportions—it is really Sara's search for herself. But because Byars's writing is so fluid, the reader doesn't feel the weight of the heavy themes. Wonderful.

Switching Well
Written by Peni R. Griffin
Copyright 1993
Cloth: Margaret K. McElderry Books
Paper: Puffin

⌒ This book came to our attention with the enthusiastic endorsement of several sixth-graders we know. Little wonder— time travel is a popular theme, and *Switching Well* gives you a double dose! In 1891 twelve-year-old Ada makes a wish to be living "a hundred years from now." She's sure things would be easier. Women would no doubt have the vote, and life would finally be fair. In 1991 twelve-year-old Amber wishes to be living "a hundred years ago." She's sure things would be simpler. Women would work only at being mothers, and families would always stay together. An imp at the bottom of a haunted well simultaneously grants their wishes, and the two girls find they've switched centuries.

There's lots of meaty stuff in this story: it will probably inspire great discussions about women's history and changing cultural standards. But the best part of this book is that it's *fun*. Ada and Amber are baffled and challenged by their shift in time. Ada, without the benefit of prior knowledge, has an especially difficult experience, but she finds an important ally in Violet, an African-American girl who helps Ada maneuver through the unfamiliar new world. Both Ada and Amber keep their heads above water, finally shunting across the years to their rightful homes. Each contrives to leave a legacy in the time she visited. The happy readers of this book recommend it again and again.

Taking Flight: My Story
Written by Vicki Van Meter
Copyright 1995
Cloth: Viking

⁓ Vicki Van Meter's accomplishments are anything but ordinary. She was the youngest girl ever (twelve!) to fly across the country and the youngest pilot to fly across the Atlantic. A remarkably focused individual, Vicki managed every technical detail of her flights: takeoffs and landings, navigation, communications, and fuel calculations. Having honed her skills so well, she was able to meet her ambitious goals. As she says, "If you can dream, you can do anything." Told in Vicki's personable voice, with many disarming anecdotes about her new celebrity status, this is a book with wide appeal.

The Talking Earth
Written by Jean Craighead George
Copyright 1983
Cloth: HarperCollins
Paper: HarperTrophy

⁓ Billie Wind is skeptical. She doesn't believe in the legends of her Seminole Indian tribe. It stretches her credulity to think that the animals can talk to her and that the earth has spirits. The elders send Billie out into the Everglades by herself to stay for two days and one night, hoping the experience will change her mind. The stay stretches into three months as Billie Wind is stranded by a fire that destroys her way home. On her odyssey back, she befriends an otter, a panther cub, and a turtle, caring for them and learning from them.

Able to take care of herself in any situation, Billie Wind is one of the most competent heroines we've come across, as well as one of the most spiritual. She embodies strength as she embraces the sacred. Brimming with Indian lore, this is a skillfull, subtle book.

Talking to Faith Ringgold
Written by Faith Ringgold, Linda Freeman, and Nancy
    Roucher
Copyright 1996
Cloth: Crown
Paper: Crown

~ In an unusual, interactive format, artist Faith Ringgold converses with the reader about the personal and historical inspirations for her work and asks related questions. For instance, Ringgold says to readers, "Analyze *The Flag Is Bleeding*. What do you see that tells you about racial conflict and discrimination? . . . What is happening in the world today that you feel strongly about? Create your own artwork that shows how you feel." In addition, she has many smart, frank things to say about life. "I am inspired by people who rise above their adversity. . . . You have to stick with it. You can't stop. That's the key. Do not stop. Continue. Persevere.

JANET RENO

~

Attorney General, United States

he book that meant the most to me was *We Were WASPs* by Winifred Wood. Winifred Wood was my aunt, and during World War II she was in the Women's Airforce Service Pilots. These women towed targets and ferried bombers to assist the war effort. I thought they were wonderful and courageous and brave. They were my heroines.

Stay in there and you will get it." Laid out in a bold, eye-catching fashion, with many full-color reproductions and family photographs, this is not a book you'll finish in one sitting—you'll want to keep dipping into it.

There's a Girl in My Hammerlock
Written by Jerry Spinelli
Copyright 1991
Cloth: Simon & Schuster
Paper: Aladdin

⁓ Handsome Eric Delong is a pretty dumb reason to go out for the wrestling team, but that's what motivated Maisie Potter. She figures this is her best chance to really grab his attention. Maisie thinks she can handle the abuse coming her way as the high school's first female wrestler, but it's tougher and lonelier than she'd counted on. Her best friend deserts her; her brother won't talk to her; her matches are forfeited because no one wants to wrestle a girl. Maisie comes close to quitting but realizes that's impossible: "First you quit wrestling. Then what? School? Life?"

Kids love the real language, the contemporary plot, and Maisie's comic voice. They find it especially gratifying when Maisie wises up to what a jerk Eric really is. Looking back on the roughest year of her life, Maisie decides that even if she wasn't a champion she was a *winner*. Our girls give this a double thumbs up.

The 13th Clue
Written and Illustrated by Ann Jonas
Copyright 1992
Cloth: Greenwillow
Paper: Dell

⁓ What is a picture book doing in this category? Pick up this challenging mystery and see if it's so easy to decipher the clues hidden in these illustrations! The book opens with a diary entry of a

KATHARINE GRAHAM

～

Chairman of the Executive Committee of The Washington Post Company

he summer between fourth and fifth grades I spent almost entirely by myself reading in a room on the third floor of Mount Kisco, where I went through all of Dumas, eight volumes of Louisa May Alcott (starting with *Little Women*), *Treasure Island*, and a stirring adventure series by a man named Knipe. I counted up at the end, found that I had read around one hundred books, and wrote my parents that I was "positively floating in books." I couldn't have been happier.

young girl complaining about her terrible day. Suddenly she looks up to find a note telling her to "find more clues." The reader follows the trail along with her as she decodes the puzzling messages that lead her to a surprising ending. Sleuths everywhere will delight in this highly original, inventive book.

Toliver's Secret

Written by Esther Wood Brady/Illustrated by Richard Cuffari
Copyright 1976
Paper: Random House

～ During the Revolutionary War, everyone seems bursting with patriotic fervor and bravery, but ten-year-old Ellen Toliver is scared, shy, and timid. When her grandfather sprains his ankle and can't deliver a secret message to the Patriot soldiers, he turns to Ellen for help. She reluctantly accepts this mission, persuaded by Grandfather's reassurance that it will be a simple and straightforward matter. Instead everything goes wrong. As each new crisis arises, though, Ellen discovers surprising strength, ingenuity, and courage in herself.

This is very exciting reading—children will race along with Ellen as she maneuvers herself into and out of danger. A fine coming-of-age story.

The Trouble with Tuck
Written by Theodore Taylor
Copyright 1981
Cloth: Doubleday
Paper: Avon/Camelot

⁓ It is a rare child who doesn't want a dog like Friar Tuck. He is a big, loyal yellow Labrador who faithfully follows nine-year-old Helen everywhere. He saves her life—not once, but *twice*—and Helen is devastated when she learns that he is going blind and that there is no surgery that can stop it. All of Helen's ingenuity and persistence are required to help Tuck. She comes up with the novel idea of getting a seeing-eye dog for her dog. Finding a guide dog is only half the answer; training Tuck to respond to new commands is the more difficult part of the solution.

Until Tuck came into her life, Helen was a shy, awkward, and anxious child. Having a real job to do pulls her out of her shell, and both she and Tuck triumph in the end.

The True Confessions of Charlotte Doyle
Written by Avi
Copyright 1990
Cloth: Orchard Books
Paper: Avon
Newbery Honor Book

Boston Globe–Horn Book Award

～ From one of our foremost storytellers comes this page-turning adventure of a prissy young miss stranded on a ship of unsavory characters. The year is 1832, and Charlotte is bound for Boston. The tension builds as Charlotte misplaces her trust in the oily captain and betrays the crew. Mutiny, murder, a trial, and ultimate redemption are only part of this incredible book. Charlotte's voyage takes her out of childhood and leads her to a surprising decision: she turns her back on a comfortable, conventional life. Our girls could barely stand the excitement, and we ourselves stayed up past midnight to finish it!

Tuck Everlasting
Written by Natalie Babbitt
Copyright 1975
Cloth: Farrar Straus & Giroux
Paper: Sunburst
ALA Notable Book
Christopher Award

～ Would you like to live forever? What would that really mean? One day ten-year-old Winnie Foster, restless and tired of being an overprotected only child, wanders into the wood. She stumbles on the Tuck family and their secret: they have drunk from the waters of eternal life and will never die. Are they blessed or cursed?

This flawlessly written book affords countless pleasures. Without giving anything away, we can tell you that the well-constructed plot offers plenty of action—a kidnapping, a murder, a jailbreak. Its finely delineated heroine, Winnie, grows up quickly as she acts to save her new friends. Deeply drawn to the Tucks, Winnie must decide if she should drink the water, too. This provocative premise is a fascinating springboard for discussion across the generations—it is a book the whole family should read.

Turn Homeward, Hannalee
Written by Patricia Beatty
Copyright 1984
Cloth: William Morrow
Paper: Troll Associates

⌒ In 1864 the invading Union Army "captured" nearly 2,000 women and children in Roswell, Georgia, because they worked as mill hands making cloth for Confederate uniforms. These "prisoners of war" were shipped hundreds of miles away to the North. Once there, they were hired out on terms little better than slavery and abandoned to their fates. When Patricia Beatty went to research this sad story of war, she discovered that nothing of what had happened to these southerners—none of them rich, none of them slaveholders—was known. Determined not to let the story disappear, she expertly crafted this historical novel.

Twelve-year-old Hannalee and her younger brother are carried off with their fellow workers, leaving behind a mother widowed by the war and a brother off fighting the Yankees in Virginia. Through Hannalee's ingenuity, they remain together through the slow journey north but are then separated and sent to distant towns. Hannalee bravely devises an escape from her involuntary servitude, rescues her brother, and finds her way homeward. Full of genuine feeling for the difficult choices faced by Hannalee on her sojourn, this novel reminds us that some of the greatest costs of war are borne by those other than soldiers.

In the equally excellent sequel, *Be Ever Hopeful, Hannalee*, Hannalee comes to the aid of her brother when he is accused of a crime he didn't commit.

Understood Betsy
Written by Dorothy Canfield Fisher
Published 1917; numerous editions available

⌐ Only Aunt Frances understands Betsy. Only Aunt Frances knows how timid, nervous, and frail she is. Only Aunt Frances can guard Betsy from the dangers of the world. When Betsy is catapulted out of Aunt Frances's protective orbit, she lands in Vermont with her taciturn Putney cousins. Because they assume she is a capable and competent child, Betsy begins to surprise herself by rising to their expectations. She is thrilled to discover what she can do!

It's easy to see why this has been a perennial hit since 1917.

Walk Two Moons
Written by Sharon Creech
Copyright 1994
Cloth: HarperCollins
Paper: HarperTrophy
Newbery Medal

⌐ Salamanca Tree Hiddle is on the run, and most of what she's running from is the truth. She's traveling with her beloved, benevolent, and endearingly dotty grandparents from Ohio to Idaho, retracing the last journey of Sal's mother. Life's been unsettled and unhappy for Sal and her father since her mother left; Sal is clinging to the belief that if she gets to Lewiston, Idaho, by her mother's birthday she'll be able to bring her mother back home.

To pass the long hours in the car, Sal's grandparents ask for a good story. Sal obliges with the long, parallel tale of her friend Phoebe and how Phoebe's mother disappeared one day. These chapters are punctuated by the interjections and observations of Gram and Gramps. As she tells Phoebe's story, Sal circles closer and closer to acknowledging the truth about her mother until, finally, she can avoid it no longer.

There is sadness aplenty in this book, and furthermore, most of its adult women are either emotionally or physically fragile. This is more than mitigated by the resilient, loving, folksy spirits of

Gram and Gramps and the incredible storytelling powers of Sal, their little "chickabiddy." The novel's clever structure allows the author to demonstrate how following a story all the way to its very end can lead you safely home. A big hit even with those who claim that they "don't like sad endings," Sal's journey from denial to acceptance is beautifully conceived, totally believable, and completely compelling.

Walking the Road to Freedom: A Story About Sojourner Truth
Written by Jeri Ferris/Illustrated by Peter E. Hanson
Copyright 1988
Cloth: Carolrhoda Books
Paper: Carolrhoda Books

⟶ This book is really two stories. The first is that of Belle Dumont, a slave woman in the early nineteenth century in New York State, struggling against hard odds to keep her family together and watching helplessly as some are sold south. The second story is that of Sojourner Truth, the woman whom Belle Dumont became in 1843, when she heeded God's call to tell her history throughout the land. In the twenty years that followed, Sojourner Truth became second only to Frederick Douglass as an orator on behalf of suffering African-Americans. The simple, moving testimony she offered, accompanied by her powerful singing, turned many against slavery and rallied the abolitionist cause across the North. A heroine to feminists as well, Sojourner Truth campaigned equally for women's rights. Her famous speech "Ain't I a Woman?" still thrills today as words of a true prophet.

The Westing Game
Written by Ellen Raskin
Copyright 1978
Cloth: E. P. Dutton

Paper: Puffin
Newbery Medal

⌐ This mystery game novel has been proclaimed by two very knowledgeable ten- and twelve-year-old sources as "one of the best books ever!" So it may be superfluous to mention that it introduces a sly, shin-kicking, stock-market-playing sleuth heroine, Turtle Wexler; is full of outrageous puns; and has an intricate plot that would challenge Miss Marple. The goal here is to find which of the sixteen heirs of Samuel Westing murdered him. Whichever character discovers the perpetrator will win the intricate "whodunit" game Westing set up in his will, thus inheriting his $200,000,000 estate. Make your kids promise not to tell you the ending so you can try your hand as well!

What I Had Was Singing: The Story of Marian Anderson
Written by Jeri Ferris
Copyright 1994
Cloth: Carolrhoda Books
Paper: First Avenue Editions

⌐ The photograph of Marian Anderson performing on Easter Sunday, 1939, at the Lincoln Memorial in front of 75,000 people will send chills down your back. This woman, the toast of Europe, with a voice that Toscanini said you hear only "once in a hundred years," was denied permission by the Daughters of the American Revolution to sing at Constitution Hall because of the color of her skin. She sang instead in the open air, dramatizing America's racial schisms. The incident was one of the seminal events in the civil rights movement.

This biography chronicles Anderson's extraordinary career, starting with her girlhood singing in the Union Baptist choir and continuing to her debut at the Metropolitan Opera in 1955. That performance broke the color barrier in opera forever. As Leontyne

Price said, "We owe her gratitude for showing that talent and dignity can prevail."

Wild Magic

Written by Tamora Pierce
Copyright 1992
Cloth: Atheneum
Paper: Random House

⌐ The legion of girls and boys who gobbled up the Lioness Quartet books (see the listing under *Alanna*) will be delighted to travel further in the country of Tortall, a kind of utopian Camelot where neither rank nor race nor gender prohibits anyone from leading the most gallant crusades against evil. Pierce's second series, The Immortals, of which this is the first title, reintroduces the favorite characters from the earlier series as well as brings us another of her striking heroines.

Daine is hired as assistant to Tortall's horsemistress because Daine clearly has a way with the horses. It turns out she has much more than just a knack for handling animals; she possesses a "wild magic" that lets her communicate with every living creature. When Tortall is besieged by malevolent, immortal monsters, only Daine can help. She risks everything she has to rescue her new homeland. Brave battles and high sorcery make this a stirring epic. Daine's saga continues in *Wolf-Speaker, The Emperor Mage,* and *The Realms of the Gods.*

Wildflower Girl

Written by Marita Conlon-McKenna
Copyright 1991
Cloth: Holiday House
Paper: Puffin

⌐ Although she's only thirteen, Peggy O'Driscoll is ready to stand up to her older sister and demand the right to leave Ireland and sail to America. After all, her sister had been only thirteen when she'd saved Peggy and her brother from the workhouse and "pushed us and made us walk and got food for us and forced us to survive the Famine." Prospects in Ireland are so bleak that her sister reluctantly gives in, and the persistent young Peggy sails off on her own to find work in Boston.

The hazardous journey is only the first hardship Peggy faces, for life as a domestic servant proves just about as brutal. The long, lonely hours, the meager pay, the unrelieved, backbreaking work are what's meant "for the likes of us." But Peggy keeps her chin held high, and though she may be fighting back tears, she counts herself a survivor. High-quality historical fiction.

A Winning Edge
Written by Bonnie Blair with Greg Brown/Illustrated by
    Doug Keith
Copyright 1996
Cloth: Taylor Publishing
⁓ Bonnie Blair is the most decorated U.S. athlete in the Winter Olympics and the first American woman to win five gold medals. Her engaging personality shines through these pages. Blair stood on skates before she could walk and has been on them ever since. There were hours of practice, setbacks and struggles, but her love of speed skating brought her honors and victories. Illustrated with warm family photos, this autobiography of a true champion hits the mark.

Winning Women: Eight Great Athletes and
Their Unbeatable Stories
Written by Fred McMane and Cathrine Wolf
Copyright 1995
Paper: Bantam/*Sports Illustrated* for Kids
⁓ Upbeat profiles of eight outstanding athletes comprise this volume. Included are Oksana Baiul, Shannon Miller, Julie Krone, Gail Devers, Bonnie Blair, Steffi Graf, Teresa Edwards, and Nancy

Lopez. Their daring accomplishments are legendary; the book focuses on their training and their many successes.

Sidebars explain how each sport is played and showcase trailblazers who paved the way. Notable quotes from each athlete are also highlighted throughout. Although no longer quite up-to-date, this remains a light and quick intro to many different and exciting sports.

Wise Child
Written by Monica Furlong
Copyright 1987
Paper: Random House
ALA Notable Book

⌐ Mystical and magical, this mesmerizing story takes place in the isolated highlands of Scotland. A girl, Wise Child, has been abandoned by her parents and taken in by Juniper, a mysterious woman who the villagers suspect is a witch. In actuality she is an educated woman, someone who knows Latin, English, music, and all the healing arts.

Wise Child begins her training with Juniper and not only is taught all that Juniper knows but also comes to love and respect her. When her mother, Maeve, reappears to claim Wise Child, the girl must choose between the luxurious, easy life her mother's "black magic" offers and the more difficult and demanding existence with Juniper.

Filled with sorcery, high drama, strong, capable female characters, *and* a nail-biting ending, this is fantasy of the highest order. Don't forget to read the prequel, *Juniper*.

The Witch of Blackbird Pond
Written by Elizabeth George Speare
Copyright 1958, 1986
Cloth: Houghton Mifflin

Paper: Laurel Leaf
Newbery Medal

～ Indulged by her wealthy grandfather in Barbados, sixteen-year-old Kit Tyler is ill suited to come live with her Puritan relatives in New England after his death. The year is 1687, and life in Connecticut is harsh. Kit's frivolous clothes, high spirits, and impulsive behavior clash with her uncle's stern and solemn household. The endless tedious chores and the rigid religious strictures of the community leave her miserable and lonely.

She finds comfort in a forbidden friendship with an old Quaker woman who lives near Blackbird Pond. Kit sees in Hannah another outcast like herself and lightly dismisses the village rumors that have branded Hannah a witch. But when political fervor and religious hysteria begin to swirl around her, Kit herself is accused of witchcraft and thrown into jail.

This dramatic turn of events causes her to grow from a heedless girl to a young woman of great compassion and understanding. Honest, independent, and loyal, Kit is a terrific heroine.

The Wonderful Wizard of Oz
Written by L. Frank Baum/Illustrated by John R. Neill
First published 1900; numerous editions available

～ There's no place like Oz, or at least certainly not to its legion of devoted fans. One of our daughters lives and breathes to read and reread this famous series. We've led off with the first title. (Baum, the original author, wrote fourteen books; after his death, the next nineteen books were written by Ruth Plumly Thompson. Their popularity is such that Oz books continue to be written by numerous authors.) Dorothy shares the spotlight with the Scarecrow, the Tin Man, and the Cowardly Lion as they follow the yellow brick road. You've no doubt seen the movie jillions of times, but you'll enjoy discovering Dorothy in print as she protects Toto and vanquishes the Wicked Witch of the West. Don't stop with this title. There are plenty of plucky heroines in *The Patchwork Girl of Oz*, *The Marvelous Land of Oz*, *Tik-Tok of Oz*, *Ozma of Oz*—just ask your bookseller!

The Workers' Detective: A Story About Alice Hamilton

Written by Stephanie Sammartino McPherson/Illustrations by Janet Schulz

Copyright 1992

Cloth: Carolrhoda Books

⌒ "There are two kinds of people in the world," Alice Hamilton's mother told her, "the ones who say, 'Somebody ought to do something about that, but why should it be I?' and those who say, 'Somebody must do something about that, then why not I?' " Alice Hamilton was the kind who took things upon herself.

In 1893 she became a doctor with a specialty in pathology. But she discovered her life's calling at Jane Addams's Hull House, where she lived, taught classes, and took the children on picnics. It was there that her keen eye noticed that the factory workers who came to Hull House had certain physical problems. The more she documented them, the more she became convinced that if conditions were improved, so would the health of the workers. Simply put, Hamilton pioneered industrial medicine. Her studies became so important that she ended up being the first female faculty member at Harvard. Her investigations of the rubber, mining, munitions, silk, and rayon industries forever changed the way factory work was conducted. As she said near the end of her long, productive life, "Taking part in a new and expanding discipline brings out the best in one."

Wren to the Rescue

Written by Sherwood Smith

Copyright 1990

Cloth: Harcourt Brace Jovanovich

⌒ Rousing adventure stories *are* being written about girls, and this fantasy tale is a terrific example.

Wren never expected to find that her best friend at the orphanage was really a princess, hidden away to keep her safe from an evil sorcerer. When the princess is kidnapped, Wren doesn't hesitate, but immediately embarks on a perilous quest to rescue her friend. It is just the sort of mission she has been longing for: she can finally be like the heroines in the plays she has read! She is joined in this endeavor by a young prince and a magician's apprentice, and the three overcome enough fearsome danger to satisfy the most intrepid reader. And—lucky us—there are equally thrilling books in the rest of the series. Don't pass up *Wren's Quest* and *Wren's War*.

A Wrinkle in Time
Written by Madeleine L'Engle
Copyright 1962
Cloth: Farrar Straus & Giroux
Paper: Dell
Newbery Mcdal

⌒ This fantasy epic of good and evil has been mesmerizing children since its publication. Shy, awkward Meg Murry and her brilliant little brother, Charles Wallace, meet three mysterious and powerful women, Mrs. Whatsit, Mrs. Who, and Mrs. Which, and are propelled on a dangerous journey through time and space searching for the Murrys' missing father.

Meg, so used to feeling at sixes and sevens about herself, is thrown into the unaccustomed role of heroine in the climactic scene when she must face alone the embodiment of evil, IT, to rescue her brother, who's become ensnared in IT's clutches. Remembering the advice of Mrs. Which, she searches her soul for what she might have that evil cannot possess: "Suddenly she knew. She knew! Love. That was what she had that IT did not have." Meg's courage and new self-knowledge bring her father and brother safely home.

Uplifting and spellbinding.

Yolonda's Genius

Written by Carol Fenner
Copyright 1995
Cloth: Margaret K. McElderry Books
Paper: Aladdin
Newbery Honor Book

⌐ Everyone is so busy thinking about all the things Yolonda's little brother Andrew *can't* do—like read and write—that no one's noticed what he *can* do. Everyone except Yolonda, that is. Yolonda knows that Andrew is a musical genius, and when Andrew starts to wither away in their new suburban Chicago school, Yolonda shoulders the task of putting things to rights. Responsibility comes naturally to this African-American girl. She's smart, does well in class, stays out of trouble, takes care of herself. She roughs up a gang of drug pushers who try to mess with her brother. Even though she's only a fifth-grader, Yolonda's got clear ambitions: "chief of police" sounds good to her. And when kids call her names because of her hefty size, she just shrugs off their jeers. In fact the person she loves most in the world besides Andrew is her aunt Tiny, a gigantic woman whose proportions match her generous heart.

How Yolonda gets the adult world to pay attention to Andrew's prodigious gift is a great story, but Yolonda herself is a true break-the-mold heroine: a queen-sized spirit in a queen-sized girl.

You Want Women *to Vote, Lizzie Stanton?*

Written by Jean Fritz/Illustrated by Dy Anne Di Salvo-Ryan
Copyright 1995
Cloth: Putnam

⌐ Leave it to Jean Fritz. She never talks down to her audience, gets right to the point, and remembers to include the fascinating little details that make a biography come alive. And, of course, in Elizabeth Cady Stanton she's got a terrific subject on which to train her historian's eye. The Cady sisters, dressed all alike in red, were little more than a constant reminder to their father that he had no sons. Lizzie vowed that she could be as smart and brave as any boy and impress her father. All he could do when confronted with her accomplishments was sigh and say "If only you'd been a boy." Lizzie took this childhood disappointment and turned her life into a crusade for women's rights. While the whole country was burning with debate over slavery, Lizzie, a staunch abolitionist, demanded that everyone, even *women*, vote. Unheard of! Unthinkable! We've come a long way since then, due in no small measure to this unstoppable woman.

A Young Painter: The Life and Paintings of Wang Yani—China's Extraordinary Young Artist

Written by Zheng Zhensun and Alice Low
Copyright 1991
Cloth: Scholastic Trade

⌐ It's not often we have the chance to follow a child prodigy as she grows up. Born in 1975, Yani began painting as a toddler. Her first scribbles quickly become recognizable images, and Yani's art instructor father realized his child possessed a special genius. At age four she had her first major exhibition in Shanghai. At fourteen she traveled to Washington, D.C., for her one-person show at the Smithsonian. Yani has painted thousands of paintings—many of them focus on the monkeys she loves. Her exuberant words will inspire you as well: "When you pick up a brush don't ever ask anyone for help. Because the most wonderful thing about painting is being left alone with your own imagination. I do not paint to get praise from others, but to play a game of endless joy."

The book is designed elegantly, with stunning examples of her art on every page. At the back you'll find a great glossary and informative notes about Chinese brush painting techniques. Yani is clearly a legend in the making, and we expect to be following her career for many years to come.

YOUNG ADULTS

AGE TWELVE AND UP

e're 180 degrees from our first books. These heroines are on their own in an uncharted world. In many cases the comforting social fabric of life is missing. The backdrop may be war or exile, or the family may be lost to death or divorce. The heroine must summon all her courage to find her way to safety.

Although the settings may be harsh, there are always achievement, triumph, and hope to be found. Girls who are suddenly seeing the world in a more complicated light are eager to explore how other girls have met their challenges. The excitement of forging new relationships—perhaps a romance—is another hallmark of this category. Many of the stories are told in the first person, and the voices range from the genuinely dramatic to the genuinely comedic. These engrossing books are sophisticated in tone and content and capture the imagination of the maturing mind.

Abigail Adams: Witness to a Revolution
Written by Natalie S. Bober
Copyright 1995
Cloth: Atheneum
Paper: Aladdin
Boston Globe–Horn Book Award
Golden Kite Award

⌒ Abigail Adams was encouraged by her father to read widely, but, despite all of Abigail's pleas, her mother refused to send her to the local dame school, for Abigail's precarious health could not be risked. For the rest of her life Abigail was sensitive about the lack of formal education available for herself and, indeed, for any woman of her day. In one of her letters to John Adams, she wrote that she hoped the country's new constitution would not neglect the schooling of its daughters. Despite her haphazard education, over 2,000 letters of Abigail's survive, amazing documents that testify to a woman of intellect, stamina, perception, and humor. Separated from her husband for months, sometimes years, at a time, she ran the family farm, managed their financial affairs, raised four children, and spoke out boldly concerning the political upheavals of the day.

This excellent biography serves Abigail Adams well. Although the author reminds us not to judge Abigail by twentieth-century feminist standards, she clearly comes across as a remarkable champion of women's rights. We see her legacy everywhere: when Sandra Day O'Connor was appointed to the Supreme Court, she said, "Abigail Adams would be pleased."

Alicia: My Story
Written by Alicia Appleman-Jurman
Copyright 1988
Paper: Bantam
Christopher Award

LINDA S. WILSON

⌒

President, Radcliffe College

ooks were constant companions when I was a girl. Books about pioneer life, biographies of women in colonial times, the Sue Barton, Nurse series as well as the classics sparked my imagination then and still stick in my memory. What made the greatest impression, however, were *Too Late the Phalarope*, by Alan Paton, and a multivolume series by Winston Churchill. I recall these not only for their content but also for the librarian's disapproval that I had strayed out of the "juvenile section."

⌒ Reading Jurman's Holocaust memoir is like looking straight into the heart of darkness.

Everything is taken from this young Polish girl. In quick succession she loses her father and four brothers. Although only a child, Alicia angrily vows to live and keep her mother safe. Caught and crammed on a train bound for one of the camps, she escapes through some loose boards. Caught again, Alicia is sent to prison (she is just twelve) and falls horribly ill; believed dead, she is taken to be buried but is rescued by a Jewish gravedigger who thinks she might still be alive. She is ensnared again and marched to the forest where a mass execution is taking place. Diversionary shooting allows Alicia to flee into the woods. Following a reunion with her mother, the two hide in the fields while Alicia, passing herself off as a Gentile, works on local farms in exchange for bits of bread and sour milk. But even Alicia's indomitable spirit cannot save her mother. When the two are cornered at last by the Nazis, Alicia's mother throws herself between the SS men and her daughter. She is murdered before Alicia's eyes—with the last bullet in the Nazi's gun.

Her story of the Nazis' relentless evil is made even more horrible by the indifference, the cowardice, or—worst of all—the compliance of people who had been friends and neighbors. Only a few moments of kindness and compassion flame up briefly. That Alicia survived at all is a miracle for which she fought every inch of the way. As she writes, "Love and hate were what motivated my young mind and heart. Love for my dear, gentle mother—and hate for the cruel murderers." Readers will be shaking with anger and awe when they put down this magnificent book.

The Amazon Papers
Written by Beverly Keller
Copyright 1996
Cloth: Harcourt Brace
Paper: Harcourt Brace

⌒ Iris Hoving is "a straight-A student, auto mechanic, hotshot athlete," but she feels like a disappointment to her mother, who was hoping for a more conventional daughter with an active social calendar. When Iris's mother flees the house to take a vacation from her intense (and intensely funny) daughter, Iris decides to "drain the cup of life, romantically speaking." She's got her eye on Foster Prizer, who, while not "heavily into education," delivers pizza and is a gorgeous hunk. From there, every step Iris takes is a hilarious misstep of increasingly gargantuan proportions. She lands herself in more trouble than she could have imagined possible. She also figures her way out of it (well, most of it) in this delirious comedy of errors. By the book's end Iris has received an apology for her mother's retrograde agenda and has decided to come up with her

own. Although the action is pure slapstick, Iris's wry voice is unexpectedly sweet and touching.

Anne Frank: Beyond the Diary
Written by Ruud van der Rol and Rian Verhoeven
Copyright 1993
Cloth: Viking
Paper: Puffin
Christopher Award

〜 This photographic remembrance, published in association
with the Anne Frank House, is a poignant adjunct to *The Diary of
a Young Girl* (entry follows). The more than one hundred photographs, many of them personal family photos, are now in the
archives of the museum. They begin with Anne's sunny childhood
days, continue through her claustrophobic confinement in the
Secret Annex, and end with the deplorable circumstances of
Bergen-Belsen. For us, finally seeing a photograph of the actual
diary that Anne received on her thirteenth birthday was particularly
chilling. Also included are essays and maps that describe the catastrophic events that trapped Anne and her family. Excerpts from
Anne's diary and reminiscences from people who knew the Franks
comprise the rest of the absorbing text; there's also a moving introduction by Anna Quindlen.

Anne Frank: The Diary of a Young Girl
The Definitive Edition
Written by Anne Frank
First published 1947; copyright 1991, 1995
Cloth: Doubleday
Paper: Doubleday

〜 We come to this book knowing the outcome. This makes it
almost unbearably painful to read, but it is an experience that
should be required of everyone. Anne was an immensely gifted

writer, and she faithfully kept this diary during the two years she
and her family hid from the Nazis in the Secret Annex. Eight people were sharing close, cramped quarters while in continual terror
for their safety. Anne, thirteen when she started the diary, confided
all the petty dramas of their daily lives, the grating tensions, the
unremitting fears, as well as the ordinary longings and feelings of
a teenage girl. She named her diary "Kitty" so that it might seem
to be the best friend she yearned for. In entry after entry, Anne
pours out her emotional turmoil, and yet her dreams for the world
never dim. Sustained by a hope we can hardly imagine, Anne was
able to write, "In spite of everything, I still believe that people are
really good at heart."

  Her diary is the most famous document of the Holocaust
nightmare and the enduring symbol for the millions who perished.
Powerful, shocking, heartbreaking, Anne's story is one that will
never leave you.

The Autobiography of Miss Jane Pittman
Written by Ernest J. Gaines
Copyright 1971
Paper: Bantam
∻ Purporting to be the autobiographical recollections of a 110-
year-old African-American woman, this is a superb, searing novel
about race in our nation. Jane's life is bracketed by the Civil War
and the civil rights movement. Loss—and the threat of it—is the
constant in her life. Her mama was beaten to death by the overseer;
she never knew her father. When the Freedom comes, Jane is about
ten or eleven (she isn't sure which), and she sets out to find the
North. Instead she finds herself one of two survivors of an ambush
and takes on the responsibility for the other survivor, an even
younger child.

  So begins the harrowing saga of Jane's life. Nearing the end
of her days, she discovers that her endurance and knowledge have
given her a new gift: power. The civil rights movement needs her.

She is asked to protest segregation by drinking at a whites-only drinking fountain. If she goes, the others on the plantation will follow. The struggle that was begun so long ago can continue.

You may know this book from the award-winning television show starring Cicely Tyson. Rent the movie. Read the book.

Beauty: A Retelling of the Story of Beauty and the Beast
Written by Robin McKinley
Copyright 1978
Cloth: HarperCollins
Paper: HarperTrophy
ALA Notable Children's Book

~ Almost everyone knows this story, but McKinley's version makes readers feel as if they're discovering it for the first time. Beauty tells this tale, and her voice is mesmerizing.

Contrary to the traditional fairy-tale version, this Beauty is not beautiful. She is the plain but scholarly youngest daughter of a prosperous, loving family. When her father's life is held forfeit by a great and terrifying monster, Beauty takes her courage in her hands and offers herself in exchange. Her bravery is equaled only by her perceptive heart. The story of growing love captivates, and the underlying moral message unfolds subtly. Both Beauty and her Beast are transformed by love in this suspenseful and beguiling novel.

Note: In an unusual move, McKinley has just published *Rose Daughter*, her second retelling of this fairy tale. After twenty years, Beauty and the Beast came back to her "dressed in a new story." She's given the traditional ending an unexpected twist; readers will enjoy comparing the two.

A Bone from a Dry Sea
Written by Peter Dickinson
Copyright 1992

Cloth: Doubleday
Paper: Laurel Leaf

⌒ Just as a paleoanthropologist may tease out information from a fossil chip, Peter Dickinson has spun an absorbing novel from a tantalizing bit of theory about our human evolution. He's packaged his intriguing book in a most atypical way—with two protagonists, separated not by place but by time. Millions and millions of years, in fact. The chapters alternate between Vinny, who has just arrived in Africa to visit her father at the site of his anthropological digs, and Li, who is a young prehuman ancestor, an apelike creature living both on the land and in the sea.

Vinny is enthusiastic about an unsupported theory suggesting that apes could have migrated from the jungle to the ocean before they began to stand upright. Her father greets this hypothesis with dour hostility, but Vinny won't back down. As for Li, she has become the unofficial leader of her tribe. She's the only one capable of real thought. When a tsunami wave destroys their familiar habitat, it is Li who turns the tribe away from the ocean and settles them on a marshy plain. She carries with her a bone from a dolphin to remind her of her former home. It is at precisely this spot that Vinny's father and his team are searching for traces of our ancestors . . . and Vinny unearths Li's dolphin talisman. These two independent heroines are thus neatly joined in this artfully constructed, intellectually challenging novel.

The Borning Room
Written by Paul Fleischman
Copyright 1991
Cloth: HarperCollins
Paper: HarperTrophy
Golden Kite Award

⌒ As one might expect from a Newbery Medal–winning poet, this polished novel shines with a serene grace. Written in some of the purest language we've come across, this is the clear-eyed reminiscence of sixty-seven-year-old Georgina Lott. She remembers all the most important events in her life as she lies on her deathbed in "the borning room," a room that her grandfather added onto his house in Ohio in 1820. Births, deaths, illnesses, and first love were all encountered there. But as Georgina grew up she was hardly unaware of the outside world. A runaway slave hides in her woods; self-righteous preachers threaten her nonchurchgoing grandfather with damnation; the modern medicine of the time cruelly fails to save her mother; Susan B. Anthony's weekly paper is read and admired. The anger and grief and joy that rush through Georgina are expressed directly and beautifully. Fleischman has given us a heroine who shows the reader how to live.

Bread Givers: A Struggle Between a Father of the Old World and a Daughter of the New
Written by Anzia Yezierska
Copyright 1925, 1952
Paper: Persea Books

~ Yezierski wrote this piercing, realistic novel as a feminist call to arms for all the young Jewish women living on Hester Street in New York City in the early 1900s.

Sara Smolinsky is the youngest of four daughters and the one who chafes the most under the restrictions laid down by her tyrannical father. He refuses to work, claiming he must study the Talmud all day, every day. He sends ten-year-old Sara out to sell herring and scrounge through the trash for coal. The poverty and dirt (they share one towel) seem impossible to escape. Their father chases away suitor after suitor for Sara's sisters and their self-sacrificing mother does nothing to help. After years of watching her sisters destroy their lives to please their father, Sara declares her independence. In a fiery scene Sara tells him, "My will is as strong as yours. I'm going to live my own life. Nobody can stop me.

I'm not from the old country. I'm American!" Sara moves into a grubby, tiny tenement room, which she prizes because it is her own. She takes a day job ironing shirts and studies at night to become a teacher.

Yezierska did nothing to pretty up the dark side of immigrant life. The confining roles for women are starkly portrayed, and Sara's triumph is revolutionary for its day. A powerful book we were thrilled to discover.

Buffalo Brenda
Written by Jill Pinkwater
Copyright 1989
Cloth: Simon & Schuster
Paper: Aladdin

～ India Ink Teidlebaum (her parents are ex-hippies) and Brenda Tuna (her parents still are hippies) become instant wisecracking, nonconformist best friends in seventh grade. Outrageous in dress, speech, and action, Brenda lives to defy authority. At first India spends her time either lost in admiration or terrified of being roped into Brenda's creative high jinks. But India comes into her own as they take over the school newspaper, invent the school booster club, and proceed to pull off one of the biggest, wackiest pranks ever. (And, oh yes, in doing so Brenda earns the name that gives this novel its title.) The humorous tone throughout is snappy and cheerfully irreverent. These two pals make a true dynamic duo!

But I'll Be Back Again
Written by Cynthia Rylant
Copyright 1989
Paper: Beech Tree Books

～ Award-winning author Cynthia Rylant has written a superior autobiography that really is a love letter—to her parents, her grandparents, her town, the children she grew up with, the boys she kissed, the Beatles. All of this became the material for her stories and characters. When she was only four, her mother took her to live with her grandparents in Beaver, West Virginia, leaving behind Rylant's alcoholic father. "That is all the loss I needed to become a writer."

Despite this painful beginning, her book is funny, wry, and perceptive. Girls just entering adolescence will love recognizing themselves as they read Rylant's anecdotes. If you came of age in the late sixties, you'll especially appreciate this poignant visit back.

The Cage
Written by Ruth Minsky Sender
Copyright 1986
Paper: Bantam

~ This is history in the raw. In May 1942 the Nazis brutally ripped sixteen-year-old Riva Minska's mother from her arms. She never saw her again. Left in charge of her three younger brothers, one of whom had tuberculosis, Riva tried valiantly to find food and shelter. But there were no options inside the barbed-wire cage of the Lodz ghetto. Time after time Riva and her brothers barely escaped being rounded up by the Nazis. One day their luck ran out: they were deported to Auschwitz and separated forever.

Sender's book is a personal criminal indictment of the Nazis. Her horrifying descriptions of their vile evildoing in the ghetto and in the concentration camp will not soon leave the reader. But what truly inspires is her constant heroic fortitude and her overriding love of books and language. In the ghetto she started a secret library. In Auschwitz, Sender's best day comes when she is given a tiny pencil and she manages to scratch out a poem. Despite every possible deprivation, hers is a voice that could not be silenced.

Sender has written two other moving memoirs, *To Life* and *The Holocaust Lady*, concerning her adaptation to the world after Auschwitz.

Cattail Moon

Written by Jean Thesman
Copyright 1994
Cloth: Houghton Mifflin
Paper: Flare

⌐ "I can't understand why my mother doesn't *want* something. Really want something, the way I want music." Julia's elegant mother spends her energy trying to remake her daughter into a carbon copy of the cheerleader she once was, but Julia has had enough. She defiantly moves out of the house to live with her father and grandmother in an isolated farming community. Although life in Moon Valley solves one problem, it immediately poses another: Moon Valley is just too small and remote to enable Julia to continue her music studies. While Julia wonders how to retune her discordant life and handle a new romance, a ghostly vision, dressed in turn-of-the-century clothes, keeps mysteriously appearing. Who is this spirit, and why does Julia feel that it has something to tell her? Torn between advancing her musical education and staying near her boyfriend, Julia must make some tough decisions. The beautiful phantom helps Julia "choose what I love and what makes me happy. . . . Choose and don't look back, no matter what."

The Changeover: A Supernatural Romance

Written by Margaret Mahy
Copyright 1974
Cloth: Margaret K. McElderry Books
Paper: Puffin
Carnegie Medal
ALA Notable Book

⌐ Laura knows Sorenson Carlisle's secret. Laura can see behind Sorry's enigmatic silver eyes to the witch he really is. No, not a cackling, Halloween-type witch but someone with special powers because of his unique sensitivity to the natural world. When the doctors are baffled by the sudden illness of Jacko, her little brother, Laura hurries to the intriguing Sorry as the only hope to save Jacko. Laura knows that Jacko has been marked by a demonic witch who is draining his life force away. Sorry informs Laura that there is indeed a slim chance to rescue her brother. Laura must "change-over" into a witch herself and then must trick the evil spirit that is possessing Jacko. The changeover will be irrevocable; the risk to herself will not be insignificant. The odds that she'll fall in love with Sorry are pretty high, too.

The repartee between Laura and Sorry is one of the prime delights of Mahy's dazzling, offbeat novel. That this supernatural romance is juxtaposed against Jacko's illness as well as some more plausible problems of modern family life simply adds to the pleasure of reading this well-constructed book. The many avid fans of this New Zealand author will also want to read *The Catalogue of the Universe*.

Children of the River
Written by Linda Crew
Copyright 1989
Paper: Bantam Doubleday Dell
ALA Notable Book
Golden Kite Honor Book

~ The class assignment is pretty straightforward: write about the topic that most deeply concerns you. The class responds with pre-dictable essays about cafeteria food and dress codes. Sixteen-year-old Sundara Sovann, a refugee from Cambodia, takes the teacher's instructions seriously and hands in a revealing poem about her feelings for her lost homeland. The class falls silent. One boy, popular football star Jonathan McKinnon, is shaken out of his compla-cency and begins looking at Sundara in a new light. That simple assignment is the catalyst for this novel about Sundara's struggle to put in perspective her Khmer heritage and her new American life.

Sundara's aunt Soka expects Sundara to live like a proper Cambodian girl; the manners and mores of America are inexplicable, if not immoral, to these new immigrants. Both Sundara and Soka must also face the tragic events that accompanied their desperate departure from Cambodia. As Sundara is drawn increasingly to Jonathan, she sees how the sweetness of her romance is offset by her unhappy knowledge of Cambodian genocide and the realities of race in America. Nicely balanced and thoughtful.

Dixie Storms
Written by Barbara Hall
Copyright 1990
Cloth: Harcourt Brace
Paper: Bantam
ALA Best Book for Young Adults

⤳ With its redemptive plot and its rich, emotionally resonant writing, this is a novel that is well worth reading. Hall is excellent at capturing the quandaries of a modern teenage girl whose roots sink deep into her native soil.

The summer of Dutch Peyton's fourteenth year is a scorcher. Crops are drying up, payments are due on their Virginia farm, and morale is withering. Dutch has lived a quiet, mostly contented backcountry life with her father, her aunt, her brother, and her brother's young son. Her mother is dead, and her brother's wife left him years ago. With the jarring arrival of her worldly and pretty cousin Norma, Dutch is forced to sort out her feelings about the ties that bind. By the summer's end Dutch is able to see more clearly what is good and beautiful and true about herself—and about those she loves the most.

Eleanor Roosevelt: A Life of Discovery
Written by Russell Freedman
Copyright 1993

Cloth: Clarion Books
Paper: Clarion Books
Newbery Honor Book
Boston Globe–Horn Book Award
Golden Kite Award

~ Eleanor's early years read almost like a sad novel, but the triumphs of her later years are very real and entirely of her own making. Despite the failure of love again and again in her life, from the alcoholism of her father to the unfaithfulness of her husband, she persisted in pursuing her dreams for humanity and worked ceaselessly to improve the lot of others. As first lady, she cast aside convention, expanding her position far beyond the traditional hostess

PATRICIA SCHROEDER

~

*President and Chief Executive Officer,
Association of American Publishers, Inc.
Former United States Congresswoman*

 s a young girl I was much more into real life figures than fiction. I loved biographies. I loved politics. My father was a pilot and I couldn't wait to get my license. My heroines were Amelia Earhart and Mrs. Eleanor Roosevelt. I spent hours in the library tracking down anything that had ever been written about them. Obviously those research skills were very valuable later in life, so I thank my heroines for inspiring me and adding to my skills bank!

role, never hesitating to express and act upon her independent opinions. During World War II, Eleanor dauntlessly traveled on fact-finding missions for the president and unstintingly supported morale at home and overseas. Later, as a delegate to the United Nations, she continued to live her ideals of service, duty, and responsibility. We find this wonderfully well-written biography, with its inviting layout and bountiful use of photographs, truly inspiring.

Note: Younger readers should check out Maryann N. Weidt's *Stateswoman to the World* (see Index).

Ellen Foster

Written by Kaye Gibbons
Copyright 1987
Cloth: Algonquin Books
Paper: Vintage

⌒ Like *The Adventures of Huckleberry Finn*, this is really an adult novel with a child at its center. And like Huck, Ellen has a backcountry southern story that you'll never forget.

After her mama's suicide, ten-year-old Ellen is left with a passel of the worst relatives imaginable: drunk, mean, crazy, lazy, spiteful, or all those things rolled up together, as in Ellen's hateful daddy. Reckoning that "maybe with God's help but more than likely without it," Ellen searches for a new home for herself. Her experiences are absolutely heart-wrenching, yet her voice is point-blank funny and never begs for sympathy. Bouncing from one place to another, she casts a cool, knowing eye on the people around her. Her blind spot, though, is race. Starletta is Ellen's only friend, yet Ellen won't eat or drink at her house—it's still dirty "colored" food. Finding a foster home with a new mama is finally Ellen's own doing, but figuring out what her friendship with Starletta means is an even more impressive accomplishment. *Ellen Foster* may owe much to the rich wellspring of great Southern novels, but it is a magnificent contemporary tour de force of its own.

BEVERLY SILLS

⌒

Chairman, Lincoln Center

 apa didn't believe in children's books, which is why I didn't read *Winnie the Pooh* until I was an adult. My father thought that if I could read, I should read real books. And I did. I read *Gone with the Wind* when I was ten years old. I'm sure I didn't know why, but I got very excited when Rhett Butler put his hand on Scarlett O'Hara's bosom. (I didn't have one yet.) I remember thinking: *Oh, my, this is the kind of book Sidney and Stanley—my brothers—hide under their beds.*

The Endless Steppe: Growing Up in Siberia
Written by Esther Hautzig
Copyright 1968
Cloth: HarperCollins
Paper: HarperTrophy
Jane Addams Children's Book Award
ALA Notable Children's Book

⌒ How to pay tribute to this magnificent book? It chronicles such a grim, violent time in the world and yet has that rare capacity to uplift and inspire. Ten-year-old Esther Rudomin's world collapses in 1941 when soldiers tear Esther and her family away from their home in Poland and deport them in cattle cars to Russia. Their only crime is that they are Jewish.

Esther spends five years in Siberia, literally living hand to mouth, eking out the most minimal existence. Food, warmth, clothing, and shelter are barely available. Esther draws inspiration from her valiant mother, taking on more and more responsibilities. Besides keeping house, studying, and scavenging for coal, she sets up a knitting business to earn more rubles. By the time the Rudomins are freed, Esther's childhood is gone. Esther's phenomenal fortitude and resilient spirit shines through the pages.

Extraordinary Women Scientists
Written by Darlene R. Stille
Copyright 1995
Cloth: Children's Press
Paper: Children's Press

⌒ Aside from Marie Curie, many people are hard pressed to name a significant woman scientist, but here are fifty who should be acknowledged widely. These brief biographies (two to six pages) are well-written sketches of fascinating women ranging from Dian Fossey to Maria Mitchell to Florence Sabin and Gertrude Elion. Their contributions are documented vividly, as are the obstacles they overcame. A handsome, attractively designed book, this would be a welcome addition to any girl's library.

Note: Stille's newest book is *Extraordinary Women of Medicine*. With the same handsome layout as *Extraordinary Women Scientists*, this book delves into the lives of fifty-five fascinating women. Girls can read about Mary Edwards Walker, the first woman U.S. Army Surgeon; Susan LaFlesche Picotte, the first Native American doctor; Margaret Sanger, the founder of the American birth control movement; and Bernadine Healy, the first woman Director of the National Institute of Health. For reference or for reading pleasure, Stille's books are first-class.

Farewell to Manzanar
Written by Jeanne Wakatsuki Houston and James D. Houston
Copyright 1973
Paper: Bantam

JANE BRODY

～

Health Columnist, Science Writer,
the New York Times

robably the most influential book of my youth was *The Story of Blood*, an account of the myriad roles played by the cells and fluids that course through our bodies and make life as we know it possible. This, in turn, inspired me to read a biography of Louis Pasteur and *Microbe Hunters*, and you can see from my career where this led me. Medical science and biology are far more complex today than in Louis Pasteur's day but are no less fascinating and still hold the promise of better health for everyone.

～ On December 7, 1941, the Japanese bombed Pearl Harbor. Two weeks later Jeanne Wakatsuki's father was taken away, suspected of spying for the Japanese military, and sent from California to a camp in North Dakota. In February her family was moved from their home near their fishing boats, and by April they had been relocated to Manzanar, an internment camp in the desert, along with 10,000 other Japanese-Americans. They stayed there until the war ended.

Jeanne is only seven when she enters Manzanar. What she witnesses is the gradual disintegration of her family, and what she absorbs unconsciously is the message that to be Japanese is to be inferior. Some of the most compelling passages deal with her conflicting cultural influences. Writing in an objective, lucid voice, with surprisingly little rancor, the author articulates the painful isolation and injustice of this cruel chapter in our history.

Fifth Chinese Daughter
Written by Jade Snow Wong/Illustrated by Kathryn Uhl
Copyright 1945, 1948, 1950
Paper: University of Washington Press

⁓ As the fifth daughter of a hardworking Cantonese family, Jade Snow Wong knows exactly where she fits in. Being female, her second-class status in the family constellation is clear and her destiny—to become a wife and a mother—is prescribed. But this unusual girl yearns to stand out and her excellent autobiography recounts a struggle for individual recognition.

Her life set against the panorama of San Francisco's Chinatown in the 1930s, the young Jade Snow absorbs the Confucian values of respect, propriety, diligence, and order. Her father makes sure that she receives a classical Chinese education by requiring her to attend Chinese school every evening after a day of American school. In fact he thinks of himself as forward thinking: "If nobody educates his daughters, how can we have intelligent mothers for our sons?" But he cannot imagine paying for college for Jade Snow as he did for her brother—if her intellectual ambitions aren't satisfied, she'll have to figure out a way to get to college on her own. Jade Snow had been working in the family's factory helping to make overalls since she was thirteen and cooking and doing housework for Caucasian families since she was fifteen. She is just able to afford junior college; then a lucky introduction to the president of Mills College results in a scholarship. Having told her astonished parents that "I am an individual besides being your fifth daughter," Jade Snow even more earnestly pursues her own interests. Her wartime research for the Navy culminates in her being asked to launch a ship, bringing great honor to everyone in Chinatown. Finding herself fascinated with ceramics, Jade Snow sets up a small pottery business in a Chinatown shop window. It is an unqualified success and brings her the sweetest accolade of all: the respect and admiration of her parents.

MAXINE HONG KINGSTON

~

Author, China Men *and* The Woman Warrior
1997 National Medal for the Humanities

 ifth Chinese Daughter by Jade Snow Wong saved my life. I learned that someone like me could be a writer. And that my life and the lives of people I know are worthy of art.

Fire on the Wind
Written by Linda Crew
Copyright 1995
Cloth: Delacorte
Paper: Laurel Leaf/Bantam Doubleday Dell

~ Based on Crew's research of the 1933 Tillamook Burn that destroyed the forests of western Oregon, this novel is a tremendously gripping read.

Fourteen-year-old Storie has grown up in the Blue Star logging camp. Confined to women's work—sewing and constant cooking for the logging crew—Storie wonders how she will spend the rest of her life. Lately, she's been questioning whether her father, whom she adores, is really right about everything. Can it be true that clear-cutting the land is good for it? Where do the animals go for food and shelter once the trees are gone? Why doesn't he want her to continue her education? Storie's anger at her father grows as she realizes his answers are no longer sacrosanct. At the same time, in the dry August heat, everyone shares a constant fear of fire sparking from one ridgeline to the next. Storie heroically puts her personal concerns aside when the flames threaten to turn Blue Star into an inferno; in the breathtaking climax, it is she who saves her father and the rest of the loggers.

Crew's forceful description of the Tillamook conflagration terrifies. And although this is fiction, her account of the ceaseless hard work in a logging camp rings true.

The Friends
Written by Rosa Guy
Copyright 1973
Paper: Bantam

⌐ Phyllisia Cathy's pretentious, domineering father calls the shots. When he sends for Phyllisia and her sister, Ruby, to join the family in Harlem, leaving their West Indian home, the girls have no choice. Phyllisia seethes with resentment. Everything about Harlem is hateful, especially school, where she is first taunted and then beaten by her classmates. They mock her West Indian accent; they dislike her academic prowess. Desperate for an ally, Phyllisia reluctantly accepts the only offer of friendship she's got, that of Edith Jackson. Edith is unkempt and poor, she steals, she pays little attention to school—but she is unstintingly kind and unfailingly loyal.

Phyllisia is surprised to find how quickly and deeply their friendship grows. However, her father condemns Edith on sight; he did not bring Phyllisia to America to associate with people who look "like that." With her thinking clouded, affected more than she knows by her father's prejudice, Phyllisia betrays her friendship, distancing herself again and again from Edith. Her painful journey to self-knowledge leads her to stand up to her father. As her mother told her, "Guilt carries its own sickness, but it also carries its own cure." Powerful stuff.

Galax-Arena
Written by Gillian Rubinstein
Copyright 1992
Cloth: Simon & Schuster
Paper: Aladdin

~ Part futuristic thriller and part *Lord of the Flies*, this novel exerts a creepy fascination that holds the reader in thrall.

Joella and her siblings, Peter and Liane, are kidnapped from an Australian train station. They are shoved aboard a spaceship and awake in a strange solar system on the planet Vexak. They are to become daredevil acrobats in the Galax-Arena for the amusement of the alien Vexa, much the way conquered people battled in the Coliseum for the Romans' entertainment. About twenty children are so enslaved, and the Vexa clearly enjoy the spectacle of pitting the children viciously against each other. Joella's brother and sister prove to be gifted gymnasts and quickly slip into the animalistic behavior that the Vexa are promoting. "Survival of the fittest" is the only rule that applies, and Joella, who can barely do a somersault, realizes that her time in the Galax-Arena will be short.

Joella says that her one gift is for telling the truth. She won't play into the children's deathly competition, and she soon begins to suspect they are all being used for something even worse than sport. As she uncovers the hideous reason for their captivity, Joella tries to use her knowledge to free her fellow captives. Joella's sanity is silhouetted against the madness of the Galax-Arena, and her lone voice crying in the wilderness is a brave one. It's a nasty tale, but with a startlingly effective heroine.

A Girl from Yamhill: A Memoir
Written by Beverly Cleary
Copyright 1988
Cloth: William Morrow
Paper: Avon/Camelot

～ "What would I have done without the library?" asks the young bookworm and budding author growing up in Oregon in the 1920s. We might ask "What would we do without Beverly Cleary?" Readers who know her books by heart will be delighted to pick up bits from her life that she wove into her famous stories, but this absolutely first-rate autobiography stands on its own merit.

By second grade she has already published a book review in the *Oregon Journal*. A discerning teacher reads one of her stories and remarks that "Beverly should write children's stories when she grows up." Later she enters an essay contest and wins two dollars. No one else had bothered to enter. "This incident was one of the most valuable lessons in writing I ever learned. Try! Others will talk about writing but may never get around to trying."

As you might expect, there are hilarious moments from her childhood that make you think of the enthusiastic Ramona, but there are painful memories, too, from the casual cruelty of teachers to the escalating tensions between Beverly and her impossible-to-please mother. This book is the all-time favorite of at least one of our daughters. Who could argue with her? It's funny and real, honest and unpretentious. Don't pass up this one or its sequel, *My Own Two Feet*.

The Golden Compass
Written by Philip Pullman
Copyright 1995
Cloth: Alfred A. Knopf
Paper: Del Rey
ALA Notable Book

～ This novel (the first of a fantasy trilogy called *His Dark Materials*; the second title is *The Subtle Knife*) was recommended unanimously by our librarians. "Of course, you'll include *The Golden Compass*," they all said, and, of course we concurred. Pullman's story, set in a world only somewhat resembling our own and studded with phantasmagorical images, is rewarding not only for its dense, complicated plotting but also for its fearless and cunning heroine, Lyra.

Always accompanied by her daemon (her creature-spirit), Lyra is "a coarse and greedy little savage." She has spent her childhood

BEVERLY CLEARY

～

Children's Book Author,
Ramona *and* A Girl from Yamhill
1984 Newbery Medalist

hen I was growing up, the library was full of such riches that my favorite book changed every few months. Two books, however, now long out of print, are still in print in my memory. The first is *Dandelion Cottage* by Carroll Watson Rankin, the story of four girls who were given the use of a parsonage for a playhouse for digging dandelions in the yard. When I was older, my favorite was *Downright Dencey* by Caroline Dale Snedeker, the story of a rebellious Quaker girl in Nantucket in whaling days. I read both books over and over. In between, I read anything that wasn't *The Story of Wheat* or *Elsie Dinsmore*.

largely unschooled, running wild with other street urchins as their unacknowledged leader. When children begin vanishing mysteriously, Lyra launches herself into the hunt to find them, allying herself with "gyptians," witches, and an armored bear. Her quest takes her deeper and deeper into the cold, distant lands of the North where the children have been imprisoned. The horrors awaiting her there are beyond anything Lyra had ever imagined. Lyra's bold deeds not only secure the fate of her world but, at the book's close, show her a bridge into a new world that shimmers within the northern lights. Can you doubt that Lyra and her daemon cross that bridge into further adventure? A thoroughly grand epic.

Having Our Say: The Delany Sisters' First 100 Years

Written by Sarah L. Delany and A. Elizabeth Delany with
   Amy Hill Hearth
Copyright 1993
Cloth: Kodansha America
Paper: Dell

～ Sadie Delany was 103 and Bessie Delany was 101 when they began writing this exhilarating and insightful book. These two sisters each bring a quick tongue, a ready wit, and a sharp mind to their reminiscences. Though their father was born a slave, they— and every other one of his ten children—were college-educated professionals. The Jim Crow laws of white America had stacked the deck against them, but this remarkable family overcame all the odds. Sadie graduated from Columbia Teachers College and "became the first colored teacher in the New York City system to teach domestic science on the high school level." Bessie received her D.D.S. degree from Columbia in 1923, "only the second Negro woman licensed to practice in New York."

Having Our Say succeeds brilliantly on two levels. First, it is an invaluable historical document, recording the feisty sisters' recollections, from growing up in the rural South at the turn of the century to the heyday of the golden Harlem Renaissance. Second, it is a splendid portrait of two very very smart and classy ladies. They've got lots of opinions, and they don't mince any words. To be in the company of Sadie and Bessie Delany for the few hours it takes to read this book is a *privilege*.

The Hero and the Crown
Written by Robin McKinley
Copyright 1984
Cloth: Greenwillow
Paper: Ace Books
Newbery Medal

～ The complexities of leadership and the ache and grit of heroism are detailed beautifully in this stirring novel, as is the portrait of a lonely girl who's spent her childhood hiding in the wings.

Everyone in the kingdom of Damar whispers and gossips about Princess Aerin. Because of her murky parentage, they mistrust everything about Aerin and are universally relieved that her cousin Tor, and not she, will inherit Damar's throne. Aerin grows up fighting this shadow of suspicion. Except for Tor, she keeps her own company and secretly begins to develop her amazing gifts. When the countryside is plagued with dragons, Aerin is the one who slips out silently to fight them. Why? "To be doing something better than anyone else was doing it." As she starts to assert herself, the challenges that confront her mount in terrifying intensity. Maur, the evil Black Dragon, nearly claims her life, but an even deadlier opponent, the mage Agsded, awaits her. Aerin persists in battling him so that she may recover Damar's stolen national treasure, the Hero's Crown.

Aerin's self-discovery is a triumphant journey. This book is the prequel to McKinley's equally elegant novel *The Blue Sword*.

Hero of Lesser Causes
Written by Julie Johnston
Copyright 1992
Cloth: Little Brown & Co.
Paper: Puffin
ALA Notable Book

⌐ Keely is as garrulous, comic, and impulsive as one might hope a girl poised on the brink of adolescence would be. One minute she's roller-skating; the next she's wondering if her best friend is more interested in boys than in her. At the center of Keely's twelve-year-old life is her teenage brother, Patrick. They spend all their time together during the long, hot summer of 1946, daring and double-daring each other to perform sillier and more outrageous acts. When Patrick is tragically stricken with polio and loses his desire to live, Keely isn't sure how to channel her grief in ways that will help him. She thinks up one distraction after the next, determined to pull him out of his misery. Her well-meaning efforts often embarrass her: she falls off a horse headfirst into a murky lake; she gets sprayed by a skunk; her rash decision to invite friends to cheer up Patrick backfires. She'll try anything before giving in to Patrick's paralyzing depression.

Always distinct and brimming with truth, Keely's words distill the essence of her rare relationship with her brother and give voice to the very real concerns of a girl whose haphazard ways finally succeed.

Herstory: Women Who Changed the World
Edited by Ruth Ashby and Deborah Gore Ohrn;
     Introduction by Gloria Steinem
Copyright 1995
Cloth: Viking

⌐ This illuminating volume offers 120 deftly written biographical sketches of women whose accomplishments were so significant

Irene R. Miller

Member, Board of Directors, Barnes & Noble, Inc.

eflecting on the most memorable books of my girlhood, the books that influenced me most as I was growing up, three come instantly to mind: *The Lion, the Witch and the Wardrobe* by C. S. Lewis, *The Secret Garden* by Frances H. Burnett, and *The Hobbit* by J. R. R. Tolkien.

 The Hobbit stays in my mind (as does Tolkien's *The Lord of the Rings*, which I fell upon later with gusto) because the hero was unusual—modest and unassuming and even a bit clumsy. Bilbo Baggins is reluctantly recruited to become part of a mission to slay a dragon who has brought misery and oppression to the land. At the beginning of the story Bilbo clearly doesn't know his own measure. As the tale unfolds, he shows cunning and courage and gains confidence as his adventures test him. Yet he remains realistic about his limitations. Ultimately the success of the venture rests with him (with a bit of help from the wizard Gandalf), and Bilbo discovers his own strength of character and the special talents only Gandalf knew he possessed. Bilbo Baggins is easy to identify with. Haven't we all secretly wondered whether we might be capable of more than we or others thought possible and thought that, deep down, we might find it within ourselves to slay dragons?

that "they managed to survive centuries of exclusion from history books."

Divided into three broad categories of time (The Dawn: Prehistory to 1750; From Revolution to Revolution: 1750 to 1850; and The Global Community: 1890 to the Present), each woman's story begins with a quotation and features a likeness. The estimable biographies are short, only two or three pages, but highlight the most salient features of that woman's life and, by placing her in the context of her time, make crystal clear her achievements. The famous and the not-so-famous, from all parts of the world, are included. We discovered and rediscovered such fascinating personalities as Cleopatra of Egypt, Artemisia Gentileschi of Italy, La Pola of Colombia, Queen Victoria of England, Margaret Sanger of America, Corazon Aquino of the Philippines, and Aung San Suu Kyi of Burma.

An intelligent and useful compendium, this is a first-class reference book as well as a pleasurable reading experience.

Homecoming
Written by Cynthia Voigt
Copyright 1981
Cloth: Atheneum
Paper: Ballantine

～ Dicey Tillerman, age thirteen, is leading her younger brothers and sister on an uncertain odyssey. They last saw their sad, fragile momma in a mall parking lot. She walked away from them and never came back. Their father disappeared years ago. The little ones have only Dicey to turn to, so she unblinkingly steps in, with no food, money, transportation, or shelter, to find a place they can call home. The four children set out on foot to find a relative who will offer them a safe harbor. Although "the whole world was arranged against kids," Dicey courageously chances their journey, navigating the children through the hazards along the way.

Every piece of this perfect novel shines: the intensity of the plot never wavers, the characters linger long after you've closed the book, and the rich, assured language envelops you completely in Dicey's world. Were Dicey the type to beg for your sympathy, each page could be blotted with tears, but Dicey, as she describes herself, is "bossy. And I lie and I fight." She needs to be tough to steer her family home. There is a whole cycle of novels about the Tillerman family. You'll especially want to read *Dicey's Song*, but honestly, anything Cynthia Voigt writes is gold.

I Know Why the Caged Bird Sings
Written by Maya Angelou
Copyright 1969
Cloth: Random House
Paper: Bantam

~ Some books are not just read; they're absorbed. They soak into your memory and never leave you. Maya Angelou's classic coming-of-age autobiography is one of those rare, fine experiences. Stamps, Arkansas, in the 1930s might seem at first glance an unlikely place and time to spawn such an amazing writer. But Angelou chronicles the tightly knit African-American community and her own family as a haven of religion, discipline, education, and affection. Her grandmother, a majestic character of biblical proportions, shaped her growing-up years with forceful dignity. Her straight-talking, beautiful, bright, and vivid mother brought a different power to Angelou's teenage years in San Francisco.

Angelou delineates the omnipresent poison of racism and its insidious effects on her family and community. There are several sexually explicit sections, the most difficult describing how she was raped as an eight-year-old child. However, you'll find this on many school reading lists. It has become an essential part of our literary canon.

In Lane Three, Alex Archer
Written by Tessa Duder
Copyright 1987
Paper: Bantam Books

⁓ Alex is a natural athlete. Tall, broad-shouldered, long-legged, she seems made to swim. She's loved it since her first lesson, feeling that she must have been a dolphin in another life. No one has to push Alex to compete. Alex pushes herself. Although often hurled up against impossibly traditional feminine ideals, she clings to her own dauntingly independent goals. Alex is hoping to represent New Zealand in the 1960 Rome Olympics, but one serious rival stands in her way. The decision will finally hinge on one crucial meet.

The novel swings between two narratives: Alex talking to herself in the present tense as she swims that last qualifying race and Alex's recounting of the events that have led her up to the starting

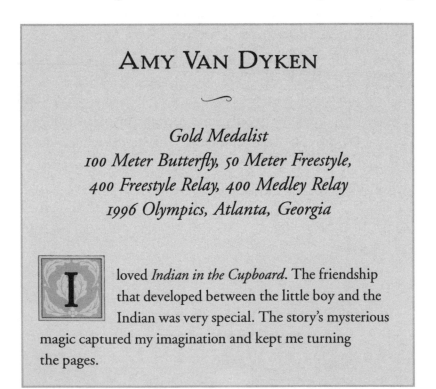

AMY VAN DYKEN

⁓

Gold Medalist
100 Meter Butterfly, 50 Meter Freestyle,
400 Freestyle Relay, 400 Medley Relay
1996 Olympics, Atlanta, Georgia

I loved *Indian in the Cupboard*. The friendship that developed between the little boy and the Indian was very special. The story's mysterious magic captured my imagination and kept me turning the pages.

block. It's an interesting structure for this book, and it works very well. Tension in the race narrative mounts steadily as more and more about Alex's watershed year—tumultuous and sometimes tragic—unfolds. Thoughtful, wonderful, not-to-be-missed. (Nor should you skip the sequel, *Alex in Rome*.)

In My Own Words: Growing Up Inside the Sanctuary of My Imagination

Written by Nicholasa Mohr
Copyright 1994
Cloth: Julian Messner

⌒ "Libraries are sometimes called colleges for the poor. Indeed, this was true in my case. . . . My access to the New York Public Library was what allowed me to pursue my thirst for knowledge. It was there that I sought out an education for myself. . . . The library became my home away from home."

The author of *Felita* (see Index) has penned her own memoir of growing up as a Puerto Rican girl in New York's Spanish Harlem in the 1940s. The youngest of seven children and the only girl, Nicholasa's boundless energy nearly exasperated her busy mother until she set the little girl to copying the comic strips. Sitting at the kitchen table, Nicholasa painstakingly drew Dick Tracy. Her mother's approval was instantaneous, and "I began my career as an artist." Drawing and reading were her sanctuaries, the necessary outlets for an imaginative intelligence to which the public school system was wearily indifferent. Nicholasa desperately wanted to attend the prestigious High School for Music and Art, but the callous guidance counselor dismissed that as being no place for a poor girl—she should learn a trade instead, become a seamstress. Because her mother was terminally ill, Nicholasa kept this distressing conversation from her, but her anxious mother's perceptive deathbed plea to Nicholasa was "Never forget what you want, never." Uncommonly fine reading.

In These Girls, Hope Is a Muscle
Written by Madeleine Blais
Copyright 1993
Cloth: Atlantic Monthly Press
Paper: Warner Books

⟶ "Girls' basketball is not boys' basketball being played by girls. It's a whole new game." And how.

In March 1992 Pulitzer Prize–winning reporter Madeleine Blais began tracing the volatile fortunes of a high school basketball team—the Amherst Lady Hurricanes—from their downfall in the state playoffs through the twelve months that followed. You will find it hard to decide what you admire most about this book: the pluck of these adolescent girls, their jivey charm, or their extraordinary athletic skills. And that is what makes Blais's saga so successful: the complete picture it draws of the hopes, fears, thrills, and chills of a wonderfully real group of girls in pursuit of a common dream.

We come to know each of the girls through their banter, their journals, their families, their individual style of play on the court. They grow ever more unified as a team in their quest for vengeance, respect, and victory. Blais excels with her large-hearted book that works as sociology, as journalism, as almost epic narrative. She pulls the reader along as if it were fiction. There isn't a dull page in it.

Izzy, Willy-Nilly
Written by Cynthia Voigt
Copyright 1986
Cloth: Atheneum
Paper: Aladdin

⟶ Izzy's typical teenage life ends when she leaves a party with her stupid drunk date and he drives their car into a tree. He doesn't get a scratch, but Izzy's leg must be amputated. In the hospital for weeks, she slowly starts to realize that nobody will ever look at her in the same way again. Her three best friends desert her, her family can't talk to her openly, and teachers aren't sure what to do with her. She's been brought up to be nice—but being nice may not work now. Out of the blue, she's visited by Rosamunde, an idiosyncratic and intelligent girl her crowd had always looked down on. Rosamunde prods Izzy into facing heartbreaking truths. And little by little, Izzy is able to assuage her grief with strength she never knew she had.

Voigt's sensitive novel displays, once again, her prodigious talent. A great writer, she makes you care deeply about her characters.

Jackaroo
Written by Cynthia Voigt
Copyright 1985
Cloth: Atheneum
Paper: Point/Scholastic

⁓ A long, long time ago, in a mythical land, lived the innkeeper's daughter, Gwyn. She knows she is different from her family. Gwyn is strong and independent and willing to take enormous risks. She knows —as does every cottager and noble—the legend of Jackaroo, the mysterious masked figure who has, from time to time, miraculously appeared to intervene on behalf of the downtrodden poor.

When Gwyn accidentally happens upon a hidden cupboard containing a set of Jackaroo's mask and clothing, she succumbs to the temptation to *become* Jackaroo. Behind Jackaroo's mask, she steps forward to right the wrongs that have been troubling her. In her disguise, Gwyn begins to see her family, her society, even herself, in new and increasingly complex ways.

Gwyn comes to realize that it is not a simple matter to don an outlaw's costume: there are many unexpected ramifications. Voigt has written a subtle, sophisticated tale of a brave and intelligent girl.

Jane Eyre
Written by Charlotte Brontë
Published 1847; numerous editions available

⌐ *Jane Eyre* was the first adult classic we read. It was one of our most memorable reading experiences. Jane still stands in our minds as proud, independent, and forthright. In Jane, Brontë created an unusual feminist heroine. As an orphan being unwillingly raised by cold, cruel relatives, she's sent away to Lowood Institution, where trials and deprivations test her. Leaving Lowood to earn her way in the world, Jane becomes a governess at eerie Thornfield Hall, where she encounters the enigmatic Mr. Rochester. Despite her forebodings, she falls in love with Thornfield's gloomy master. The dark secret that awaits Jane at the center of this book has never lost its dramatic power. Amid the passionate romance and the thrilling mystery, Jane is guided unfailingly by her stern inner moral compass. Readers, you would be remiss not to give this book to your daughters.

Little by Little: A Writer's Education
Written by Jean Little
Copyright 1987
Cloth: Viking
Paper: Puffin
Boston Globe–Horn Book Honor Book

⌐ This is an honest, affecting autobiography of a bittersweet childhood.

Almost blind from birth, author Jean Little suffered through years and years of torment from classmates. It wasn't just because she had to hold a book right up to her face to see it, but because her eyes were badly crossed as well. Luckily, though, she had two of the world's greatest parents, patient, understanding people who nonetheless refused to coddle her. Jean was sent to school with

JUDY MCGRATH

⟅

President, MTV

dove into *Jane Eyre* and found a fascinating world. Here was a plain young woman, with great integrity, determined to find her way in a culture that valued wealth and lineage above all else. She had perseverence—a most essential quality, in my mother's opinion—honesty, singularity—I was an only child—and she created a good life on her own terms. I was struck by the contrast between the harshness of her life in England and my comfortable home in America, and felt great sympathy.

"normal" children and was not excused from any work because of her disability. Her imagination and her love of books were her salvation. "From the first sentence, *The Secret Garden* seemed especially mine. I did not wonder what Mary Lennox looked like. I knew. She looked exactly like me. . . . She, too, was selfish and bad-tempered and lazy. She even tried to get Martha to put her shoes on for her. I wasn't the only one who had done such a reprehensible thing. Yet little by little, she grew into somebody quite different. And the way it happened made perfect sense. I knew that I, too, would be different if I could find a hidden garden and friends like Dickon and Colin and the robin."

Ultimately she finds those friends, publishes a poem in a national magazine at age seventeen, and wins the dance prize at the prom. While teaching handicapped children, it occurs to Little that no one has written a story that has "a happy ending without a miracle cure." With the 1962 publication of her first book, *Mine for Keeps*, that person would be her.

Living the Dream
Written by Dot Richardson with Don Yaeger
Foreword by Bob Costas
Copyright 1997
Cloth: Kensington Publishing
Paper: Kensington Publishing
⌒ The 1996 Olympic Gold Medal Winner for women's softball has written an engaging, forthright, and patriotic autobiography.

When Richardson was ten, she was spotted by a coach as she pitched to her brothers. He wanted her to join his Little League team, on the condition that she cut her hair and call herself "Bob." Richardson replied, "If I have to hide who I am, I don't feel it's right." Luckily she was discovered (on the very same day!) by the Amateur Softball Association Women's Fast-Pitch Class A team. This cemented her love for the game and through high school and college she garnered award after award for her incredible prowess. When it was announced that softball was going to be a sport at the Olympics for the very first time, Richardson was in medical school but leapt at the chance to take a year off and represent her country.

Dr. Dot's enthusiastic memoir covers all the highlights and sacrifices she's made in her amazing dual careers. Her simple words "The truth is, I just wanted to compete" sum up a life which serves as an exhilarating role model for all.

Lyddie
Written by Katherine Paterson
Copyright 1991
Cloth: Lodestar Books

Paper: Puffin
ALA Best Book for Young Adults

～ The Lowell mill girls present a fascinating chapter in the story of America's industrialization. In this novel, Katherine Paterson, a Newbery Award–winning author, has created a powerful feminist character set in a troubling yet historically important period.

Lyddie Worthen's driving ambition is to buy back the Vermont family farm she and her family were forced to leave after their father abandoned them. She finds her way to Lowell, Massachusetts, to employment in the textile mills, grim, dangerous factories where young women worked grueling thirteen-hour days. Although she is unschooled, Lyddie's innate common sense tells her how to survive in this rough, menacing environment. A new world of understanding is opened to her when she discovers a sympathetic, educated coworker who helps her learn to read and begins to kindle her sense of justice. Lyddie at first rejects involving herself with the stirrings of a labor movement for safer working conditions— she is afraid of losing her salary. But when she is dismissed summarily for "moral turpitude" after sexual harassment by the overseer, Lyddie takes another hard look at her life. Putting off an offer of marriage from a fine young man, Lyddie decides to head west to progressive Oberlin College, where she's heard they will educate women.

Exceptionally fine reading.

Mama's Girl

Written by Veronica Chambers
Copyright 1996
Cloth: Putnam
Paper: Riverhead Books

～ This is one of the rougher real-life books we recommend. We have read that this book is a favorite of mother-daughter book clubs. If you can handle it, this would be a remarkable choice.

Chambers's mother is from Panama and her father from the Dominican Republic. She grows up on the edge of poverty in Brooklyn and suffers bitterly through the demise of her parents' marriage. Her father is violently abusive. Her brother ends up in jail for dealing drugs. During her teenage years Chambers tries living with first her mother and then her father—her mother is dismissive of Chambers's academic ambitions; her father's household is a hellish minefield of tension. Chambers hangs tough, though, and at sixteen gets herself admitted to Simon's Rock College. She's named one of *Glamour* magazine's top ten college women of 1990. Currently she contributes articles to many important publications.

This intense book unsparingly describes the narrow world of poor African-American women who have yet to experience the rewards of the civil rights movement. (When Chambers makes enough money to give her mother a gift certificate to Elizabeth Arden, her mother asks her if they allow African-Americans in there.) It is also explosively honest about the anguished, often tangled, emotions between mothers and daughters. Chambers spent her whole childhood reeling from her feelings of abandonment and betrayal. When she and her mother begin to resolve them, Chambers writes, "All my life, I'd hoped to meet someone upon whom I could unload everything. It never occurred to me that my mother was the person I wished for. . . . I'd assumed she'd known everything I'd felt and just didn't care. But I was wrong and I was thrilled to be wrong."

Margaret Bourke-White:
Photographing the World
Written by Eleanor H. Ayer
Copyright 1992
Cloth: Dillon Press
～ This biography does a terrific job of pulling readers into famed photographer Margaret Bourke-White's fast-paced, fearless life.

When Henry Luce launched *Life* magazine, a photo by Bourke-White was on the cover. She'd already made journalism history with her industrial photographs for *Fortune* magazine, her pictures revealing for the first time the inner workings and the beauty of some of America's biggest factories.

She was born in 1904 and her individualistic parents taught her to value absolute truth, total perfection, and hard work. Bourke-White first picked up a camera at age fifteen and then went on to photograph some of the most memorable scenes of our century. She clung to her camera in gale force winds to photograph a dust storm during the Great Depression; she was the first female military photographer of World War II and took the eyewitness photos of Patton's liberation of Buchenwald; her image of Gandhi at his spinning wheel is the most famous picture of India's spiritual leader ever taken. The action never lets up in this amazing woman's story.

The Mozart Season
Written by Virginia Euwer Wolff
Copyright 1991
Cloth: Henry Holt
Paper: Scholastic

⟋ Twelve-year-old Allegra Shapiro is the youngest finalist in a statewide music competition. She spends the summer trying to find her own interpretation of Mozart's Violin Concerto in D. While she practices and practices, she discovers her past—her Jewish past—and the unresolved troubles and grief of people around her. These discoveries bewilder and upset Allegra, leaving her wondering whether anyone's efforts to make a better life ever change anything. What really matters?

Allegra's intelligence and persistence, with the support and wisdom of a loving family, lead her not only to decide that *"everything matters"* but to a version of the concerto that is uniquely her own. A triumphant conclusion to a beautiful novel.

My Brilliant Career
Written by Miles Franklin
First published 1902
Paper: HarperCollins

⌒ This Australian turn-of-the-century novel reads like an unguarded memoir by a heroine who is always at full throttle.

In a torrent of words, fifteen-year-old Sybylla Melvyn decries the miserable outback life she's subjected to. Denied any crumb of art, music, or literature on which to sustain herself, this blisteringly

PAULA ROBISON

⌒

Flutist

 read *Dancing Star* as an eleven-year-old idealist, sure I was meant to *do* something, but without a clue as to what it was. I loved music, but the piano was my instrument then and I just couldn't make it sing.

Dancing Star presented Pavlova and her era to me in such vivid detail that I felt I was watching her at the barre, listening to her conversations with Sergei Diaghilev, Michel Fokine, and Isadora Duncan, feeling her pain as she worked, and experiencing her joy in performance.

. . . That was it! I wanted to bring joy to people too! But how? Then one day someone gave me a flute. I had found my path, and the light Anna Pavlova's story kindled in my heart guides me still.

forthright young woman sees nothing on the horizon but the weariness of her existence. This, she sardonically remarks, is "my life—my career—my brilliant career!" Her grandmother offers her rescue: Sybylla can live with Grannie and Aunt Helen in their comfortable, cultured home. She leaves Possum Gully in a flash, intent on pursuing a *true* brilliant career and determined to channel her pent-up energies into writing. Temptation steps in her path in the person of Harold Beecham: rich, handsome, intelligent, kind, and head-over-heels in love with Sybylla. When Sybylla must return to the parched, pinched outback life, Harold looks even more like a white knight. But Sybylla knows her own wild heart best. "He offered me everything—but control." Stirring feminism from prefeminist days.

JILL KER CONWAY

⁓

Author, The Road from Coorain
First Woman President, Smith College

y favorite books as a child were all Australian. I loved *My Brilliant Career* because its heroine was so feisty and so full of the dream to become a writer. It was also full of the sounds and smells of the Australian bush so it seemed to fit my experience as a child in outback Australia.

National Velvet
Written by Enid Bagnold
Copyright 1930, 1949
Cloth: William Morrow

Paper: Flare

⁓ "I'm a girl with a Chance," Velvet Brown pleadingly tells her mother. The chance is the surreptitiously obtained opportunity to ride her piebald horse in England's prestigious (and male-only) race, the Grand National. Mrs. Brown has already been a renowned champion, swimming the English Channel; now it could be Velvet's turn to shine. Velvet has inherited all the great qualities—vision, perseverance, stamina, faith—that marked her mother as a winner. Araminty Brown unstintingly backs her daughter all the way: "If Mrs. Brown had been asked what her hope and expectancy in life was for Velvet she . . . would have answered 'guts.'"

This book is usually eclipsed by the more famous movie, but both are worth spending time with. Although Velvet is fourteen at the time this story takes place in 1930, she is still deep in the throes of childhood, playing with her paper horses, in a way that seems improbable, if not impossible, these days. Her dream of glory is a child's dream. Yet the novel's rich language and its complicated, quirky characterizations require an older reader. Perhaps that means that it is hard to find the right audience for this book today, but you'll rarely meet two more memorable heroines than the indomitable Mrs. Brown and her ardent daughter, "National Velvet."

Nothing to Do but Stay: My Pioneer Mother
Written by Carrie Young
Copyright 1991
Cloth: University of Iowa Press
Paper: Dell

⁓ You will part from Carrie Young's gallant mother with respect bordering on awe. In 1904, when she was twenty-five, Carrine Gafkjen staked out a 160-acre homestead on the North Dakota prairie by herself. Her tiny cabin had room for a potbellied stove, a shakedown bed, a table, and a chair. Her only food was potatoes.

She shrewdly kept working and reinvesting until she became a woman of independent means. Then, at thirty-four, she married and raised six children, all of whom appear to have inherited her remarkably tenacious temperament.

A tribute to our vanished past, this vigorously affirmative memoir records the stoic struggles of Gafkjen's prairie life as well as her simple joys. The author recalls the high standards her mother set: neither a sickly husband nor backbreaking farm work kept her from sending her children to school during blizzards, dressing them in perfectly laundered clothes, or creating feasts laden with Norwegian delicacies for the traveling minister. For lovers of the American pioneer story, this wonderfully written, nostalgic book makes a bountiful gift.

Plain City

Written by Virginia Hamilton
Copyright 1993
Cloth: Scholastic
Paper: Scholastic

⌒ Buhlaire Sims is a mixed-race twelve-year-old living way on the wrong side of the tracks. Her classmates taunt her for both reasons. Her mother, Bluezy, a singer and fan-dancer, is gone much of the time, in and out of Buhlaire's life. She believes that her father died in Vietnam until the school principal gently explains that this could not be so: the war ended years before she was born. Furthermore, he tells her, Buhlaire's father is alive and back in Plain City.

This astonishing news turns Buhlaire's already shaky world upside down. She's bitterly resentful of how Bluezy has kept Buhlaire's history from her, and she's suspicious of Bluezy's motive—could it be because of the "vanilla" blood she's tainted with? Wandering about the snowy city, Buhlaire becomes lost in a white-out and is unexpectedly rescued by her father. However, there is no fairy-tale ending. Buhlaire must confront her dad's mental illness and recognize the supportive family around her. Hamilton's strong, sweeping prose takes us from Buhlaire's anger to her awakening and acceptance.

Postcards from France
Written by Megan McNeill Libby
Copyright 1997
Cloth: HarperCollins
⌒ This charming book does for middle-schoolers what *My Year in Provence* did for adults!

Originally composed as monthly letters to her local paper while the author was living as a fifteen-year-old foreign exchange student in Valence, France, these twelve chapters make up an extremely readable, highly entertaining memoir. Megan's observations of the differences between our cultures from a teenager's perspective are sharp and funny. School, rock climbing, cooking, and travel are all part of her exciting year abroad. It's not all a breeze, though. The beginning is particularly rough, until she experiences a Proustian moment and realizes she can truly understand the language. "I fantasized a lot about running away. . . . I understood that if I gave up and went home, my friends and family would forgive me and soon forget, but I would not forgive myself—and I would never forget. What I have now that I didn't have before I left home is the belief that I can do anything I set my mind to do. . . . I'm glad I made the journey."

The Primrose Way
Written by Jackie French Koller
Copyright 1992
Cloth: Harcourt Brace
Paper: Gulliver Books
ALA Best Book for Young Adults

⁓ This book offers exciting historical fiction about an outspoken young woman longing for freedom from narrow Puritan strictures.

When sixteen-year-old Rebekah Hall arrives from her comfortable home in England to join her father in the New England settlement of Agawam, she is shocked to discover that she will be living in a dirt cave with no furniture, no fireplace, no light. Weep though she might, Rebekah stirs herself to assist her father and the struggling colonists. When she discovers that no one in the little village can speak Algonquian, Rebekah convinces her reluctant father to let her learn the language by inviting a young Pawtucket girl to live with her. Headstrong Rebekah is never afraid to act according to the dictates of her heart and finds herself increasingly drawn to Mishannock, a powerful young leader in the tribe. Through war and sickness, their regard for each other grows until Rebekah realizes she must choose between the clashing cultures.

Koller has done extensive research on this era. At the back of the book, you'll find a useful glossary of Puritan and Algonquian terms and a complete bibliography. Koller also shares her historical sources and inspirations in a fascinating afterword.

Rainbow Jordan
Written by Alice Childress
Copyright 1981
Paper: Avon

⁓ Rainbow is fourteen. She is an African-American girl in an unnamed city. She's capable, valiant, bright, perceptive—and pretty much alone. Her mother is around, but only sometimes, and Rainbow is already more competent than her twenty-nine-year-old parent. When her mother isn't there and the caseworker discovers the situation, Rainbow is put in foster care, mostly with Miss Josie. She allows that she'd like to get close to Miss Josie, but life has taught her to be guarded, to be careful. "I am lonesome so regular till it's like a job I gotta report to every day."

Rainbow is under pressure—pressure from school, her friends, her boyfriend. (Parents should be aware that there is quite a bit of frank sexual discussion between Rainbow and her boyfriend.) She's too smart not to realize she can't hold it together by herself but uncertain as to how best to get help. She needs someone in her corner: "Wish I could tell somebody how I feel. . . . That's been the toughest thing. . . . I went to the circus and saw a man walkin the high wire and keepin his balance. . . . Ha! Ask me about it. I do it every day."

There is no single defining moment of heroism in this book. Rather, readers will be impressed with Rainbow's courage as she accumulates one small victory after another in her struggle to survive.

The Ramsay Scallop
Written by Frances Temple
Copyright 1994
Cloth: Orchard Books
Paper: HarperTrophy

⌐ This contemplative and polished novel is set in 1299. Even then, there would have been independent thinkers such as Elenor.

Elenor is only fourteen, but resents her longstanding betrothal to Thomas of Thornham, who has been away with the Crusades. She complains that this engagement is nothing more than a "conspiracy of papas" to unite adjoining properties and that only men have any choices in this world. When Thomas returns, sore at heart from the fighting and brooding over the injustices he's seen, neither he nor Elenor is remotely interested in this marriage. Ramsay's village priest wisely counsels them to postpone the wedding and instead attempt a pilgrimage to Spain. Both leap at the chance to delay their nuptials, even though they will be saddled with the other's company.

As in *The Canterbury Tales*, they meet other pilgrims, each with an instructive story to tell. Their journey, sometimes hazardous, always challenging, brings them new insights. Thomas discovers that he is capable of love and leadership. Elenor understands that marriage can, after all, offer equality. "She would have love and companionship and encouragement and would give these, too. At the same time, she would be living her own life, trying to act and think for herself no matter what Thomas thought."

The Return
Written by Sonia Levitin
Copyright 1987
Cloth: Atheneum
Paper: Ballantine
ALA Best Book for Young Adults
National Jewish Book Award

⌒ Oppressed, shunned, and cursed by other African tribes because they are Jews, Desta, her brother, Joas, and their little sister, Almaz, take a dramatic leap of faith. They decide to escape from Ethiopia and make their way to Israel, the promised land they've read about in their scriptures. They've arranged to travel with Desta's betrothed, Dan, but immediately their plan goes horribly wrong and the three children flee alone from their village. Joas is killed by robbers, and Desta must take charge. Without food, without drink, Desta and Almaz trek through the wilderness. At last they do catch up with Dan and slowly, painfully continue their exodus across to Sudan, where they are detained in a refugee camp. Weeks and weeks go by until finally they learn about a secret airlift that is flying persecuted Jews out of Africa to Israel.

This fictionalized account of "Operation Moses," which rescued more than 8,000 African Jews, is told by Desta in a voice filled with longing: longing for the African childhood she misses, longing for the salvation she seeks in Jerusalem. Never forgetting that she is a descendant of the magnificent Queen of Sheba, Desta conducts herself throughout with honor and valor. This is a compelling book for any reader.

The Road from Home: The Story of an Armenian Girl
Written by David Kherdian
Copyright 1979
Cloth: Greenwillow
Paper: Beech Tree Books
Newbery Honor Book
Boston Globe–Horn Book Award
Jane Addams Children's Book Award

⮡ Upon giving his orders to his Death Units to exterminate without mercy all Polish-speaking men, women, and children, Hitler wrote, "After all, who remembers today the extermination of the Armenians?" By faithfully re-creating his mother's voice in this powerful memoir, David Kherdian has ensured that the devastating story of the Armenian people will not be forgotten.

Born into a tight-knit, prosperous family, Veron Dumehjian was only eight in 1915 when she learned firsthand the meaning of the words *deportation, massacre,* and *annihilation.* Forced from their home by Turkish soldiers, her family was marched to the desert, where Veron watched her young brothers and sister die of cholera. Her father was taken from them and never seen again. Her mother died of heartbreak. Veron's ordeal continued. She made her own way, in and out of orphanages and hospitals, witnessing one horror after another, waiting for the day she could be reunited with the remnants of her family—one lone aunt and a grandmother. During all these dark, traumatic events, Veron retained her sanity and faith; her story gives us a picture of personal suffering and triumph.

Roll of Thunder, Hear My Cry
Written by Mildred D. Taylor
Copyright 1976
Cloth: Dial Books for Young Readers
Paper: Puffin

Newbery Medal
～ Savagery, compassion, and truth infuse this novel.

Nine-year-old Cassie tells the heartwrenching story of the Logan family and how they try to break the suffocating chain of rural Southern racism during the Depression. Cassie records the degradation of having to walk while the white kids ride school-buses, of getting dirty hand-me-down textbooks, of having to apologize to a cruel white girl for something she didn't do. And the Logans are luckier than most; although they still have a mortgage, they have land. It gives them an edge when dealing with the seedy, contemptible white men who relentlessly manipulate the African-American community. When these men don't get their way, they lynch and burn. The terror builds in one frightening incident after another, but Cassie and her strong, sheltering family always hold on to their dignity and pride. A lacerating story, presented with conviction and intensity.

Rosa Parks: My Story
Written by Rosa Parks with Jim Haskins
Copyright 1992
Cloth: Dial Books for Young Readers
Paper: Scholastic

～ "People always say that I didn't give up my seat because I was tired, but that isn't true. . . . No, the only tired I was, was tired of giving in." On December 1, 1955, when Rosa Parks refused to give up her seat on a Montgomery, Alabama, bus so that a white person could sit down, she launched a revolution. The famous bus boycott followed, segregation on buses ended, and the civil rights movement took off. In her engrossing narrative, which is a model of thoroughness and balance, we learn Parks's whole life story. She endured racism as a child in Pine Level, Alabama, finished high school only after she was married, was active in protest marches and voter registration for African-Americans. She lived in fear of violent reprisals from the Ku Klux Klan. Her strong marriage to Raymond Parks, her close friendship with Dr. Martin Luther King, Jr., and her deep relationship with her mother sustained her. Despite the highly emotionally charged content of the book, this is a careful, dispassionate reconstruction of events. Without question, it belongs on every bookshelf devoted to American history.

The Ruby in the Smoke
Written by Philip Pullman
Copyright 1985
Cloth: Random House
Paper: Random House
ALA Best Book for Young Adults

⌒ The audacious plot of this hair-raising Victorian melodrama is packed with every hyperbolic element imaginable: a stolen jewel, secret Chinese triads, dastardly murders, the vile opium trade, piracy on the high seas, rank London slums, a wealthy Indian maharajah . . . And it works! Every chapter in *The Ruby in the Smoke* ends in a cliffhanger that just won't let you put this book down. The author's introduction to his smart and savvy heroine is unforgettable: "Her name was Sally Lockhart; and within fifteen minutes, she was going to kill a man."

Sally Lockhart is sixteen and recently orphaned. She receives a poorly printed message that appears to have been dictated by her late father, warning her of an imminent, but unspecified, danger. Sally is no fool. As she carefully and courageously navigates her way through the perils that threaten her life, Sally never forgets her father's motto: "Keep your powder dry." She unravels every clue and faces every fact, as well as using her good head for business to find herself an accounting job with an enterprising (and attractive) young photographer. Mystery. Romance. Danger. It's all here— plus a refreshingly atypical nineteenth-century heroine.

Note: Sally goes on to have more adventures in *Shadow in the North* and *The Tiger in the Well*. Pullman has written another fine book, *The Tin Princess*, drawing on characters from his Sally Lockhart trilogy and giving them their own dashing adventures in a tiny European kingdom. His sterling heroines are always worth reading about.

Sarny: A Life Remembered

Written by Gary Paulsen
Copyright 1997
Cloth: Bantam Books

~ Gary Paulsen, a gifted writer of numerous award-winning novels, has created a heroine who commands your respect.

Being taught to read as a young slave girl changes Sarny's life. She can read the newspaper and tell that the South is losing from the long list of slain soldiers. When her children are wrenched from her arms and sold away, Sarny reads the bill of sale and knows she must make the treacherous 350-mile journey to New Orleans. Along the way, she meets the enigmatic Miss Laura, who becomes her benefactor and mentor. Working for Miss Laura gives Sarny the chance to really educate herself. From her first bubble bath to *Hamlet* to finance, Sarny "started learning on the world." With Miss Laura as a silent backer, Sarny decides to open a school for black children. After it is burned, Sarny rebuilds. When her husband is lynched, she moves to Texas and begins teaching again. Over and over Sarny proves herself to be a resilient, indignant, intelligent woman.

Selma, Lord, Selma: Girlhood Memories of the Civil-Rights Days

Written by Sheyann Webb and Rachel West Nelson as told to
Frank Sikora

Copyright 1980
Cloth: University of Alabama Press
Paper: University of Alabama Press

⌐ "If you can't vote, then you're not free; and if you ain't free, children, then you're a slave."

When eight-year-old Sheyann Webb heard those words at Brown Chapel AME Church in 1965, she knew there was nothing more important than being part of the civil rights movement. She told her best friend, nine-year-old Rachel West, about the meetings at the church, and soon the two were Dr. Martin Luther King's loyal participants in the voter registration drive in Selma, Alabama. For three months Brown Chapel was the focus of their lives. The girls often led the singing of spirituals and kept prayer vigils as the movement grew. Fear and death stalked them: Sheyann prepared her own obituary; Rachel was devastated when a white seminary student who had lived with her family was murdered. The culminating confrontation came on March 7, 1965, when America watched police troopers teargas and beat hundreds of peaceful marchers on their way to Montgomery.

Based on more than forty interviews with Sheyann and Rachel, this is an incredible firsthand document of the civil rights battleground. As Sheyann says, "We were just people, ordinary people, and we did it."

Seven Daughters and Seven Sons
Written by Barbara Cohen and Bahija Lovejoy
Copyright 1982
Paper: Beech Tree Books
ALA Notable Book

⌐ Princess Shahrazad herself could not have told a more hypnotic tale than the one in this novel.

A long, long time ago, there lived in Baghdad a poor man with seven daughters. He is pitied by all for this misfortune, especially since his wealthy brother brags loudly about his seven sons. Nevertheless, this poor man loves his daughters dearly, particularly Buran, the cleverest of them all.

Buran longs to end her father's melancholy, brought on because he cannot provide his daughters with dowries. She proposes the most fantastic, the most outrageous remedy: disguised as a boy, she will leave Baghdad and set herself up as a merchant, buying and selling goods from the sailors and caravans along the coast. Buran ambitiously promises to make her family rich, richer than her boastful uncle and his seven wastrel sons. It is not a woman's place to do this, but Buran knows her worth. As "Nasir," her brisk trade in herbal medicines and her keen business - acumen soon make her famous throughout Tyre. Famous enough to befriend Mahmud, son of the Wali of Tyre, a friendship that quickly becomes complicated as Buran finds herself falling in love.

Based on an eleventh-century Iraqi folktale, this is a spellbinding romance of a worthy daughter who brings honor and fortune to her family.

Shabanu: Daughter of the Wind
Written by Suzanne Fisher Staples
Copyright 1989
Cloth: Random House
Paper: Random House
Newbery Honor Book

∽ This novel will sweep you away. Absolutely.

Shabanu lives in the Cholistani desert in Pakistan. She and her family are camel breeders. With no boys in the family, Shabanu has known a modicum of independence helping her father, but, at age eleven, she is already betrothed to a young man she is fond of. Although she has always thought of her parents as kind and loving, when a series of catastrophic events forces her into a different arranged marriage without her consent, Shabanu bitterly sees that she has no more freedom than their camels.

There is very little room for Shabanu to maneuver in this tightly controlled world. As more and more freedom and happiness is taken from her, you'll be impressed with her grit and determination to hold her soul sacred and inviolate.

The sequel, *Haveli*, is every bit as good.

The Smithsonian Book of the First Ladies: Their Lives, Times and Issues
Edith P. Mayo, General Editor; foreword by Hillary Rodham
    Clinton
Copyright 1996
Cloth: Henry Holt

⁓ Editor Mayo is curator of the First Ladies exhibition at the Smithsonian Institution. This fun-to-read collection of their biographies, forty-three in total, is illustrated with 127 photographs and paintings, bringing to life the achievements of the diverse women who have held this unofficial title. Many were outgoing, involved campaigners, who relished their public prominence and exhibited a great flair for politics. We never knew, for instance, that Julia Grant loved every minute in the White House, that Sarah Polk edited her husband's speeches, or that Lou Hoover (the first woman to earn a geology degree from Stanford) was the first First Lady to make a radio broadcast. Others, such as Jane Pierce and Eliza Johnson, couldn't wait to leave.

This thorough book also includes one of our favorite quotations from Barbara Bush who, when addressing a Wellesley commencement, told her listeners, "Who knows, somewhere out there in this audience may even be someone who will one day follow in my footsteps and preside over the White House as the president's spouse. And I wish him well." And who knows? Perhaps one day there will even be a book entitled *The Smithsonian Book of the First Gentlemen*!

So Far from the Bamboo Grove

Written by Yoko Kawashima Watkins
Copyright 1986
Cloth: William Morrow
Paper: Beech Tree Books

⌒ "I competed with life and death when young. . . . And I won." This autobiography is the victorious result of that heroic effort.

Yoko was only eleven in 1945 when she, her mother, and her sixteen-year-old sister, Ko, became refugees. They were Japanese, living in northern Korea, and war was everywhere. When the Russians arrive in their little village, the three escape in the middle of the night. Disguised as Koreans, they flee through the dangerous countryside. Bombs explode everywhere; Watkins walks for miles and miles with shrapnel lodged in her ear. When they finally reach Japan, the war is over, but hardship and hunger are still their lot. Living in a train station, foraging through garbage cans for food, they hope to find a safe haven with the sisters' grandparents. But after discovering that they, too, have been killed, Watkins's heartbroken mother collapses and dies in her arms. The sisters must now survive on their own. Their endurance and courage dignify an abysmal, wretched time.

Jean Fritz writes in her foreword that this story is "so grim, so tragic that [Watkins] would spend years of her adult life trying to get it down on paper." You'll also want to read the completely compelling sequel, *My Brother, My Sister and I*.

Sorrow's Kitchen: The Life and Folklore of Zora Neale Hurston

Written by Mary E. Lyons
Copyright 1990
Cloth: Atheneum
Paper: Aladdin

⌒ Zora Neale Hurston, novelist, playwright, anthropologist, was born in Eatonville, Florida—the first incorporated African-

American community in America—in 1891. She wrote, "Mama exhorted her children at every opportunity to 'jump at de sun.' We might not land on the sun, but at least we would get off the ground." Her favorite place in Eatonville was Joe Clarke's store, where the adults would hang around swapping "lies" and tall tales. Young Zora was entranced and began making up her own stories; she never lost her love for the folklore and African-American culture of the South. She headed north after her mother's death, obtaining a high school education (remarkable in itself for that time) and later going on to Howard University and Columbia University. She became part of the fabled Harlem Renaissance, but where others were seeking to join the mainstream of white America, Hurston stubbornly clung to her interest in the folkways of her people. She collected their stories, studied voodoo practices in Haiti, and wrote novels in Southern African-American dialect. Determined, outrageous, funny, brilliant, she nevertheless died in poverty, obscure and alone, in 1960. Her reputation has been resurrected since then, and this excellent biography makes clear her remarkable contributions.

Squashed
Written by Joan Bauer
Copyright 1992
Cloth: Delacorte
Paper: Laurel Leaf

⁓ So many of the novels we've come across for this age group deal with serious issues in very serious language. This one takes a different tack with refreshing results.

Some kids just drift around, but sixteen-year-old Ellie has big dreams: she plans to win the blue ribbon for her pumpkin, Max, at the Rock River, Iowa, Pumpkin Weigh-In and Harvest Fair. This is a significant event in Rock River, and Ellie has set her sights high. Ellie's single-minded determination is the despair of her father, whose fond hopes center on her losing weight and studying harder in school, but Ellie classifies the world into two types of people, "growers" (of which she is one) and "non-growers" (which includes her father).

Ellie's wisecracking, comic voice is the highlight of the hilarious (and unique!) pumpkin plot. When she meets Wes, the past president of the Gaitherville High Agricultural Club, she's found a kindred "grower." Romance blossoms as these two work to ensure a blue ribbon for Max. Fresh, funny, and original.

The Story of My Life
Written by Helen Keller
First published 1902; numerous editions available
⁓ "From *Little Lord Fauntleroy* I date the beginning of my true interest in books. . . . I cannot remember what they all were, or in what order I read them; but I know that among them were *Greek Heroes*, La Fontaine's *Fables*, Hawthorne's *Wonder Book*, Bible stories, Lamb's *Tales from Shakespeare*, *A Child's History of England* by Dickens, *The Arabian Nights*, *The Swiss Family Robinson*, *The Pilgrim's Progress*, *Robinson Crusoe*, *Little Women* and *Heidi*, a beautiful little story which I afterward read in German. . . . I did not study or analyze them—I did not know whether they were well written or not; I never thought about style or authorship. They laid their treasures at my feet, and I accepted them as we accept the sunshine and the love of our friends."

As all the world knows, at nineteen months of age Helen Keller was struck by an illness that left her deaf and blind and with almost no power of speech. Four years later her phenomenal teacher, Anne Sullivan, entered her life, and language and learning again became real. Written in 1902 during her sophomore year at Radcliffe, this exceptional autobiography traces, without an ounce of self-pity, her early family life, her epiphanies with words and speech, her daily struggles to "practice, practice, practice." She also describes her many profound friendships with famous men of the day such as Dr. Alexander Graham Bell, Dr. Oliver Wendell Holmes, and John Greenleaf Whittier. Fascinating letters to and from them all are included.

Reading *The Story of My Life* is an experience no one should miss. This is a luminous book, one that lifts the reader up and leaves her awed and grateful.

Summer of My German Soldier

Written by Bette Greene
Copyright 1973
Paper: Laurel Leaf
ALA Notable Book
Golden Kite Award

⌐ One thing is true: the jarring plot of this novel will make you uncomfortable. During World War II, twelve-year-old Patty Bergen, living in Jenkinsville, Arkansas, aids Anton, a young German soldier, in escaping from the nearby POW camp. Her treason seems particularly sharp—she is betraying both her country and her Jewish religion. But Patty's disquieting actions are not the stuff of mere melodrama. Like a good parable, this story pokes and prods, challenging us to examine the conventions on which we base our lives.

Patty is an outcast within her own family. Her mother overtly disdains her, and her father habitually ignores or beats her. Patty's desperate efforts to win attention from them are fruitless. She depends on her only ally, Ruth, the family's African-American housekeeper, to offer the one thing Patty craves: unconditional love. When Patty meets Anton, she immediately recognizes a pariah like herself and never stops to think about her actions. Unaccountably, she finds that this prisoner rewards her by being the first person, besides Ruth, to acknowledge the remarkable girl she is. The stifling society of Jenkinsville and her family try to cripple

Patty's natural humane impulses, but she refuses to live in their narrow world. This demanding novel and its complicated heroine are not afraid to question any assumption or stereotype.

Sweet Creek Holler

Written by Ruth White
Copyright 1988
Cloth: Farrar Straus & Giroux
Paper: Sunburst
ALA Notable Book

⌒ Ginny Carol narrates her growing-up story and the lives and events of her neighbors in this poignant, finely crafted novel.

Her tale begins in 1948. Tucked away in the coal-mining hills of Virginia, in a little hollow along Sweet Creek, the Shortt family struggles to get by. Ginny's voice has the ring of truth as she remembers her childhood adventures: the joy of swinging on a vine over a ravine, skirting the ghosts that haunt the big house around the corner, the climbs on the forbidden firetower. Her best friend, Lou Jean, the sweetest and prettiest girl around, boldly assures Ginny, "We are special, you and me. . . . We will live forever!"

But as the girls grow up, Ginny sees that life in the holler is marred by poverty, isolation, and something even more treacherous—the limited expectations for women and the suspicious community that makes sure nobody steps out of line. The neighbors regard Ginny's mama as too beautiful to be trusted and Ginny's sad neighbor, Mrs. Clancy, as unnatural for grieving in solitude. When Lou Jean becomes pregnant, she is lambasted up and down Sweet Creek. Her pliant nature can't bear the strain. Lou Jean's suicide leaves Ginny with an ache that will never go away.

Unlike Lou Jean, Ginny has always refused to base her life on other people's opinions. Her mama has encouraged Ginny to read, to write stories, to think for herself. She is grief-stricken by her best friend's death, but Ginny's path long ago veered from Lou Jean's.

White's writing soars amid all the heartbreaking events that lead Ginny Carol out of childhood.

Thwonk
Written by Joan Bauer
Copyright 1995
Cloth: Delacorte
Paper: Laurel Leaf

⌐ The slings and arrows of outrageous fortune fly fast and furious in this hilarious novel.

Allison Jean (A.J.) McCreary is a talented photographer whose artistic vision is clear but whose romantic eye is blind. For five months she's had a hopeless crush on Peter Terris, *the* classically handsome hunk in her high school. When Cupid intervenes on her behalf just in time for the St. Valentine's Day Dance, A.J. can't believe her good luck. But after Peter's heart is pierced (thwonk!), A.J. learns the timeless lesson that true love and infatuation don't amount to the same thing. Or, as A.J. herself puts it, "There's a lot more to life than genetic perfection."

A.J.'s sardonic voice, with her many comments on the current adolescent scene, and the capricious, comedic plot make this a book your daughter will want to pass from friend to friend.

To Kill a Mockingbird
Written by Harper Lee
Copyright 1960
Cloth: HarperCollins
Paper: Warner Books
Pulitzer Prize

⌐ " 'You want to grow up to be a lady, don't you?' I said not particularly."

Everyone in Maycomb, Alabama, with the possible exception of her father, Atticus, expects Scout Finch to eventually cast aside the blunt, tomboy days of childhood and join the circumscribed life

CASSANDRA DANZ

~

Comedienne and Gardening Writer,
known as "Mrs. Greenthumbs"

hen I was a little girl, my head was always in a book. My mother would come into my room and yell, "What, reading again? Why don't you go out and play? You're going to ruin your eyes." With such encouragement, naturally I became a prolific reader.

My favorite heroine was in a book by Kathleen Winsor. *Forever Amber* whisked me away to Restoration London. The book was risqué but well researched.

Amber was a tramp. When I was twelve, I thought she was really something. She has amber eyes and natural amber-colored hair. Imagine, the same color as her name! How, I wondered, did her parents know that she would turn out that way? But that was a feeble quibble. Here was a girl who was unstoppable. Yes, she slept her way to the top, but she really loved only one man. Yes, she stole from her elderly Puritan husband as he lay dying, but she saved her boyfriend from the Great Bubonic Plague of 1665 by lancing his buboe with a kitchen knife. She then contracted the plague herself and survived. She escaped from the great fire of London, slept with the king—and enjoyed it!

My life has not resembled Amber's. But I still admire Amber's spunk, her ability to survive in the face of fire, plague, and a male chauvinist society, not to mention a nagging mother.

where "fragrant ladies rocked slowly, fanned gently and drank cool water." But Scout is in no hurry to do so. The ladies of the Maycomb, Alabama, Methodist Episcopal Church South seem hypocritical to Scout as they sit over tea, sanctimoniously discussing missionary efforts in Africa without acknowledging the racial injustices in their own backyards. Even as Scout feels the grip of this conventional world close upon her, though, she begins to glimpse that, at least for a few of these ladies, social graces merely mask an iron will: Miss Maudie minds her p's and q's, but speaks her mind when called for; Aunt Alexandra, the stuffy model of propriety, reveals unexpected grace; even the vile Mrs. Dubose shows a gallant side as she fights to rid herself of morphine addiction.

Scout's unpretentious narration of the grim events that take her and her brother out of innocence is beautifully written. This tragic story of race, with its bitter consequences, is a beloved classic. In the face of ignorance and anger, Scout and her family comport themselves with decency, sympathy, and honor.

Toning the Sweep
Written by Angela Johnson
Copyright 1993
Cloth: Orchard Books
Paper: Scholastic
Coretta Scott King Award

~ Three generations of strong-willed African-American women gather at the grandmother's desert home in this lyrical novel. Theirs is the very human, universal tale of the shifting of generations, of mothers and daughters, of letting go. It is also the very particular story of African-American grief.

Fourteen-year-old Emmie's grandmother Ola is a woman whose creed has always been "I do what I want." Now Ola has cancer and must relinquish her cherished independence to live with Emmie and Emmie's mother, Diane. While Emmie and Diane help

Ola pack up her house, each of the women lend their unique voices to the novel.

This is particularly Emmie's story, however. She has learned about an old Southern tradition of hammering upon a plow—called "toning the sweep"—that was a way of letting people know when someone had died. As more and more of the painful details

SHERRY LANSING

⌒

Chairman and CEO, *Paramount Pictures*

hen I got a little older, I found that one of my favorite books was *To Kill a Mockingbird* by Harper Lee. This is such a rich, multilayered story that one can read it again and again and always find something new in it. Chicago, where I grew up, was a long way from the small Southern town where Scout lived, but racial injustice is an issue that translates to any location and any time period. The values that Scout picked up from her father and from those around her (some by negative example)—fairness, justice, honesty, and kindness—are values that are vital to all civilized society. The horror of what happens when these qualities are absent from our lives is strikingly revealed through the eyes of this young girl who found herself growing up amid events both commonplace and extraordinary. From this fascinating book, I learned to judge people by their character, and not by their appearance, and to treat all people with compassion and dignity.

of her granddaddy's murder so many years ago emerge, Emmie begins to wonder if his soul might not be restless. She brings this idea to her mother and together they tone the sweep for her grand-daddy. As a result of Emmie's insistence on exposing the truth and creating family rituals, the tensions between Diane and Ola recede. Ola looks carefully at Emmie and sees that "she's got more courage than she can use."

A Tree Grows in Brooklyn
Written by Betty Smith
Copyright 1943, 1947
Paper: HarperCollins

⌒ Dozens of women we know get lumps in their throats when they talk about this book. A sprawling novel of tenement life in Brooklyn beginning in 1912, it teems with vivid thumbnail charac-ter sketches and unforgettable vignettes of urban poverty.

At the center of this book, sitting on her fire escape under the shade of the one type of tree hardy enough to grow in the city, is eleven-year-old Francie Nolan. She is always reading, writing, or dreaming. She needs her dreams, for her life is harsh. Her father, Johnny, is handsome, charming, and an alcoholic. Her hardwork-ing mother, Katie, scrubs floors for a living but can barely keep the family fed. Katie fiercely clings to the hope that her children will have a better life and religiously follows the advice her mother gave her: "Every day you must read one page from some good book to your child. Every day this must be until the child learns to read. Then *she* must read every day. I know this is the secret."

Despite the fact that Francie and Katie are made of "thin invisible steel," we think this book depicts a particularly bleak world for women, a world where women dance in attendance to their men. Jo March has more choices and freedom than Francie Nolan! Yet Francie emerges as determined to flourish as the tree growing behind her home. She will be off, at just over sixteen, to begin at the University of Michigan, but she leaves her Brooklyn childhood with more than just a pang of regret. She must close that chapter of her life as reluctantly as the reader closes this absorbing book.

Under the Mermaid Angel
Written by Martha Moore
Copyright 1995
Cloth: Delacorte
Paper: Laurel Leaf
ALA Best Book for Young Adults
～ Life in Ida, Texas, can be summed up by saying that the most exciting thing to do is visit the wax museum. Thirteen-year-old

OPRAH WINFREY

～

Talk Show Hostess, Producer, Entrepreneur

 think the book that moved me most when I was growing up was a *A Tree Grows in Brooklyn*. I had a tree in my backyard too, so I identified with her. I just thought, "Oh, this is my life." And then I discovered Maya Angelou's *I Know Why the Caged Bird Sings*. Well, first of all, it was the first time I had ever encountered another woman who had been sexually abused. I could not believe it, that someone had put this in writing. It was unbelievable.

Jesse Cowan lives in Ida, in a run-down trailer park, with her parents, a whiny little sister, Doris Ray, and young twin brothers, Jimmy and Roy Dean. She is fairly sure that her boring teenage life is never going to get better. When Roxanne, with her flowing long red hair and wild clothes, moves in next door, Jesse starts to have fun. Roxanne is over twice her age, but she treats Jesse like an equal. They lie out under the stars, watching for meteor showers; they confide important, sad secrets. Jesse's secret is that she hasn't been able to properly mourn the death of her littlest brother, William III. Roxanne's is that she has moved to Ida to find the baby boy she'd given up for adoption years ago. Roxanne is relying on Jesse to bring them together. By the end of the novel Jesse has worked through her grief and has contrived a way for Roxanne to meet her son.

Reading this reminded us of *A Thousand Clowns*—the funny episodes, the eccentric characters, the pungent lines about truth and miracles and enjoying whatever life hands you. Jesse tells her growing-up story in a likable, believable voice that we know will warm you inside.

Upon the Head of the Goat: A Childhood in Hungary, 1939–1944

Written by Aranka Siegal
Copyright 1981
Cloth: Farrar Straus & Giroux
Paper: Puffin
Newbery Honor Book
Boston Globe–Horn Book Award

Grace in the Wilderness: After the Liberation, 1945–1948

Written by Aranka Siegal
Copyright 1985

Cloth: Farrar Straus & Giroux
Paper: Puffin

〜 We've heard Aranka Siegal speak passionately about her concentration camp years to eighth-graders. The middle-class American kids were all well fed, well dressed, and safe. Listening to Siegal's horrifying narrative, we just kept praying that our children would *always* be safe. Siegal's award-winning book and its haunting sequel are meant to help us. These books teach the meaning of the biblical expression *scapegoat* so that readers can never be tempted again to put their own sins and fears on someone else's head.

The first of Siegal's books begins when she was nine years old, spending the summer in the remote countryside with her beloved grandmother. The ominous rumblings of war are heard even there, and when Piri (the fictionalized name Siegal gives herself) returns home, the noose begins to tighten. Her resourceful, intelligent mother grows ever more desperate. She sends Piri out disguised as a Christian peasant to search for food and for messages about relatives. But with every hope of escape blocked, the Jews in the city are forced into a ghetto and then herded into a train. The book ends as the still uncomprehending passengers hear the name of their destination: Auschwitz.

Grace in the Wilderness tells Siegal's story after liberation. Piri and an older sister, Iboya, kept each other alive throughout their captivity and now must endeavor to live with their nightmares and find a purpose to their lives. Piri and Iboya are relocated by the Red Cross to Sweden, finally emigrating to America. These two books are dramatic, dark, and effective documents of a young child's pain and terror and the wrenching struggle to rebuild a life.

Wait Till Next Year: A Memoir
Written by Doris Kearns Goodwin
Copyright 1997

Cloth: Simon & Schuster

⌒ Pulitzer Prize–winning historian Doris Kearns Goodwin begins her memoir with the day in 1949 when her father gave her a bright-red scorebook that "opened my heart to the game of base-ball." With her loving father as her eager audience, Goodwin began to record for him every inning of every game that the Brooklyn Dodgers played. It was a magical era in baseball, when the great Jackie Robinson, Roy Campanella, and Pee Wee Reese were local heroes to the kids, girls and boys alike, in the congenial neighbor-hood of Rockville Center, Long Island. From recounting the games to her father, Goodwin learned how to fasten together a dramatic narrative. From her mother, whose world was circumscribed because of ill health, Goodwin learned the language of great liter-ature. They shared wonderful times together, reading *Just So Stories*, *Little Toot*, *Nancy Drew*, Louisa May Alcott, and Robert Louis Stevenson.

Besides baseball, the historic events of the 1950s made their mark on Goodwin. The Rosenbergs, McCarthyism, Korea, Little Rock—all were as closely followed as the games. The golden age of baseball comes to an end when the Dodgers and the Giants leave New York for California; Goodwin's childhood comes to an end shortly thereafter when her mother dies and she and her father move away from their tightly-knit community.

Girls will admire how Goodwin strove to live up to the high standards her father set for her. He "never accepted the cultural con-ventions that crushed the ambition and imagination of so many girls. He did not agree that girls should subdue their competitive instincts, or alter their behavior to make themselves attractive to men. He urged me to run for class office, try out for school plays, and speak up in class if I had something to contribute." Now a famed biographer of the Roosevelts, the Kennedys, and Lyndon Johnson, Goodwin here blends a terrific sportscasting story with an unpretentious personal portrait.

Warriors Don't Cry: A Searing Memoir of the Battle to Integrate Little Rock's Central High

Written by Melba Patillo Beals

Copyright 1994, 1995

Paper: Pocket

~ This is an unflinching, riveting memoir by one of the eight teenagers chosen to integrate Little Rock High School in 1957.

Every day Melba Patillo walked into a war zone: angry white mobs screamed at her as she entered the school. Once inside, she braved one physical assault after another. Her eyes were sprayed with acid. Dynamite flew at her in the halls. Flaming pieces of paper struck her. Policemen turned their heads. The National Guard soldiers sent to protect the "Little Rock Nine" were pulled out too soon. Time after time Patillo relied on the support of her mother and grandmother. But they, too, were under attack: her mother lost her teaching job and had to fight to get it reinstated. They ran out of food and lived on apples a friend gave them.

Throughout it all, Patillo's faith that the wheel would turn, that someday the sacrifice would be worth it, never really wavered. Even though you think you may know much about this vicious chapter of our history, you'll have to brace yourself for the impact of this story.

Welcome to the Ark

Written by Stephanie S. Tolan

Copyright 1996

Cloth: William Morrow

~ This altogether fascinating novel poses many thought-provoking questions in a most original manner.

"A private nuthouse." That's where Miranda Ellenby's parents have placed her after Miranda, deemed the smartest girl in the world, started telling people she was an alien. "Did I believe the alien story? It isn't such a bad explanation, given how different I am from them—from everybody." For Miranda *is* phenomenally different: she's brilliant beyond almost anyone's power to understand. She and three other prodigies are invited to try living in an experimental group home they dub "The Ark." It will be the first real home for some of them. Because society doesn't know how to handle their genius, these four have been subject to continual exploitation or abuse. They now have a chance to reach out to one another and, through state-of-the-art computers, to other extraordinary young minds around the world.

When these gifted children begin to connect, they find themselves sharing one another's dreams, acquiring one another's memories, sensing one another's thoughts. Thinking and working together, their powers are heightened far beyond the normal. Miranda believes that they have been brought together for some higher purpose and begins to explore what their mission might be. By the final chapter, it is plain that Miranda will play a pivotal role in altering world events.

What Every American Should Know About Women's History: 200 Events That Shaped Our Destiny

Written by Christine Lunardini
Copyright 1997
Cloth: Adams Publishing
Paper: Adams Publishing

◦ This pocket-sized book offers short, lively views of 200 seminal events in American women's history, from 1607, when the first European women arrived in Jamestown, to 1993, when Maya Angelou read her poetry at President Clinton's inauguration. Laid out in chronological order, it pulls from many varied areas: science, literature, politics, art, family life, athletics. A few pages are devoted either to individually significant women or to milestones in feminist history. Some sample headings should suffice to spark your interest: "1790: Judith Sargent Stevens Murray Argues for Equal Education for Women," "1872: Victoria Woodhull Runs for President of the United States," and "1931: Jane Addams Is Awarded the Nobel Peace Prize." A highly useful and engagingly informative resource.

When I Was Puerto Rican
Written by Esmeralda Santiago
Copyright 1993
Cloth: Addison-Wesley
Paper: Vintage

~ This complex, unsentimental coming-of-age autobiography is a book for experienced readers.

Santiago was happiest as a *jibara*, a country girl, and the first home she remembers is a metal dwelling with a dirt floor. The tastes, sounds, and scents of *jibara* life are distinct and carry a delicious magic for the little girl. We watch her parents fall in and out of love, arguing, separating, reuniting, and the family's moves that result from these upheavals, all filtered through a child's eyes. Despite the turmoil that her battling parents sometimes cause Santiago, Puerto Rico is home. Nothing could have prepared young Esmeralda for the shock of moving to Brooklyn. She hates it—hates the dark, fearful streets, hates the concrete, hates being confined to the apartment. She hates Brooklyn so much she knows she must get out. When a guidance counselor tells her about the School for the Performing Arts, she seizes the chance to try out and, although her spoken English is poor, memorizes a difficult monologue phonetically. Santiago is admitted because everyone admires the chutzpah it took for her to audition. She went on to attend Harvard and then to record the memories of her two worlds so effectively.

Where the Lilies Bloom
Written by Vera and Bill Cleaver
Copyright 1969

Cloth: HarperCollins
Paper: HarperTrophy
ALA Notable Book
New York Times Outstanding Children's Book

⌒ Mary Call is at her wit's end. She is only fourteen, but she has more responsibility than someone twice her age. Her pa is dying, and she has promised him that, no matter what, she will keep the family—her ten-year-old brother, Romey, her five-year-old sister, Ida Jean, and her eighteen-year-old sister, Devola—together. They live in a flimsy, ramshackle house high up in the Appalachians. There's no money to speak of and not much food. Devola, particularly, is a worry. She's cloudy headed, and their neighbor Kiser, who is also their landlord, is after Devola to make her his wife.

Miraculously, despite her crazy, desperate situation, Mary Call crackles with spirit, humor, and unflagging courage. She refuses to fail. Her voice positively sings of life's pleasures: honest work, the rhythm of seasons, the love of relatives, the kindness of friends, and the stubborn persistence of hope when it should have vanished. A beautiful book.

A Whole New Ball Game: *The Story of the All-American Girls Professional Baseball League*

Written by Sue Macy
Copyright 1993
Cloth: Henry Holt
Paper: Puffin
ALA Best Book for Young Adults

⌒ For all you who cheered through *A League of Their Own*, here is the definitive story of the real women who made up the All-American Girls Professional Baseball League. Started during World War II to keep the game going while the men were away fighting, the league took off. Over its twelve-year existence, more than 550 women played the sport, gaining hundreds of thousands of fans.

This nicely written account features tons of inspirational quotes from the players. "We were pioneers, you know. I didn't realize it then, but we were. And every one of us values the opportunities we had." With wonderful photos and baseball memorabilia (don't miss the reproductions of the baseball cards), this is a lively celebration of a too-short chapter in baseball history.

Note: Macy has also written *Winning Ways: A Photo-History of American Women in Sports*. Its fascinating pictures document women and athletics over the last century.

Women of the World: Women Travelers and Explorers

Written by Rebecca Stefoff
Copyright 1992
Cloth: Oxford University Press
Paper: Oxford University Press

~ During the nineteenth and early twentieth centuries, these nine women explorers led the kind of lives that, even today, would amaze most people. Without a thought for how others might judge them, they left comfortable homes and trekked to far-flung, exotic lands. Often they were the first women to visit from the West. Some wrote travelogues that financed their next trip; some became public speakers. All were devoted to the very idea of travel, and none were deterred by roughing it. Stefoff writes, "The more distant and dangerous the destination, the more eager these women to make the trip." Florence Baker sailed down the Nile, Fanny Bullock Workman explored the Himalayas, Freya Stark traveled through Persia, Alexandra David-Neel entered the forbidden city of Tibet, and Louise Arner Boyd led an expedition to the Arctic. Enlivened with maps and photographs, this readable text liberates these intrepid women from obscurity.

Year of Impossible Goodbyes

Written by Sook Nyul Choi

Copyright 1991
Cloth: Houghton Mifflin
Paper: Yearling/Dell
ALA Best Book for Young Adults

⁓ The horror of war and occupation hits ten-year-old Sookan's Korean village not once but twice. In 1945 Sookan and her family are living under harsh Japanese rule. Fear is everywhere. There are cruel reprisals for the slightest infraction of the military regime. Sookan, her mother, and her young brother, Inchun, work endless hours in their front-yard factory, constantly subject to humiliation and in terror for their lives. When the Japanese leave, there is only a brief rejoicing, for soon the Russian Communists arrive and a new reign of fear begins. Sookan's mother determines that they must flee to the South. Sookan and Inchun are separated from their mother at the border and must finish the brutal journey alone.

Love, evil, and courage are here in equal parts. Sookan's bravery is riveting as she leads her brother to safety. An intense, amazing record of a savage piece of history.

Z for Zachariah
Written by Robert C. O'Brien
Copyright 1974
Paper: Aladdin
ALA Notable Book
Edgar Allan Poe Award

⁓ After a totally annihilating world war, Ann Burden believes herself to be the only person left on the planet. The nuclear radiation has somehow left her isolated valley home untouched. Her family had left to seek out other survivors, but they never returned, and fifteen-year-old Ann has been living alone, farming, fishing, and tending the animals, for over a year. When at last she spies a person making his way to her valley, she should be overjoyed. Good sense makes her cautious, though, and, unseen, she watches the stranger carefully before making any overtures of friendship. When he falls ill, she comes out of hiding to help him. John Loomis is a scientist who's been protected from radiation by a "safe-suit." Instead of finding a companion and ally, Ann is confronted with a dangerous, unbalanced menace, someone intent on taking over her farm—and herself. Their cat-and-mouse game is frightening, and Ann realizes she must end this deadly contest. Remembering her chess games with her father, she also remembers his advice: taking the offensive is the way to win.

RESOURCES

HOW TO FIND THE BOOKS
WE'VE RECOMMENDED

our absolute best friend in chasing down books is your librarian. Librarians are kept up-to-date about new books, and—a big plus—books have a nice long shelf life at a library. You can often order books through a cooperative lending system from another library, browse to your heart's content, sign up your toddler for story hour, seek out the advice of a passionate bibliophile, *and* pay nothing at all. It is the best deal around. Use it!

Bookstore quality varies, in both selection and knowledgeable staff, but even a poorly stocked store will order a book for you at no extra charge. A good store will have not only a large collection of titles but also staff whose opinions you can come to rely on. Many stores, such as Barnes & Noble and Borders, offer author appearances that can be quite captivating. Two of our favorite New York City children's bookstores are Books of Wonder (1-212-989-3270) and the Bank Street Bookstore (the number outside New York State is 1-800-724-1486; inside New York State, use 1-800-

439-1486). Each will take your order and ship directly to you. The staff at both stores is extremely knowledgeable, and both put out small catalogs as well.

A direct-mail book company specializing in children's literature is Chinaberry Books (1-800-776-2242). The estimable catalog *Common Reader* (1-800-832-7323) carries several classic children's selections each month. In addition, *Cricket Magazine* (1-800-827-0227) and *New Moon Magazine* (1-218-728-5507) usually recommend a few titles by authors whose work they publish. These are not separate catalogs; you'll find them bound with the magazine.

The Internet is now a viable choice for ordering books. You might want to try Amazon (www.amazon.com) or Barnes and Noble (www.barnesandnoble.com) The selection is vast and often includes some editorial brief as well as comments from readers for each title.

FUTURE EDITIONS

s you can tell, we love reading and talking about books. It would be wonderful to hear what books you would suggest for future editons. Please write to us at:

Contemporary Books
220 East 42nd Street, Suite 400
New York, New York 10017

Or you can E-Mail us through our home page:
www.booksforgirls.com

INDEX OF TITLES, AUTHORS, AND CONTRIBUTERS

(Note: Contributers' names are set in boldface type.)

Revolutionary Poet: A Story About Phillis Wheatley, 110
Richardson, Dot, 292
Ride on the Red Mare's Back, A, 110
Rimonah of the Flashing Sword: A North African Tale, 111
Ringgold, Faith, 40, 237
Road from Home: The Story of an Armenian Girl, The, 304
Robison, Paula, 296
Roll of Thunder, Hear My Cry, 304
Roop, Connie, 79
Roop, Peter, 79
Root, Phylis, 35
Root Cellar, The, 213
Rosa Bonheur, 214
Rosa Parks: My Story, 305
Roucher, Nancy, 237
Rubinstein, Gillian, 277
Ruby in the Smoke, 306
Rumpelstiltskin's Daughter, 111
Running Girl: The Diary of Ebonee Rose, 214
Running Out of Time, 215
Rylant, Cynthia, 96, 264

Sakurai, Gail, 85
Saller, Carol, 57
Sally Ann Thunder Ann Whirlwind Crockett, 37
Sally Ride: Shooting for the Stars, 216
Samuelson, Joan Benoit, 99
Samurai's Daughter: A Japanese Legend, The, 112
San Souci, Robert D., 112
Santiago, Esmeralda, 42, 327
Sarah, Plain and Tall, 112
Sarah and Me and the Lady from the Sea, 216
Sarny: A Life Remembered, 307
Sauer, Julia L., 160
Saul, Wendy, 201
Savitri: A Tale of Ancient India, 113
Schaefer, Carole Lexa, 39
Schecter, Ellen, 127
Schlank, Carol Hilgartner, 60
Schmidt, Annie M. G., 194
Scholastic Encyclopedia of Women in the United States, 217
School Mouse, The, 114
Schotter, Roni, 95
Schroeder, Patricia, 269
Schwartz, Joyce R., 194
Scieszka, Jon, 192
Scooter, 217
Season of Comebacks, A, 218
Secret Garden, The, 219
Secret of the Old Clock: A Nancy Drew Mystery, The, 220
Secret Soldier: The Story of Deborah Sampson, 114
Selma, Lord, Selma: Girlhood Memories of the Civil-Rights Days, 307
Sendak, Maurice, 117
Sender, Ruth Minsky, 265
Separate Battle: Women and the Civil War, A, 228

Seven Daughters and Seven Sons, 308
Seven Kisses in a Row, 115
Seven Ravens, The, 116
Shabanu: Daughter of the Wind, 309
Shark Lady: True Adventures of Eugenie Clark, 116
Sheila Rae, the Brave, 38
Sheldon, Dyan, 45
Shemin, Margaretha, 84
Shepard, Aaron, 89, 113
She's Wearing a Dead Bird on Her Head!, 116
Shoeshine Girl, 229
Shura, Mary Francis, 164
Siebert, Muriel, 108
Siegal, Aranka, 322
Sign on Rosie's Door, The, 117
Sikora, Frank, 307
Sills, Beverly, 271
Sills, Leslie, 176
Silver, 117
Silverman, Erica, 74
Sing, Sophie!, 38
Sisters, 38
Sky Pioneer: A Photobiography of Amelia Earhart, 230
Sleeping Ugly, 118
Small, David, 18
Smith, Betty, 320
Smith, Doris Buchanan, 212
Smith, Lane, 192
Smith, Lee, 53
Smith, Sherwood, 152, 250
Smithsonian Book of the First Ladies: Their Lives, Times and Issues, The, 310
Snyder, Zilpha Keatley, 154
So Far from the Bamboo Grove, 311
So Young to Die: The Story of Hannah Senesh, 231
Sophie's Tom, 118
Sorrow's Kitchen: The Life and Folklore of Zora Neale Hurston, 311
Speare, Elizabeth George, 248
Spinelli, Jerry, 238
Spinner, Stephanie, 84
Squashed, 312
Squiggle, The, 39
Stamberg, Susan, 186
Stanley, Diane, 111, 166, 167
Staples, Suzanne Fisher, 309
Star Fisher, The, 232
Stateswoman to the World: A Story About Eleanor Roosevelt, 232
Stefoff, Rebecca, 329
Steig, William, 57
Steinem, Gloria, 185, 282
Steinke, Ann E., 188
Stellaluna, 39
Stephanie's Ponytail, 40
Steptoe, John, 92
Stevens, Carla, 82
Stewart, Sarah, 24
Stewig, John Warren, 104
Stille, Darlene E., 272
Stop the Presses, Nellie's Got a Scoop! A Story of Nellie Bly, 233
Story of Holly & Ivy, The, 119
Story of My Life, The, 313
Story of Ruby Bridges, The, 119

Story of Stagecoach Mary Fields, The, 120
Stranded, 233
Stratton-Porter, Gene, 165
Streatfeild, Noel, 140
Street, Picabo, 7
Strug, Kerri, 170
Summer of My German Soldier, 314
Summer of the Swans, The, 234
Swamp Angel, 120
Sweet Clara and the Freedom Quilt, 121
Sweet Creek Holler, 315
Switching Well, 235
Swoopes, Sheryl, 109, 146
Sybil Rides for Independence, 122
Szabo, Corinne, 230

Taha, Karen T., 72
Taking Flight: My Story, 236
Talking Earth, The, 236
Talking to Faith Ringgold, 237
Tam Lin, 123
Tar Beach, 40
Tatterhood and the Hobgoblins: A Norwegian Folktale, 123
Taylor, Mildred D., 304
Taylor, Theodore, 240
Tell Me a Story, Mama, 41
Temple, Frances, 302
Thee, Hannah, 124
There's a Girl in my Hammerlock, 238
Thesman, Jean, 266
They Led the Way: 14 American Women, 124
13th Clue, The, 238
This Time, Tempe Wick, 125
Thompson, Kay, 63
Thousand Oaks California Branch Inc. of the American Association of University Women, 206
Three Days on a River in a Red Canoe, 41
Three Little Pigs and the Fox: An Appalachian Tale, The, 125
Thunder Cake, 41
Thwonk, 316
Tiegs, Cheryl, 83
Tillie and the Wall, 43
To Climb a Waterfall, 44
To Kill a Mockingbird, 316
Together, 44
Tolan, Stephanie S., 325
Toliver's Secret, 239
Tomlinson, Theresa, 160
Toning the Sweep, 318
Totenberg, Nina, 224
Travers, P. L., 191
Tree Grows in Brooklyn, A, 320
Trivas, Irene, 13
Trouble with Trolls, 44
Trouble with Tuck, The, 240
True Confessions of Charlotte Doyle, The, 240
Tuck Everlasting, 241
Tumble Tower, 45
Turn Homeward, Hannalee, 242
Turner, Robyn Montana, 214
Tye May and the Magic Brush, 126

SUBJECT

INDEX